THE
ADVOCATES
OF
PEACE
IN
ANTEBELLUM
AMERICA

Religion in North America

Catherine L. Albanese and Stephen J. Stein, editors

Valarie H. Ziegler

THE
ADVOCATES
OF
PEACE
IN
ANTEBELLUM
AMERICA

*Indiana
University
Press*

BLOOMINGTON & INDIANAPOLIS

The paper used in this publication meets the minimum requirements of American
National Standard for Information Sciences—Permanence of Paper for Printed
Library Materials, ANSI Z39.48-1984.

Library of Congress Cataloging-in-Publication Data

Ziegler, Valarie H., date.
    The advocates of peace in antebellum America / Valarie H. Ziegler.
        p.   cm. — (Religion in North America)
    Includes bibliographical references and index.
    ISBN 0-253-36864-2 (alk. paper)
    1. Peace movements—United States—History.   2. American Peace
Society—History. I. Title. II. Series.
JX1961.U6Z54   1992
327.1′72′0973—dc20   91-16318

                1 2 3 4 5   96 95 94 93 92

To the Ziegler girls of the LPSA—
Making a place for women in whiffleball
and everywhere else

CONTENTS

FOREWORD

The antebellum years in nineteenth-century America were anxious and troubled times. Dramatic changes brought by industrial and transportation revolutions, by rapid urbanization and immigration, by the movement of population westward, and by economic cycles of speculation and crash were unsettling. Foreign and domestic conflict marred American lives. The fact of slavery gnawed equally at the social infrastructure and conscience of the nation. In an era that Alice Felt Tyler memorably described as the time of "freedom's ferment," reform movements flourished. Indeed, in their midst, a series of ultraisms swept the social landscape as Americans matched what they felt as the extremity of the age's problems with the extremity of their proposed resolutions. Among the social reform movements, temperance, abolition, and woman suffrage crusades have no doubt attracted the most attention. But concern for Indian rights, movements for health reform, and experiments in communal living were all part of the ferment. So, too, as Valarie Ziegler so forcefully reminds us, was peace reform.

In a work that is a complex choreography of personalities, motivations, and ideological maneuvers, Ziegler shows that one major faction of the peace movement, the American Peace Society, distinguished between the evil of war and the relative good of state restraint of domestic crime. The other major faction, nonresistants who were also closely bound to the abolition movement led by William Lloyd Garrison, rejected any contact with what they regarded as the corruptions of statecraft. As incisively, Ziegler's narrative exposes another, and more ironic, division. This division cut both groups away from their earlier rhetorics of reform as the screws were tightened in the tense atmosphere of the Civil War. Both the American Peace Society and the nonresistants, Ziegler demonstrates, moved from an ethic of "love," in which the Sermon on the Mount was primary, to an ethic of "coercion" in which they endorsed the Northern war effort in the context of antislavery. They did so by denying that the Civil War was in fact a war and by viewing it instead as a Northern police action against the recalcitrant states of the South, or by defining the Civil War as a divine crusade in which God led his hosts against the Southern slave empire.

This is an intricate argument, and Ziegler develops it with care and rich historical contextualization. Beginning with the early part of the nineteenth century and the inception of both groups, she tracks their encounters with the challenges to peace that each decade brought, showing the nuances that gradually meant change for each side of the movement. And Ziegler thoroughly convinces as she explains. She knows the secondary literature on the peace and antislavery movements, and she uses it to effect. Even more, she has thoroughly immersed herself in the primary materials, and she has a gift for exposing the logic of each position with analytic skill and, at the same time, wit and grace. As she does so, Ziegler walks a fine line between the purely descriptive and the overtly normative. She succeeds by, as it were, getting inside each position and looking at the world from the stance of its presuppositions. That she does succeed is a measure of her evenhandedness in exposing the commitments and ideals as well as the self-serving rationales that each side of the peace movement lived within.

At a late-twentieth-century moment when our own nation struggles with issues of war and peace, Ziegler's reconstruction of the rhetorics and debates of an earlier century's small and self-conscious peace movement is timely. And that her strongest conclusion is one of cooptation provides, perhaps, warning and instruction.

Catherine L. Albanese
Stephen J. Stein
Series Editors

ACKNOWLEDGMENTS

I am grateful to see this book in print. To Indiana University Press for having the confidence to publish it and to Rhodes College for giving me a sabbatical to work on it, I am appreciative. No scholar can begin a career without institutional support.

I have been sustained throughout this project by many friends, and it is a pleasure to have the chance to thank them. My mentor at Emory University, Brooks Holifield, was everything an adviser should be. He had both a critical eye and a real enthusiasm for my work. He understood my fears and frustrations, and without discounting either, he helped me find a place for myself in the academic world. Kris Kvam and Linda Schearing, trusted colleagues in the Emory graduate program, walked with me every step of the way.

My friends in Memphis have been wonderful. As new faculty members, Carol Danehower and I shouted encouragement to one another in the basement of the physics tower at Rhodes while we pounded out lectures and puzzled over publications. Michael McLain, my department chair and cherished friend, made me feel like a hero as I wrestled with this manuscript. He also did much more than his share of departmental work so that I had time to write. Robert Pugh listened to me agonize for hours over a manuscript that he's never even seen, and Anisa Cottrell copied articles for me at every Xerox machine in Memphis. The Rhodes women of the Society of Saint Beatrice de Silva met weekly in my office amid much hilarity, and I was nourished by the sisterhood. Cheryl Cornish, pastor of First Congregational Church and my best friend, helped me choose stories for the text that were interesting as well as informative. And Carol Devens—that intrepid historian—and I spent a remarkable year pulling things out of footnotes and putting them into the text, both in our manuscripts and in our lives. I hope we got it right.

I am conscious, finally, of the debt I owe my family. I was lucky to have parents who surrounded me with books and taught me to love them. Jim Combs, my uncle, was the first writer in our family and my role model as an author. My four grandparents helped raise me, and though they were not scholars, they created a nurturing environment that made it possible for me to be one. Three of my grandparents are now dead, and it is their absence that I feel keenly at this time. Thus, I am sorry that Clarence Combs, Audrey and Harold Ziegler didn't live to see this book, for they surely helped inspire it.

THE
ADVOCATES
OF
PEACE
IN
ANTEBELLUM
AMERICA

INTRODUCTION

In 1823, Henry Clarke Wright left Andover Seminary in the middle of his senior year to pastor a Congregational church in Westbury, Massachusetts. During his studies, Wright had devoted ten to sixteen hours a day to his books, fashioning a desk that allowed him to work standing up. Shunning all social life, he sought to "have as little intercourse with the students as possible; not calling at their rooms, nor seeking intimacy." He could not, however, avoid contact with his roommate, who, he complained, "ate and ate and ate, without intermission or limitations. . . . Chairs, desks, and beds, converted into tables at once! Even the floor ever strewn with edibles, and the refuse; bones, crusts, potato-skins, clam-shells, oyster shells, etc. . . . He was ever groaning in agony from indigestion, and ever loading his poor goaded stomach with what the stomach of a wild elephant would groan under." In response to such gluttony, Wright subsisted on crackers, milk, and water—a diet guaranteed by its ease of digestion and lack of excitement not to divert him from his work.

When Wright took the pulpit to deliver his first sermon at West Newbury, he posed the following question: "Am I to become your enemy, because I tell you the truth?" Warming to his task, the new minister warned his congregation:

> So far from being my duty to make you think well of yourselves, it is my duty and wish to make you odious in your own estimation, so long as you live in the practice of evil. . . . Should I see faults in anyone, I shall not whisper them behind his back; I will meet him face to face, and tell him what I think. Will you do the same? If so, we can live in peace.[1]

Both Wright and his congregation survived what was surely one of the more contentious sermons ever to launch a pastorate. Earnest and demanding, Wright went on to become a professional reformer, but his style never changed. As in his first sermon, he ever after insisted that people could live in peace only as they acknowledged and repented their moral shortcomings. Wright's job was to confront people with their sin, convert them, and then lead them into the millennial age. As a reformer, he sought nothing less than the eschaton.

Significantly, he was not alone. Though few in nineteenth-century America were more confrontational than Wright, his certainty that Americans could and should bring about the millennium did not make him unique. Antebellum culture was replete with Christian reformers intent upon instituting Christ's reign on earth. In the free North and the slave South, the settled East and the frontier West, Americans labored to perfect the social structures around them. Frequently they worked at cross purposes with one another, following different visions of the New Jerusalem. Armed with Bible and conscience, they were suspicious of compromise. In time, those variant versions of the good society led to bloody conflict, first on the plains of Kansas, and later on the battlefields of Shiloh, Vicksburg, Manassas, and Gettysburg. Ultimately, the political settlement they engineered fell immeasurably short of the divine realm they sought. Sherman could march to the sea, but he could not lead the saints into the millennium.

If Henry Clarke Wright shared a reformer's zeal with other Americans, however, there was one commitment that set him apart. Wright belonged to a small network of pacifists convinced that the path to the millennium necessarily passed by way of the cross of suffering love rather than by the battleground of violence. These advocates of peace— by and large Northerners convinced of the superiority of life in the free states—formed the first peace societies in American history in 1815. Advocating a variety of positions from absolute pacifism to just war theory, the various state and local societies united in 1828 under the leadership of William Ladd, a retired Maine sea captain, to create the American Peace Society. With Ladd at their head, the members of the new organization continued to allow for a range of opinions on war and peace.

That toleration seemed more like indecision to the group's more radical pacifists, however, and as time passed they lobbied the society to define its position more precisely. In the late 1830s, the American Peace Society split asunder over the issues of defensive wars and personal self-defense. Responding to the pressure of those who wanted to take a more stringent stance, a majority of the society agreed in 1837 to condemn all war as contrary to the gospel, but it refused to make that view a prerequisite for membership. Nevertheless, the designation of all war as contrary to the gospel prompted Bowdoin College's William Allen, the most conservative just war advocate, to withdraw from the society and from peace advocacy in protest. In 1838 a radical contingent led by William Lloyd Garrison also withdrew and formed the New England Non-Resistance Society. For this band of radical abolitionists, nonresistance entailed not only renouncing all wars (offensive and defensive), but also abjuring self-defense, lawsuits, and participation in coercive governments as well. The Non-Resistance Society had an institutional life of only a few years, but its adherents continued vocally to identify themselves as nonresistants and to distinguish their beliefs from those of the American Peace Society throughout the antebellum period.

From 1838 on, two different groups composed the peace movement in America. The American Peace Society understood itself as the champion of Christian civilization. It sought to educate Christian nations to reject the barbarities of war and turn instead to peaceful methods of resolving disputes between nations. The Garrisonian nonresistants, on the other hand, envisioned themselves as sectarian radicals. They considered so-called Christian nations disobedient to the rule of Christ. Rather than seeking to persuade governments to substitute peaceful methods for warlike ones, they strove to persuade individuals to dissociate themselves from the state and to adopt the nonresistant lifestyle exemplified by Jesus. Each group found positions in Christian tradition and Scripture to support its argument,[2] but underneath their debates lay two different reforming temperaments. Members of the American Peace Society were cultural Christians who assumed that all institutions worked together to create a Christian civilization. The nonresistants believed that institutions were corrupt and that reform occurred only when righteous individuals separated themselves from the fallen world.

Despite those differences, the groups shared a common theological ethic. Along with the nonresistants, the members of the American Peace Society believed that God had revealed in Jesus a definitive model for Christians to exemplify. God called believers to obey the Sermon on the Mount, living in love for their neighbors. Like Jesus, Christians should offer goodness and kindness to all, even if their neighbors scorned them, took advantage of them, or killed them. Trusting in God's redemptive love to convert others, they should, like Jesus, refuse to return evil for evil. An ethic of love, which in rejecting violence called upon believers to emulate Jesus regardless of the consequences, was thus the foundation of each group's peace activism.

The advocates of peace preached this message throughout the antebellum period. Ironically, the culmination of their efforts was not the kingdom of God, but the Civil War. Rather than creating a society that lived in peace before God, the friends of peace labored in vain in a world intent upon violence. When the war came, the advocates of peace had to confess that Americans preferred an ethic of coercion to an ethic of love. Yet they did not despair. They deplored the slaughter that the war created, but they were Northerners who despised the Southern "slaveocracy." Though their Northern compatriots had chosen violent means, at least they were sacrificing themselves for worthy causes: liberty and Union. There would be time to preach peace after the slave power had met defeat. The advocates of peace approved of the war aims, if not of the war.

That approval, however, struck many people as odd. Most Americans had never been sympathetic to pacifism in the first place, and now its advocates seemed to be equivocating. How could the pacifists claim that obedience—regardless of the consequences—to the nonviolent love ethic of Jesus was an end in itself at the same time they tacitly supported the Union war effort? How could they preach peace when they applauded war?

It was clear to their contemporaries that they could not. Historians on the whole have agreed. Yet the antebellum pacifists believed that the path to the millennium required them to support liberty and Union. The peace that passed mortal understanding was unattainable as long as half the nation stood mired in sin. Ultimately, Christ's ethic of love would prevail, but for now God's "terrible swift sword" must bring an unrepentant South to its knees. In thus reconciling violent means with peaceful ends, the advocates of peace conceded that sometimes the best way to love their neighbors was to coerce them.

Two Reforming Temperaments

The temperamental differences dividing the American Peace Society from the nonresistants were not unique to the peace reformers. Pacifism was a minor movement in a century obsessed with reform activities. Determined to rid society of sin, Christian activists sponsored a bewildering array of voluntary societies, laboring for, among other things, temperance, women's rights, colonization, abolitionism, Sabbath observance, manual labor, vegetarianism, the evangelization of sailors, the conversion of the West, prison reform, educational improvements, and the distribution of Bibles and evangelical tracts. Once a person caught the reform fever, she or he typically toiled on behalf of a number of causes. Convincing people to work hard was not difficult, but determining the proper strategies—particularly the appropriate degree of "ultraism"—was.[3] Ought the reformer seek to mend society's flaws or to replace the present order with a new one? Just how much perfection could be achieved? Was it legitimate to use political means? The advocates of peace were not the only ones who found themselves torn by such questions; any Christian serious about applying his or her faith faced the same dilemmas.

No movement was more divided than the one that came to overshadow all the other campaigns for reform: the antislavery effort. The first group to organize was the American Colonization Society. Formed in 1816, this society was dedicated to freeing slaves and sending them as colonists to Africa. In the late 1820s and early 1830s a number of antislavery reformers came to believe that the American Colonization Society was racist. Rejecting colonization as a strategy and arguing instead for the creation of an egalitarian biracial nation, these reformers turned against their elders in the American Colonization Society and proposed immediate emancipation as the proper goal of the antislavery movement.[4] The immediatists were generally young reformers born between 1780 and 1810. Almost uniformly they had been raised by strict, orthodox parents who had taught them to be acutely sensitive to sin and wrongdoing. Encouraged to think of themselves as persons with a special calling, the immediatists typically experienced religious conversions in their teens and then in their twenties faced vocational crises that they resolved by choosing benevolent careers. Spurred on by fears of falling short of God's glory, yet buoyed by a concomitant conviction of special grace, the immediatists brought to their work an extraordinary zeal.[5] Their fervent agitation for emancipation produced shock waves in the North—where proslavery mobs of "gentlemen of property and standing" publicly assaulted them[6]—as well as in the South—where state legislatures outlawed the distribution of abolitionist literature while calling upon Northern lawmakers to gag its authors.[7]

Most of those working to create world peace were also involved in the campaign to free the slaves, and most abolitionists, at least initially, chose to use moral suasion rather than violence to effect emancipation. Thus, the disagreements about means and ends debated in the peace movement generally found expression in the antislavery movement as well. Some pacifists like William Ladd had supported colonization and were surprised at the vehemence with which many younger pacifist immediatists rejected the American Colonization Society in the 1830s. It was not long, moreover, before the immediatist abolitionists were divided among themselves. Like the advocates of peace, the antislavery immediatists disagreed about the morality of political involvement. Moderate immediatists favored using political means to abolish slavery, reasoning that such action would preserve and strengthen an already sound body politic. Radical immediatists, however, branded political involvement as morally compromising and sought to replace the fallen social order with a regenerate, apolitical one. Pacifist immediatists like William Jay, Lewis Tappan, and Gerrit Smith[8] favored political antislavery, while Garrisonians like Henry C. Wright and Garrison himself denounced both colorizationists and political immediatists as halfhearted reformers. Insisting that a government founded upon military might and dedicated to the preservation of slavery was immoral, the Garrisonians refused to vote or hold office. Unwilling to employ methods lower than the ethical standard they were seeking to implement, the Garrisonians used perfectionism as both a means and an end in their reforming activities.[9]

The debate between moderate and radical immediatists reached a crisis in the late 1830s over the question of allowing women to join voluntary societies as full members. In the antebellum period, only the Quakers permitted women to address "promiscuous assemblies" of men and women. Typically, if women wanted to direct a voluntary society, they formed a ladies' auxiliary, did their talking there, and sat quietly through meetings of the men's groups. The Garrisonians changed all that in 1838 at the organizing convention of the New England Non-Resistance Society. The moderates walked out after the Garrisonians pushed through a measure allowing women to join the nonresistance society and speak at its meetings. That schism anticipated a similar split among antislavery immediatists in 1839, when, in protest against admitting women as full members, moderates under the leadership of Arthur and Lewis Tappan left the Garrisonians in control of the American Anti-Slavery Society and created the American and Foreign Anti-Slavery Society. In both schisms, the moderates were distressed at the Garrisonians' ultraism. They believed the Garrisonians were driving respectable people away from antislavery and peace reforms by incorrectly presenting them as movements to overthrow the foundations of society.[10]

The debate over women's participation was for both movements a warmup to the more prolonged dispute over the legitimacy of using political means to achieve the groups' moral ends.[11] Predictably, moderates thought political participation was both moral and effective, while the Garrisonians condemned it as unethical. In the antislavery movement, moderates worked to outlaw slavery and participated in political organizations like the Liberty party, the Liberty League, and the Republican party. In the peace movement, they petitioned Congress to create an international League of Nations and to include arbitration clauses in treaties with foreign powers. The Garrisonians, on the other hand, held themselves aloof from the work of government—though they energetically labored to influence voters and officeholders who did find it in their hearts to participate in politics.

Peace activists in both immediatist camps, as well as pacifists sympathetic to colonization, were determined to use peaceful methods to abolish slavery. That resolve, however, became more difficult both to uphold and to define after 1850 with the enactment of the Fugitive Slave Law and the escalation of violence over the slavery question. The Fugitive Slave Law was so abhorrent that many nonresistants could not resist using violence to defy it, and even moderates began to question the utility of a political process that could produce such legislation. Open warfare in Kansas between slavery and antislavery forces prompted more doubts about the efficacy of either nonviolent or political strategies for social change, and it was, by 1861, at times tempting to think that John Brown had adopted the most effective means to address the issue. The bombardment of Fort Sumter confronted both antislavery and peace advocates with the futility of using either political or peaceful means to settle the slavery question. No matter what the reformers decided, the rest of the country would put the issue to rest through methods so terrible in their scope and destructiveness that the result could only be, as Lincoln noted, "fundamental and astounding."[12]

Undoubtedly, then, confusion often reigned when antislavery and peace activists devised strategies for reform. The antislavery groups were the most conspicuous of all the nineteenth-century voluntary societies, and even they spent a dismaying amount of time working at cross purposes with one another. Yet the most remarkable thing about the voluntary reform societies of the antebellum period was not their success or failure, but the energy that countless Americans threw into them. Reform activity on such a mass scale was unprecedented in American history.

Scholars have offered a number of theories to account for the exceptional devotion to reform evidenced in the nineteenth century. The most prominent discussions have suggested that the period's religious benevolence was the result of the reformers' anxiety about loss of social status. The impetus for reform, this argument goes, was the reformers' desire to exert social control, not to achieve social improvement. Classically stated by David Donald in his essay "Toward a Reconsideration of the Abolitionists," the social control and status anxiety theories have also received compelling presentations by, among others, John R. Bodo, Charles C. Cole, Jr., Charles I. Foster, and Paul E. Johnson.[13] Other scholars, such as John L. Hammond, have contended that the benevolent impulse was not so much an effort to impose unity as an expression of that unity already achieved by the religious revivals that swept the country in the train of the Second Great Awakening.[14]

Accompanying all of this analysis has been a preoccupation with the psychology of reform, particularly a fascination with uncovering the motivations that animated antislavery reformers. Lively debate has also focused on the question of which group of abolitionists was most effective. In 1933 Gilbert Barnes argued that political emancipationists were practical and effective reformers, as opposed to the impractical Garrisonians, who were too frequently lost in a world of abstract ideas. David Donald and Stanley Elkins agreed with Barnes's assessment, and a number of historians in the 1970s, such as Eric Foner, Hans Trefousse, and Richard Sewell echoed the contention that political antislavery reformers were the most effective emancipators.[15] On the other hand, revisionists such as Aileen Kraditor, Lewis Perry, Bertram Wyatt-Brown, and Ronald G. Walters have denied both that the Garrisonians were ineffective reformers and that the categories of practical and impractical were helpful in evaluating abolitionists.[16]

Scholarly discussions of the peace reformers have centered on two questions: were the advocates of peace really pacifists, and what did they accomplish? In addressing the first question, most historians have argued a declension theory, contending that the peace societies were originally founded in a "true" spirit of pacifism but gradually lost that fervor as political events forced them to choose between liberty (freeing the slaves) and peace. Forms of this theory appear in the works of Charles DeBenedetti, John Demos, Jane Pease and William Pease, and Alice Felt Tyler.[17] Two important studies—Merle Curti's *The American Peace Crusade, 1815–1860* and Peter Brock's *Radical Pacifists in Antebellum America*—presented a significant variation of the declension theory. Defining pacifism in an absolute sense as complete nonresistance, Brock and Curti maintained that the American Peace Society, in rejecting the Garrisonians and limiting its efforts to eliminate international war, had ceased to be a pacifist organization by the 1840s. The nonresistants then emerged as the true party of peace but betrayed the cause in the 1850s, when concerns for freeing the slaves began to outweigh their commitment to peace. The nonresistants' support for the Union in 1861 then completed their fall from grace.[18]

In answering the second question—what did the peace societies accomplish?—scholars have offered largely negative assessments. A few have managed to speak enthusiastically about the contributions to pacifist thought made in the nineteenth century. Devere Allen, for example, argued that "these men and women, their aims and deeds, their splendid loyalties and their betrayals, their cautious compromises and their daring ventures, should be indelible."[19] Most accounts, however, have concluded that the peace societies accomplished little. The small number of peace reformers who labored prior to the Civil War converted few, and with the coming of the war even those who had been enthusiastic abandoned peace for other values.

In this study of antebellum pacifism, I analyze the underlying assumptions that formed the peace activists' worldview. I do not evaluate the activists according to some ideal scale to determine whether they were "truly" pacifists or not. Recognizing that pacifism is a multifaceted phenomenon and that no single position can be designated pacifist, I am more concerned to distinguish different types of peace activism.[20] Neither is it my primary intention to consider the psychological motivations that lay behind the reformers' actions. In his study of antislavery, Ronald Walters contended that "antislavery is a structure of perception," noting that "we do not need to know what brings individuals to a movement in order to understand the movement itself. We can suspend the question of motivation and ask, instead, what there was in a social and cultural situation that gave a reform its style, its particular set of concerns and solutions."[21] In this work, I will seek to reveal the "structure of perception" that prompted two different groups of antebellum reformers to work for peace. In particular, I will analyze the role that theological assumptions played in forming antebellum attitudes toward peace and war.

In characterizing one theological position as an "ethic of love" and another as an "ethic of coercion," I have attempted to use phrases that are descriptive rather than normative. I do not intend for the term *ethic of love* to indicate moral superiority, nor do I use the term *ethic of coercion* pejoratively. In the context of antebellum pacifism, an ethic of love connotes the reformers' desire to obey the Sermon on the Mount literally—to love their enemies and refuse to return evil for evil, regardless of the consequences. Modern ethicists designate such a moral stance as deontological. An ethic of coercion, in this context, implies the reformers' willingness, under certain conditions, to use violent means as they sought to order society according to their perception of God's will. Some reformers refused to concede the legitimacy of violent means; others limited its use to the police function of the state; and still others were willing to use violence to defend the state from external aggression as well. Modern ethicists designate moral reasoning that takes consequences into account as teleological. My goal is not to identify or defend any of these positions as correct but to describe the logic and development of the peace reformers' thought.

I am arguing that certain features of nineteenth-century evangelical theology provided a set of presuppositions about the nature of reality that formed the context for peace activism. Without understanding that context, it is impossible adequately to assess the antebellum peace movement. As Lewis Perry observed, "it should be clear that nonviolence was less important than the theology in which it was couched."[22] Scholars such as Lewis Friedman, Donald Mathews, James Brewer Stewart, Bertram Wyatt-Brown, and Walters have also noted that the antislavery movement was in part an expression of Protestant evangelical theology. In this study, I analyze the antebellum peace movement in light of the theology that provided the medium in which the pacifists moved, breathed, and understood their world.[23] In particular, I seek to demonstrate the theological shift from an unconditional ethic of love to a qualified acceptance of an ethic of coercion that occurred in both groups of peace activists.

A Theology of Reform

Though the peace movement ultimately supported reformers of two different temperaments—the American Peace Society and the nonresistants—the two groups shared a number of theological presuppositions. Notions of disinterested benevolence, millennialism, and personal responsibility formed an ethos in which selfless love in service of God's coming kingdom was a routine expectation. Being a Christian meant achieving personal holiness as an individual and working with other Christians to create a holy society. Certainly many Americans resisted the call, but anyone familiar with antebellum culture would have understood it, and reform-minded Christians embraced it. In response, they created an unprecedented system of benevolent enterprises. As historian James H. Moorhead has observed, "benevolence provided a model for the externalization of self-doubt into cleansing action and, in view of the open-ended definition given to unselfish service, was a powerful psychological mechanism for the inducement of radical commitments."[24]

The elements that went into the reform ethos were a long time in the making. In attempting to trace the theological sources of reform activity, historians usually start with the eighteenth century and Jonathan Edwards. Along with others who used the same concepts and vocabulary, Edwards helped popularize two ideas that came to be decisive for nineteenth-century reformers. He suggested, first of all, that genuine ethical behavior, or "true virtue," was benevolence to Being in general. Having received the divine and supernatural light that God communicated to the elect, the converted Christian could revere the excellence of Being in general. This appreciation, or sense and taste of the infinite, prompted in the believer a disinterested love for all being that found fulfillment not in self-centered pursuits but in abandoning one's self to love for God and for God's end in the creation.[25] Edwards also pushed believers to serve the cause of Being in general by promoting a second theological observation that was to have considerable impact in the nineteenth century. He argued that the millennial age would not interrupt history with a cataclysmic blast but would "be gradually brought to pass" by "the preaching of the gospel, and the use of the ordinary means of grace."[26] "A happy change is nigh," he told his listeners; it was their task to bring it to completion in the New World, the land that God had chosen for the dawn of the millennial day.[27]

In the nineteenth century, with Arminian theology and the "new measures" of revivalism typified in the ministry of Charles Finney, millennialism and the notion of disinterested benevolence were incorporated into a distinctive form of popular piety. Evangelical Protestantism had enormous cultural influence. For the ordinary American Christian, the millennium was not merely an eschatological doctrine. It was a reality so tangible that it made sense to watch for it, long for it, and work for it.[28] As Francis Wayland, president of Brown University and the most influential moral philosopher of the age, noted in 1830,

> Perhaps before the youth of this generation be gathered to their fathers, there may burst forth upon these highly-favored States the light of Millennial Glory. What is to prevent it? I do believe that the option is put into our hands. It is for us . . . to say, whether the present religious movement shall be onward, until it terminate in the universal triumph of the Messiah, or whether all shall go back again. . . . The church has for two thousand years been praying, "Thy kingdom come." Jesus is saying unto us, "It shall come if you desire it."[29]

At times their belief in the proximity of the kingdom degenerated into the assumption that its progress was both easy and inevitable. But in any case—except for a few groups like the Millerites, who eschewed the postmillennialism of the age for premillennial visions of a catastrophic interruption of history—most antebellum Christians agreed with Wayland that the kingdom would come if they desired it.

Inseparable from their belief in the coming kingdom was their understanding that they were morally obligated to help bring it about. Orations about disinterested benevolence had an unmistakable tinge of Wesleyan holiness in them by the nineteenth century, but the vision of Christians working selflessly for the glory of God remained. Both Calvinists and Finneyites insisted that the highest good in the universe was the glory of God. Sin was selfishness and willful disobedience to the laws that God as moral governor had prescribed. Happiness, on the other hand, was living in perfect obedience to God's will. And religion was not simply something to experience, but also something to do—and to do vigorously.[30]

In the first place, that meant developing personal holiness. Antebellum reformers knew that the cosmic struggle between good and evil that engulfed the outer world was mirrored in each person's soul. But if an individual could conquer selfishness and throw him or herself into the service of the gospel, then the millennium would begin, at least in that person.[31] As William Ladd explained, "Let a man adopt the pacific principles of the gospel to their whole extent. Let him love his enemies, and be prepared to render always good for evil, and the millennium has come *to him*."[32] The reformers struggled with inner desires that ran counter to the perfection they sought to achieve. Like everyone else, they were tempted to hate their enemies rather than love them and to indulge sensual appetites that their theology told them to control. But their theology also informed them not only that they could win such struggles, but also that they should. Entire sanctification was a matter of will. The perfection of the eschaton was theirs if they would only choose it—again, and again, and again, as they conquered the exigencies that each moment tempted them to live for the self rather than for God.

This battle for sanctification meant controlling the body. It was no coincidence that movements for dietary reform, temperance, manual labor, exercise, and sexual asceticism arose in the antebellum period. The manual labor movement, for example, strove to incorporate physical labor into school curricula, as well as to encourage older individuals to work with their hands because of the widespread fear that overworking the mind would lead to an imbalance of blood in the brain, thus depriving and eventually disabling the body. Manual labor could cure that ill. It could also fill up free hours that people might otherwise spend on sensual indulgences such as alcohol, tobacco, or sex. Intellectual activity that was not balanced by healthy manual labor, Finneyite Theodore Dwight Weld contended, would "destroy the symmetry of human proportion and make man a monster." Significantly, when Northern evangelicals in 1830 endowed Lane Seminary in Cincinnati—a Western site they described as part of "the great battlefield between the powers of light and darkness"—they insisted the seminary be a manual labor institution.[33]

Sexual expression was another domain that the reformers sought to control in themselves. They assumed that indulging sexual desire set loose forces of passion that were insatiable. Sylvester Graham designed his famous diet—which for a time became required fare at Finney's Oberlin College—as a method of combatting passion. Regular consumption of unseasoned lukewarm vegetables and "Graham crackers," would, Graham claimed, save the individual from the ravages of uncontrolled passion such as tuberculosis, insanity, and cancer of the womb.[34] Indeed, the individual who wished to attain sanctification could not be too careful about mastering bodily desires. As Finney noted in his *Systematic Theology,*

Unless the bodily appetites and powers be consecrated to the service of God . . . permanent sanctification as a practical thing is out of the question. . . . Few people seem to keep the fact steadily in view, that unless their bodies be rightly managed, they will be so fierce and overpowering a source of temptation to the mind, as inevitably to lead it into sin. If they indulge themselves in a stimulating diet, and in the use of those condiments that irritate and rasp the nervous system, their bodies will be of course and of necessity the source of powerful and incessant temptation to evil tempers and vile affections.[35]

Reform-minded parents stressed to their children the importance of sexual self-control, urging them to substitute prayers and benevolent deeds for the certain ruin of carnal thoughts and practices.[36] As Lewis Tappan warned, "youthful lusts" presaged a life of "idiocy, insanity, disfigurement of body, and imbecility of mind."[37]

Seeking bodily sanctification led reformers into lifestyles that to later generations seem unthinkably repressed. One of the goals abolitionists Angelina Grimke and Theodore Dwight Weld set for their marriage was self-mastery over animal passions. Apparently they succeeded, for when their abolitionist colleague James G. Birney visited, he remarked that he envied them "their self-denial—their firmness in principles puts me to shame."[38] Henry Clarke Wright, always zealous for virtue, spent his first pastorate getting up at two in the morning. He would run for miles in the dark along the Merrimac River, then take a cold bath, and settle in for hours of work in his study. Refusing all stimulants, he drank nothing but water. In an 1855 book entitled *Marriage and Parenthood*, Wright created a couple named Nina and Earnest who were so controlled that they waited for five years after their wedding to consummate the marriage.[39] William Lloyd Garrison stressed self-control so strongly that he inadvertently killed his son Charley. When he was six, Charley fell sick with a fever, and Garrison arranged for him to undergo a medicated vapor bath. The steam was so hot that after twenty minutes Charley screamed in pain. Thinking his son was overreacting, Garrison "appealed to his little manhood" and convinced Charley to finish the treatment. When at last he lifted Charley off the steam chair, Garrison saw to his horror that the skin on his buttocks had been burned away. Charley became delirious within the hour and died four days later.[40]

In addition to securing personal holiness, the iron will that evangelical theology cultivated in believers was also a remarkable spur to social action. Nineteenth-century reformers never limited holiness to individual piety. Individual conversions were only the first step in eliminating sin and preparing the world for the eschatological age; the next task was to develop a system of benevolence that would mold social and political institutions into a form consistent with the demands of the gospel. If the kingdom were to come, it would find a resting place only among holy individuals dwelling amid regenerate social institutions.[41]

Unfortunately, it was never simple to determine the exact shape a regenerate society ought to take, although the antebellum reformers assumed that, guided by intuition, they could propose an accurate blueprint. Finney's doctrine of moral government posited the existence of, in historian D. H. Meyer's words, a "hypothetical, frictionless uni-

verse" in which individuals and institutions by nature lived in harmony.[42] In practice, however, that ideal universe was elusive. Different
people pondered different ideal social orders, and the appeal to intuition
as an arbiter of morality inadvertently established the individual conscience as the ultimate authority in moral matters. As Richard Hughes
and Leonard Allen have shown, one of the ways antebellum Americans
attempted to overcome the surfeit of utopian visions that emerged was
by pointing to some primordial order as normative. Decades earlier,
when Jefferson wrote the Declaration of Independence, he had made the
same move, appealing to "the laws of Nature and Nature's God" as his
authority for standing in judgment on the British government.[43]

Primitivism, however, was no better guarantor of social unity than
individual intuition, for antebellum Americans found variant primordial
orders attractive. In the South, Christians combed Scripture and tradition and discovered that God had ordered society in a hierarchical
arrangement with white male planters on top and enslaved Africans on
the bottom.[44] Social reformers in the North disagreed with that assessment but were unable to find consensus among themselves about what
primordial vision should replace the Southern plantation patriarchy. In
the peace movement, the members of the American Peace Society
pointed to the early church as their model. The early church had been
both pacifist and respectful of government, and that suited the peace
society's purposes. The nonresistants cited the early church as well but
pointed primarily to the perfection of the pre-Fall creation. Using Eden
as a model, they worked to return society to the original "government of
God," an ideal order in which human institutions were unnecessary
because regenerate individuals would spontaneously know and obey
God.

Though the advocates of peace might debate the details, underlying
their visions was a common understanding that God called and expected
each individual to be radically committed to constructing a holy society.
Notions of disinterested benevolence, millennialism, and personal responsibility came together to form a theological worldview where individual sanctification and social service went hand in hand. As they
measured the distance between their present surroundings and the
godly society they sought, however, the peace reformers found themselves disagreeing over just how much needed to be changed. The
sectarian nonresistants wanted to turn the world upside down, whereas
the cultural Christians of the American Peace Society were content to
fine tune it.

Nevertheless, in their peace advocacy the two groups appealed to a common ethical insight: the conviction that God called the peace re-former to practice peace without regard for the consequences. No matter what evil the world dealt them, they were determined not to return evil. Simply by being faithful to the love ethic of Jesus, they trusted that they would be effective witnesses for the gospel of peace. By 1861, however, the nation was moving into war, choosing violence rather than love to settle the political and moral issues of the day. In reaction, both groups elected to temper their ethic of love with an ethic of coercion. Separated by temperament, the American Peace Society and the nonresistants paradoxically became tied by a common impulse to subordinate their witness for peace in order, through violent means, to create social conditions conducive to peace. The genteel cultural Christians of the American Peace Society and the radical anarchists of the New England Non-Resistance Society at last met on common ground after the bombardment of Fort Sumter.

Admittedly, many Americans were unconcerned about the dilemmas the friends of peace faced. The peace advocates' struggles to think and act in a manner consistent with the gospel of peace were always the endeavor of an elite. The New England Non-Resistance Society was a tiny group. It met irregularly. Most people, North or South, barely knew it existed—though people in both sections certainly knew and con-demned the "no-government" and "come-outer" abolitionists who tirelessly strove to throw American society into turmoil. Without non-resistance to provide the philosophic underpinnings, radical aboli-tionists would never have been so extravagant. The members of the American Peace Society, on the other hand, hoped to work through institutional channels to persuade mainline Americans of the sensibility of their cause. They claimed to have reached hundreds of thousands, and it is true that many literate Americans of the period read something written by the American Peace Society. The society was constantly send-ing its journal to the clergy, scattering its pamphlets about passenger trains, and submitting short moral lessons on the horrors of war to the journals and newspapers of the day. The society's two- to three-para-graph newspaper articles were, at times, so ubiquitous as to be un-avoidable. Welcome or not, the ideas of the advocates of peace were a part of the public consciousness.

Most Americans, however, remained uninterested in the technical debates that rocked the peace societies throughout the antebellum pe-riod. At times those debates were highly abstract and hopelessly cir-cular. Nevertheless, to discuss antebellum pacifists without reference to their ideas is to overlook something that the advocates of peace themselves considered immeasurably important. For the sake of their ideas, they were willing to create schisms, break friendships, suffer public ridicule, and even, on occasion, risk their lives. In studying their ideas, we take them on their own terms—we take them seriously in a way that they themselves would have recognized as significant. In studying their ideas, we come to understand the peace activists' consciousness as they chose to articulate and defend it. Certainly many factors other than theological ones were involved in the antebellum peace movements, but at the core was an impetus to seek peace because it was an idea whose millennial time had come.

In working for the millennial kingdom, both the American Peace Society and the nonresistants labored to follow Jesus without regard for the consequences. Each group struggled, in addition, to convert the world. They assumed the kingdom would come if they could just convince others to obey the Prince of Peace. Ultimately, events not only proved them wrong, but also revealed the tension between means and ends that plagued both groups from the start. These were pacifists confident both that their theology accurately depicted reality and that that theology rightly applied could change the world. By 1865, however, few people but the advocates of peace themselves found either of those assumptions convincing, and even their thinking had undergone significant modifications. To tell their story is to unfold those developments.

1

EARLY

ADVOCATES

OF

PEACE

In the year 1805 a young merchant journeying to Boston stopped at a tavern in Providence to spend the night. He carried a considerable sum of his own money, with which he intended to buy goods in Boston. As a favor to his bank, he also carried a bundle of its money to deposit in Boston. Since a number of robberies had occurred in the area, he was understandably nervous.

When he retired to his room for the night, however, he was not without protection. A Christian for five years, he had asked Christian friends whom he respected whether he should arm himself during his business travels. All agreed that it was his duty to do so. "I decided," he explained, "if it was duty, to arm effectually was also duty. I obtained large double barrel pistols, with a spring dagger. I exercised myself with my pistols until I became expert in suddenly discharging them. As I commenced travelling armed, I was constantly looking out for robbers." When he went to sleep for the night, David Low Dodge had already securely locked his door, examined his pistols, and placed them care-fully under his pillow.

As he slumbered, a packet ship landed in town, bringing many lodgers to the tavern. Forgetting that Dodge had already rented the room, the landlord jarred the door open, bursting the lock. Half asleep yet alarmed by his intruder, Dodge reached for his pistols. It was only "by a kind of providence I so far awoke as to recognize him by the light of his candle; by which means I just escaped taking his life. We were both frightened at the occurrence; and I do not know that I slept any more that night."

As he drove on to Boston the next day, Dodge found that the incident had disturbed more than his slumber. He could not cease wondering how God would have regarded him had he taken the innkeeper's life. Determined to study the matter by the light of revelation, Dodge ex-plored the role of armed self-defense in Christian tradition. What he found disturbed him. "When I turned to the spirit, and the examples of Christ, and the precepts of the Gospel," he explained, "they appeared against it; but when I turned to the theologians and moral philosophers, they generally appeared to favor it, except some of the early Christians, and those in the days of the Reformation, as Martin Luther, Erasmus, and a few others, until the times of the Moravians, Quakers, and some other denominations." He spoke with pious persons who argued in favor of self-defense, but he found their arguments unconvincing. Fre-quently they tried to prove their point by citing heroic persons—par-ticularly from the American Revolution—who had chosen to defend themselves or their country. Dodge was unconvinced, preferring "to test the question by Gospel authority" rather than by appealing to the char-acter of those who had resorted to armed defense. Others appealed to supposed consequences asking, "shall we stand still and let assassins into our houses, and let them murder ourselves and families?" Dodge rejected that reasoning, answering that Christians must trust in God's promises to protect them. Obeying Jesus' command not to resist evil with evil, they must give up their weapons and proceed upon faith alone.

Following his own advice, Dodge laid aside his pistols. He pursued the issue no further until 1808, when an attack of spotted fever laid him so low that his physician advised him he was dying. Once again, his thoughts turned to the problem of violence and Christian faith:

> When time appeared to be receding, and eternity opening with all its infinite importance, my mind being serene as the rising morning, this subject passed before it, when I had no more doubt, from the spirit and

example of Christ and the precepts of the Gospel, that all kinds of carnal warfare were unlawful for the followers of Christ, than I had of my own existence. At this solemn moment the Word of God appeared a reality; a sure foundation on which to rest my eternal hopes. From this period, my war spirit appeared to be crucified and slain; and I felt regret that I had not borne some more public testimony against it.[1]

From the moment of Dodge's recovery, the nineteenth-century American peace movement commenced.

Dodge was born on June 14, 1774, in Brooklyn, Connecticut, to a struggling farm family. His earliest childhood memories were of the Revolutionary War. Against his parents' wishes, both of his brothers enlisted in the colonial army, and both died in the war. Dodge recalled that one of them, William Earl, came home in 1778 on sick leave. He also remembered a Brooklyn farmer named John Baker, who declared that warfare was contrary to the gospel and who subsequently suffered the taunts of his neighbors that he was a coward or a Tory. When Baker was drafted in the autumn of 1779, he fled to the woods. His neighbors, however, pursued him "as hounds would a fox" and delivered him, bound hand and foot, to the troops at Providence. Somehow Baker was able to cut himself free during the night. He hastened back to Brooklyn, where he spent the winter hiding in the woods, frightened even to light a fire to warm himself. No one but Baker's brother and Dodge's parents knew that he had returned. David remembered being terrified that "wild Indians" were attacking one day when he inadvertently discovered Baker sneaking up to the Dodge farm house, where Dodge's mother provided him food and clothing.[2]

Despite these experiences, Dodge did not become a pacifist in his youth. In 1792, when he was a few months underage, he received his parents' permission to join a company of grenadiers in Hampton, Connecticut, and later he served without objection in the state militia. In June of 1798 he married Sarah Cleveland, whose father, Aaron, was a Congregational minister later known for his opposition to slavery. After discussions with his father-in-law, as well as after reading Jonathan Edwards, Samuel Hopkins, and Joseph Bellamy, Dodge experienced a religious conversion. He also became involved in the dry goods trade and was soon prospering economically. In 1805 he had his memorable meeting with the Providence innkeeper and turned his thoughts toward peace.[3]

By 1808, Dodge was a partner in the Boston dry goods firm of Higginson, Dodge, and Company and had moved to New York City to open his own branch office.[4] An active Presbyterian layperson, in that same year he gathered a number of "earnest and evangelical spirits" at his house. Calling itself a "Christian Society for the Promotion of Morals and Religion," the group distributed tracts and Bibles, and provided the organizational foundation from which the New York Bible Society and New York Tract Society would emerge.[5] It was from this group that Dodge would also recruit members for the New York Peace Society, the first peace society in America.

Dodge made his peace sentiments public in the spring of 1809 when he published *The Mediator's Kingdom Not of This World: But Spiritual.* Within two weeks about two thousand copies sold.[6] The book's radical pacifism angered as many people as it intrigued. One historian writes that Manhattan congregations "sprang to arms, and in the name of the Nazarene poured execrations on the aristocratically poised and dark-haired head of the thirty-five-year-old dry goods merchant."[7] Three literary men, including a minister, attempted to refute him in a letter published as *The Duty of a Christian in a Trying Situation.* Dodge answered their protests in his 1810 *Remarks upon an Anonymous Letter* and then in 1812 published *War Inconsistent with the Religion of Jesus Christ.* Rumors that Dodge was a Quaker began to circulate, as some critics hoped to discredit his pacifism by attributing it to a fringe denomination. When the 1814 edition of the *Mediator's Kingdom* appeared, Dodge included a statement denying that he was a Friend. He continued to be active in the Presbyterian church, energetically engaged in the emerging benevolence empire. Between 1809 and 1812, he attempted to organize other evangelical Christians in his campaign against war, corresponding with leaders such as Lyman Beecher, John B. Romeyn, and Walter King.[8] By 1812 he had enlisted enough friends of peace to form a society.

Unfortunately, the imminence of war persuaded Dodge's supporters to postpone an official incorporation of their society. During the War of 1812 they concentrated on disseminating peace information as individuals rather than as a society. When the war finally ended, a group of about thirty men at last met together on August 16, 1815, to create the New York Peace Society. The society elected Dodge as its president, a post he would not relinquish for years. Future recruits, the society decided, must be members in good standing of evangelical churches and would be admitted only by unanimous vote. Though some in the group fell short of Dodge's absolute pacifism, Dodge himself was certain that the society ought to remain unswerving in its rigor. As he wrote in his autobiography,

Our object was not to form a popular society, but to depend, under God, upon individual personal effort, by conversation and circulating essays on the subject; and I remain fully satisfied to this day that this is the true gospel mode of procedure, and I am persuaded that other societies have abridged their usefulness by adopting a popular course, and confining their active services almost wholly to one object while neglecting other important duties.[9]

The "other societies" to which Dodge referred principally meant the Massachusetts Peace Society. Dodge was not the only person in 1815 who longed to form an organization dedicated to peace. Working independently of Dodge, Noah Worcester, a Unitarian minister in Massachusetts, was putting together a peace society in Boston. Born in 1758, Worcester had grown up on a farm in New Hampshire and received little formal education. In 1776 he joined the colonial army as a fifer and narrowly escaped capture at the Battle of Bunker Hill. His experiences in the army did not incline him to oppose militarism, though he did note with alarm that army life had hardened him emotionally. As a child, he said, "my sympathetic affections or passions were remarkably tender; so that I was easily moved to tears." After coming home from the army, however, he attended a funeral and "was shocked to find myself so changed and so unmoved."[10]

After the war Worcester married and worked as a farmer and part-time school teacher. He moved to Thornton, New Hampshire, in 1782, where he experienced conversion at the Congregational church pastored by the Rev. E. Estabrook. In response, Worcester adopted the theory of disinterested benevolence advocated by Samuel Hopkins, the noted disciple of Jonathan Edwards, resolving that "it is the duty of every Christian to seek for that situation in life in which he may probably be the most useful, or do the most good." Estabrook was a pacifist, and he loaned Worcester a book that "had a powerful influence on my mind" so that "I could no longer take pleasure in any thing of a military nature." After guiding himself through a course of theological studies, Worcester was ordained in the Congregational church in 1787. When asked to pray before local militia drills, he discovered that the popular dictum that the best way to prevent war was to be prepared for it no longer persuaded him. "In praying on such occasions," he said, "I ever felt deeply, that the business of war was horrible, and opposed to my own feelings as a christian." By 1810 Worcester was publishing works on the Trinity that were sympathetic to Unitarianism, and in 1813 he accepted a position as editor of the *Christian Disciple,* a monthly periodical for Unitarians.[11]

By the time he moved to the Boston vicinity to assume his new position, Worcester had already begun to put his peace principles into action. The War of 1812 was extremely unpopular in New England, at least in part because of the havoc it wrought in the Yankee shipping industry, but Worcester condemned the war on religious grounds. In 1812, while still a minister in New Hampshire, he had preached two sermons opposing the war, and then, on the day appointed by President Madison for national fasting, he had refused to pray for the success of American arms. Instead, he gave a sermon lauding Abraham and Lot for settling their differences peaceably. By 1814 he was so convinced that war was "the effect of delusion, totally repugnant to the Christian religion, and wholly unnecessary" that he wrote a book to that effect called *A Solemn Review of the Custom of War.*[12] Unable to find a publisher to produce such a book while the war with England raged, Worcester covered half the costs out of his own pocket. The book became one of the most influential works of the peace movement. In May of 1815, at his own expense, he began publishing a quarterly journal called *The Friend of Peace.*[13]

Worcester managed to persuade a number of Christians to join together on December 28, 1815, to create the Massachusetts Peace Society. Some of the members were influential. William Phillips, the governor of the state, served as president, and other members included Thomas Dawes, a deacon at the Old South Church and a judge; Joshua P. Blanchard, an affluent Boston merchant; Abiel Holmes, father of Oliver Wendell Holmes; Henry Ware, professor at Andover Academy; and William Ellery Channing, one of the most famous clergymen in the nation.[14] From its inception, the Massachusetts Peace Society was more lax than Dodge's organization. Its first publication—a circular letter containing the society's constitution—argued that Christians could work together to overcome the spirit of war even if they disagreed about the right of self-defense. "We intend," the constitution explained, "that this society shall be established on principles so broad, as to embrace the friends of peace who differ on this as well as on other subjects."[15] The Massachusetts Peace Society sought to enlist the aid of anyone who opposed any aspect of war for any reason. It never made opposition to defensive war and self-defense either a prerequisite for membership or an object of its platform. From the first, radicals like Dodge found its philosophy of peace reform lacking in gospel rigor.

Neither of the peace societies took the public by storm. Quakers lent support, but this was a period of theological dispute and schism for the Friends. Divided among themselves over the Hicksite controversy and suspicious that the peace societies were too secular for their liking, the

Friends never played a significant role in the antebellum peace movement.[16] Commenting ruefully on the apathy the cause of peace had
encountered, Thomas Dawes noted in an address to the Massachusetts
Peace Society on its second anniversary, "It has been triumphantly
enquired why we do not found a society to regulate the winds: as if the
phenomena of nature were as much within our control as our moral
propensities."[17] Nevertheless, of the two societies the Massachusetts
Peace Society was by far the more influential. Though never wealthy or
teeming with members, it did send missionaries to start auxiliary societies in neighboring communities and states. Through the influence of
Worcester's literature, by 1817 four branch societies had been established
in Ohio, and there were hopes of starting a society in Indiana.[18] Though
the majority of the members of the Massachusetts Peace Society always
lived within twenty miles of Boston, by 1823 the society had established
nineteen auxiliaries in Massachusetts, at least four in New Hampshire,
two in Connecticut, and one in Nova Scotia.[19]

Both the New York Peace Society and the Massachusetts Peace Society
attracted professional people, particularly from the clergy. Peter Brock
described the membership of the New York Peace Society as "eminently
respectable, decidedly bourgeois, with its Wall Street brokers, merchants and businessmen, clergymen and philanthropic gentlemen active
'in the most benevolent enterprises of the day.' " The membership of the
Massachusetts Peace Society was no less well-to-do. Clyde Winfield
McDonald, the only social historian to analyze an antebellum peace
society, has argued that the Massachusetts Peace Society was primarily a
"Federalist-clerical-mercantile organization." The society, he claimed,
consisted of greater Boston clergymen, merchants, bankers, and educators who not only belonged to the Federalist party but who also were
sympathetic to evangelical reform. The society established auxiliaries
primarily in coastal towns; where inland chapters existed, the members
were generally clergymen. The typical member was a middle-aged male
Protestant with a college education. The Congregational clergy was
especially active, but few of Boston's uppermost economic and political
leaders joined. Most of the leaders who did not join the society had
economic interests similar to those who did, prompting McDonald to
conclude that a blend of social, political, and religious motives determined which Federalists chose to belong to the Massachusetts Peace
Society.[20]

Until 1828 Noah Worcester edited the *Friend of Peace*, the official
journal of the society. Peace activist Frederick Holland recalled in his
1861 "History of the Peace-Cause" that the society's distribution of peace
literature was at best uneven: "Many parts even of N. England never saw

a peace tract during those thirteen years of Worcester's agency," he noted, "while, in Boston, the blue covered pamphlets were a drug, and Worcester's shelves groaned with printed sheets, many of which perished as waste paper."[21] The New York Peace Society, however, had no journal, no auxiliaries, and even less money than its Massachusetts counterpart. The New York Peace Society subscribed to two hundred copies of the *Friend of Peace* for several years but eventually found the cost prohibitive.[22] From 1823 on both societies lost members and money as the initial momentum generated by public reaction against an unpopular war dissipated. The Massachusetts Peace Society boasted one thousand members in 1818, but by 1822 it was in debt. The New York Peace Society found its existence to be even more precarious. From 1815 to 1828, it had enough money to print only two of its annual reports. By 1826 it listed only fifty-four subscribers, and its seventy-dollar indebtedness prompted it to appeal to the Friends for aid.[23]

Despite such difficulties, Dodge never reconciled himself to cooperating with the Massachusetts Peace Society. Yet most people regarded Noah Worcester as a saint. Samuel J. May, a Unitarian minister active in the peace and antislavery movements, remembered Worcester as "the most holy man I ever knew." Reflecting on the paltry annual contributions that the Massachusetts Peace Society managed to raise, Frederick Holland confessed that "the Society was made to hang its life upon the sublime poverty of this bravehearted Apostle—who, to publish his never praised periodical, was content to live on bread and water, make his own shoes, and deny himself most of those comforts which are to other men necessities. A more contented . . . exemplary life was never lived."[24] From 1815 until 1828, Worcester worked tirelessly on behalf of peace. He tempered his zeal with a personality so genial that admirers insisted that "he did not *fight* for peace. . . . He breathed the spirit which he inculcated."[25] In 1828, at age seventy, he resigned all of his offices so that new leaders could direct the movement. Holland's admiration was unbounded:

> Worcester's example is one of those many proofs with which our country abounds that no disadvantage of imperfect education, obscurity of position, destitution of means, lack of influential connections, unpopularity of opinions can keep a man down who wills to be up! that nothing else determines a man being remembered after he is gone so much as . . . the triumph with which he wins over every selfish motive and worldly consideration in promoting the real progress of the world.[26]

Even so, Dodge could not bring himself to approve of Worcester's work. He believed that Worcester had tried to correct Dodge's own radicalism in *The Mediator's Kingdom* by adopting a less rigorous approach in his *Solemn Review of War*. He fretted that the *Friend of Peace* not only drained the New York Peace Society's coffers, but also corrupted its membership:

> This publication not only involved the New York Peace Society in debt, but the lax doctrines advocated in it, decreased the zeal of our members. The investigation of the question upon secular principles turned away the thoughts of some of our members from the divine prohibition of war, to the mere question of its expedience and utility. Doubts began to arise whether, under the light of the gospel, its precepts were equally binding on nations as on individuals.[27]

In short, Dodge experienced the ambivalence about a moderate approach to pacifism that radical pacifists after him would face repeatedly as they tried to cooperate with less extreme advocates of peace. Such tensions would eventually split the movement, and the questions raised never ceased to create controversy.

More than anything, it was temperament that divided Dodge and Worcester. Though Worcester was moderate compared to Dodge, both Dodge and Worcester were exceedingly ambitious reformers. Each was a perfectionist. Each shared the notions of disinterested benevolence, millennialism, and personal responsibility that provided the theological background for antebellum religious reform. Each believed that the New Testament ethic of love made pacifism mandatory for Christians, regardless of the personal risks that might be involved. Nevertheless, like the more well-known peace activists who came after them, Worcester and Dodge disagreed on just how much distance lay between the present world order and the eschatological age to come. Worcester and other moderates who followed him found significant continuity between this world and the millennium. Christendom, in his mind, was basically sound, though it needed to mend its imperfections. Dodge, however, took the more radical position that the world was depraved and needed to be overturned before the millennium could begin. Like the radicals who came after him, he lacked the conciliatory nature and instinct for compromise that was characteristic of moderate peace activists.

From 1815 to the formation of the American Peace Society in 1828, then, the peace movement in America consisted of the activities of local peace societies. The debates waged during this period raised issues that peace advocates would continue to address until at least 1865. The principal positions later articulated in the nonresistant schism from the American Peace Society found spokespersons in the two key figures of this period: David Low Dodge and Noah Worcester. Like the later nonresistants, Dodge was impatient with Worcester's willingness to desert the high ground of radical pacifism. And like the moderates of the American Peace Society, Worcester was eager to establish an organization that could unite all the opponents of war in a common cause.

Nevertheless, despite their opposing temperaments, Dodge and Worcester shared a number of theological assumptions. Those common themes allowed them to join together in the American Peace Society in 1828. But behind those mutual theological understandings lay significant disagreements. Their distinctive personalities and predispositions led them, within a common theological framework, to develop interpretations of Scripture, the state, the nature of regeneration, and strategies of reform that diverged at significant points. Those disagreements foreshadowed the schism that eventually divided the nonresistants from the American Peace Society. Since many of the arguments were repeated over and over—never less heatedly for being redundant—in the next forty years, it is worthwhile to examine each position systematically.

David Low Dodge: Forerunner of the Nonresistant Position

The first advocate of peace to gain notoriety, Dodge articulated a number of theological positions that later nonresistant radicals would reiterate. Not all of his ideas, however, were controversial. Like all peace reformers, radical and moderate, his first priority was to obey the gospel of peace regardless of the consequences. Understanding peace as an absolute duty, he insisted that all moral persons, whether they were private individuals or corporate institutions, were bound by the gospel. There would be no "moral person, immoral society" distinction in the nineteenth-century peace movement. The advocates of peace insisted that the self-sacrificing love of the gospel ethic was possible for nations as well as institutions.

Dodge's exegesis of Scripture also struck a theme common in antebellum pacifism. In concord with other peace reformers, he contended that the gospel message of love abrogated the Old Testament tradition of holy wars. Thus, in explicating peace as a duty incumbent upon individuals and nations alike and in concluding that the New Testament's ethic of peace surpassed and replaced the holy war tradition of the prior dispensation, Dodge was unremarkable among the nineteenth-century peace workers. It was other aspects of his theology that made him distinctive—above all else the conviction that the Christian was a regenerated individual, ill at ease in the sinful environment of his or her culture, characterized the tone of Dodge's work. From Dodge onward, those sympathetic to the nonresistant position never failed to describe themselves as a regenerated minority determined to convert others through the strength and purity of their witness to peace.

This peculiar temperament of the distressed outsider allowed Dodge to share certain convictions with moderate peace reformers yet retain a separate identity. Fundamental to every peace reformer was a passionate conviction that Jesus had ordained an ethic of love that was incumbent on both individuals and nations. That ethic, Dodge was convinced, was none other than the ethic of the millennium. "The nature and precepts of the gospel," he asserted, "are the same now as they will be . . . in that glorious reign of righteousness and peace, and . . . it is our duty constantly to be influenced by the same spirit now which will then be manifested by the followers of the Lamb." To be true to the spirit of Christ meant acting by faith upon the promises of God; it meant being obedient without regard for the consequences. Christians, Dodge claimed, "ought to have nothing to do with consequences, but only duties. 'Thus saith the Lord,' should be their warrant and only guide."[28] That call to obedience made no distinctions between the behavior required of nations and that required of individuals. "These precepts of the gospel," Dodge insisted, "appear to be binding universally without any limitation. . . . It does not appear and cannot be shown that God has restricted the precepts of the gospel to individuals."[29]

In this formal description of Christian behavior as dutiful obedience to the millennium's ethic of love, Dodge and other peace reformers concurred. As Christians who regarded the Bible as authoritative, they also agreed that Scripture provided the specific content of that ethic. That conclusion was significant in that it ran counter to customary interpretations. American Christians had typically held to some form of just war theory, regarding wars as unfortunate yet inevitable and judging the righteousness of particular conflicts according to their goals, their consequences, and the means used to pursue them.[30] In 1815, for example, Alexander McLeod, minister of the Reformed Presbyterian Church of New York City, published a book defending the War of 1812 on the grounds that the Westminster Confession permitted Christians to make war on "just and necessary occasions." In fact, McLeod argued, it was sinful *not* to support a just war.[31]

In depicting the Bible as a book that commanded peace, then, the antebellum pacifists were advocating a novel interpretation. Admittedly Quakers, Mennonites, and Brethren had read the text similarly, but mainline Christians had often regarded the faith of the historic peace churches, in McLeod's words, as fanaticism, not religion.[32] Seeing God's hand in war—whether against the Native Americans or the British—was an American tradition. The peace reformers' insistence that Scripture forbade Christians to fight thus marked their exegesis as odd. In arguing, however, that believers ought to interpret the Bible not according to tradition or creed, but by their own reason, the advocates of peace had hit upon a method of interpretation that other groups would also use to argue against conventional understandings of the Christian message.

Since the eighteenth century, in fact, Unitarians had been using what they considered "free, impartial and diligent" examinations of Scripture as justification for rejecting orthodox doctrines—such as total depravity or the Trinity—that they found objectionable. When Worcester, in his last pastorate as a Congregational minister, became disenchanted with the orthodox doctrine of the Trinity, he wrote a book urging people to rise up from their "passive state of mind" to use the Bible in forming theological conclusions for themselves. "The scriptures were designed for the great mass of mankind," he insisted, "and are in general adapted to their capacities."[33] Having gone to the Scriptures to renounce the Trinity, Worcester turned to the Bible in his campaign against war as well. In 1816 he devoted two articles in the *Friend of Peace* to a critique of McLeod, complaining that in justifying war McLeod had altered all the precepts of Scripture.[34]

Unitarians were not alone in turning to Scripture for support against traditional theological authorities. Revivalists also claimed that the Bible was a book that ordinary people could interpret for themselves without the help or stricture of creeds. When Charles Finney experienced conversion and commenced his ministerial studies, he rejected the Westminster Confession and the doctrine of predestination taught by the Presbyterian church. Rather than preaching doctrines he could not believe, no matter how historic, he turned to the Bible and to his own mind. The theology he devised was democratic, rejecting the prevailing doctrine of the bondage of the will and arguing instead that anyone who chose salvation could receive it. Like Worcester and the Unitarians, Finney was convinced that his theology was "unequivocally taught in the Bible."[35]

It is easy to see, then, why the antebellum pacifists appealed to the Bible for authority in grounding their peace claims. Like other Americans who had been unhappy with historic doctrines, they could use the Bible to reject traditional teachings. Thus, Dodge in 1810 defended himself from his detractors by arguing: "The commands of the Gospel are *universally binding,* unless limited by some other precept. . . . Until it is proved, from the Scriptures, that destroying an enemy is inconsistent with forgiving him, we cannot admit the principle of war as a gospel doctrine."[36] Proving that Scripture commanded people to be peaceful, however, was not without its difficulties, particularly in light of the holy war tradition in the Old Testament. It was hard to argue that Jesus' words bidding his disciples not to resist evil with evil were the definitive statement of Scripture when gory stories of divinely ordained conquest and slaughter dotted the Old Testament. To overcome this difficulty, the advocates of peace argued that the age of holy wars was a bygone dispensation, abrogated by the gospel age of peace.

Dodge was the first peace reformer to use this argument. Defenders of defensive war had traditionally maintained that God was always moral. If God had once permitted warfare, they reasoned, then warfare must continue to be permissible.[37] Dodge granted that God's laws were moral but insisted that God intended some of those laws to be temporary. The Old Testament, Dodge said, was a literal and temporal dispensation that was a type of the New Testament age to come. As the New Testament replaced Old Testament practices like animal sacrifice with the pure worship of the risen Christ, so the spiritual armor and warfare of the new dispensation replaced the literal warfare of the patriarchal period. God had once commanded armies to fight in order to execute the divine vengeance; now God no longer commanded armies to do so. Therefore, Christians had no authority to fight. Rather, they were to obey the gospel ethic of the new and everlasting covenant. That ethic forbade returning evil for evil and demanded instead that Christians love their enemies and suffer persecution patiently. "It is sinful to exercise any affection towards enemies short of that benevolence or mercy that invokes the advancement of their best good," Dodge explained. And the willingness patiently to endure unjust treatment distinguished Christianity from all other religions and moral systems on earth. "The spirit of martyrdom," he said, "is the true spirit of Christianity. . . . The spirit of martyrdom is the crowning test of Christianity."[38]

Though the advocates of peace agreed that the New Testament dispensation abrogated that of the Old Testament, they were at odds over how to correlate Paul's claim in Romans 13 that God had ordained the magistrate to punish sinners with Jesus' words in the Sermon on the Mount that forbade returning evil for evil. Paul's discussion of the state had given Christians pause for centuries:

> Let every person be subject to the governing authorities. For there is no authority except from God, and those that exist have been instituted by

God. Therefore he who resists the authorities resists what God has appointed, and those who resist will incur judgement. For rulers are not a terror to good conduct, but to bad. Would you have no fear of him who is in authority? Then do what is good, and you will receive his approval, for he is God's servant for your good. But if you do what is wrong, be afraid, for he does not bear the sword in vain; he is the servant of God to execute his wrath on wrongdoers. (RSV)

Moderates, along with most Christians who had ever read that passage, believed that God had mandated the state to maintain law and order. The magistrate's power to punish the wrongdoer, they argued, came from God and must be valued as highly as Jesus' command to love one's enemies. When the state demanded obedience from citizens or punished criminals, it was not declaring war on them. It was simply creating social conditions that allowed persons to live in peace with one another. The moderates, in short, refused to define the state's power to govern as a form of violence prohibited by the gospel. As William Ellery Channing noted in a sermon to the Congregational ministers of Massachusetts in 1816, "the very end and office of government is to *resist* evil. For this the civil magistrate bears the sword; and he should beware of interpretations of Scripture which would lead him to bear it in vain."[39]

Dodge disagreed. For him, as well as for the nonresistants who came later, the Sermon on the Mount was the hermeneutical key to interpreting the New Testament. Jesus' command to love one's enemies and to return good for evil, Dodge insisted, prescribed an absolute rule of behavior. It limited the Romans 13 text, where Paul advised Christians to obey the magistrates because they were ordained of God. The gospel prohibited war in every form, and whenever the government asked Christians to do something—such as take up the sword in its defense—that the gospel forbade, Christians must obey God rather than the government. Scripture, he explained, "utterly forbids compliance with such commands as are inconsistent with the gospel." Thus, Dodge conceded that God ordained the state but denied that Christians were obliged to obey when it strayed from gospel precepts. "I would have it understood," he concluded, "that I consider every act of mankind which is palpably contrary to the spirit and precepts of the gospel criminal."[40]

In Dodge's view, obedience to the Sermon on the Mount entailed rejecting both offensive and defensive warfare. He noted that there were many reasons to condemn war. It was inhuman in that it abused the creation, oppressed the poor, snuffed out the youth of a nation, and turned soldiers' wives and children into grieving widows and orphans. War was also unwise in that it destroyed property, deprived soldiers of their civil liberties, and rarely if ever achieved the ends for which it was waged. But the primary reason that Christians must condemn all warfare was that it opposed the spirit of the gospel, which "absolutely requires the exercise of love, pity, and forgiveness, even to enemies." Both offensive wars and defensive wars required soldiers to kill one another. Thus, Dodge noted, "soldiers must be metamorphosed into something besides moral and accountable beings in order to prosecute war." The spirit of returning evil for evil, of seeking to harm one's neighbors rather than humbly enduring persecution and suffering at their hands, was a mockery of the gospel. Since soldiers in defensive wars tried just as hard to kill their enemies as soldiers of an aggressor nation did, Dodge refused to make a moral distinction between the two types of warfare. In his opinion, both were scandalously unfaithful to the example of Jesus, who accepted death rather than disobey the gospel of love.[41]

Once Dodge rejected defensive war on the grounds that it returned evil for evil, it was inevitable that he would reject personal self-defense as well. He did not rule out the possibility that a Christian might be able to run away from an attacker, but he did insist that Christians sinned if they used violence against an assailant. Returning evil for evil was always wrong, and it would be particularly bad to strike and possibly kill someone whose spiritual well-being was so deranged that he or she would seek to assault others in the first place. No one who cared for an assailant's salvation would be eager to send a soul in such a pathetic condition hurtling into eternity. And no one concerned for their own soul would want to face the day of judgment with murder on their conscience. It was, moreover, sinful to seek to injure an attacker when the believer should trust in God's providential care. "God's children are dear to him," Dodge argued. "He shields them by his protecting care, not suffering any event to befall them except such as shall be for his glory and their good." Occasionally, Dodge reasoned, God might call upon Christians to be martyred, just as in the days of the early church. In that instance, faithful believers could be certain that God honored their sacrifice. In any case, to answer an assailant with anything but nonresistant love would be to disobey the ethic of the kingdom, which refused to return evil with evil.[42]

Not surprisingly, many readers thought Dodge was crazy. Self-defense, they insisted, was a law of nature; how could Dodge ask people to be nonresistant in the face of horrible danger? "Shall we stand still and suffer an assassin to enter our houses without resistance and let him murder ourselves and our families?" they demanded. Dodge's answer was twofold. In the first place, he replied, the very form of the question revealed inappropriate ethical reasoning. Christians were to be obedient to the gospel because it was their duty to follow Jesus; they were not, as his questioners did, to choose their actions on the basis of presumed consequences. Second, he conceded that self-defense did seem to be a law of nature. It was, however, only the law of humanity's present corrupted nature. As God originally created it, the human race was not subject to violent passions. Only after the fall did violence and a concern for the self above others come to seem natural. Thus, Dodge contended, the so-called natural reflex of self-defense (or national defense) was only a sign of humanity's fallenness. [43]

If the spirit of war was a product of humanity's sinfulness, then the answer to the war spirit was the regenerating power of the Holy Spirit. Dodge did not believe, as more moderate peace reformers did, that humanity could turn away from war simply by deciding not to be violent any longer. Instead, because he regarded war as an outer expression of a fundamental spiritual flaw, he believed that only a resolution of humanity's sinfulness could answer the problem of war. Such a resolution required divine grace, not human will power. God, he contended, redeemed the church and set it apart as a peculiar people so that it might show forth God's praise. Its members were transformed by the renewing power of the Holy Spirit. Called apart to live in obedience to the gospel of love, they were citizens of the heavenly Zion, a "holy nation in the midst of a wicked and benighted world." [44]

If God had called Christians out of the world to be a holy people, Dodge was certain that they needed to separate from the work of government. Because he respected the witness of Scripture, he accepted Paul's declaration that government was ordained of God. But the state for Dodge could never be anything more than an institution of preservation. He conceded that God chose to use the state to contain sin and to establish a rough kind of order in society, but he denied that the state was a willing servant of the divine plan of redemption. "The Mediator's kingdom," he asserted, "is not of this world, but spiritual, heavenly, and divine." Dodge considered the church, "under the gospel dispensation," to be "in a special manner the kingdom of heaven," but he regarded the state as alien to that kingdom since the state operated according to an ethic of coercion rather than the gospel of love. At creation, Dodge argued, God had governed humanity directly. It was only because of the Fall that human beings came to have authority over one another, and the governments that emerged from the Fall worked to perpetuate their own glory rather than to serve God. [45]

For Dodge this meant that the state was opposed to the "mediator's kingdom," for the state deliberately chose to live by its own laws rather than by the gospel of love. Invoking the sectarian mindset that typified his worldview, he concluded that the state must therefore be at war with Christ—for if the state did not promote the kingdom, then it must oppose it. "If it is a fact," he said, "that the nature and laws of the Mediator's kingdom are diametrically opposite to the kingdoms of this world, then the inference is irresistible that the kingdoms of this world belong not to the kingdom of our Lord, but to the kingdom of Satan; and however unsavory the truth may be, it ought not be disguised." Because they were a redeemed and peculiar people, Dodge argued, Christians ought to avoid the political wranglings of the state, for "when they thus mingle with the world and unite in its pursuits, they may spiritually be styled adulterers."[46]

The answer, Dodge concluded, was to follow the example of the early church. "As virgins are pure and undefiled," he noted "so were the disciples of Christ in the first age of the church when they had not impure intercourse with the kingdoms of this world." Dodge was convinced that the church fell from its original purity when it failed to understand that it was a people called out from the world. In fact, whenever Christians forgot their peculiar calling, they ceased to be members of the Mediator's kingdom:

> It evidently appears . . . [that] that mystical Babylon, that mother of harlots and abominations of the earth, is just as extensive as the union of the church with the kingdoms of this world; and just in that proportion in which an individual Christian, or a single church, or a number of churches united in one body, engage in the honors, profits, and fightings of the kingdoms of this world, just in that proportion they may be said to be guilty of *spiritual whoredom*. . . . How inconsistent is it, then, for the citizens of the heavenly Zion to be mingling with the politicians of this world and uniting in their processions, feasts, and cabals, when they ought rather to be praying for them, that the very sins they commit in these scenes may be forgiven them!

To be true disciples of the gospel of peace, Christians must withdraw from the world, refusing to stain themselves by a political ethic that differed from Christ's example of vicarious love and sacrifice. Rather than ruling the world, the faithful Christian lived in readiness to be martyred by it. By thus offering an example of the redeemed community to a world sunk in sin, the church lived the life of the coming kingdom even in the present age.[47]

In delineating this position, Dodge set the tone for the radical peace reformers who would follow him. Like him, they would stress points characteristic of the nonresistant mindset—they would consider the

Sermon on the Mount the key to interpreting the New Testament, they would denounce all acts of violence, and they would urge Christians to separate from the state. By insisting that Christians were a people redeemed from the sinful world, Dodge expressed the temperament that would distinguish nonresistants from other peace reformers. Above all else, the conviction that Christians were regenerated persons called to separate themselves from the sinful world colored every theological judgment and strategy for action that the nonresistants devised.

Noah Worcester: Forerunner of the Moderate Position

The moderate position, as typified by Noah Worcester, could not have differed more in temperament. Though he agreed with Dodge that nations and individuals were duty-bound to obey the gospel of love and that the New Testament abrogated the Old Testament just war tradition, Worcester refused to imagine that Christianity and culture were at war with one another. Rather than regarding the Christian as a regenerated individual set in the midst of a depraved world, Worcester believed God had created the institutions of Christian civilization to work together to bring about the millennial age. For Worcester, the difference between Christians and other people was not that Christians were regenerated while the rest of the world was mired in sin. Rather, what set Christians apart from the world was that the gospel had educated them to reject coercion and violence and embrace Christ's ethic of love. The task of the peace reformer was to instruct those addicted to war of their error. Feeling at home in the world and trusting that God had designed Christian civilization as an instrument of the gospel, Worcester was confident that the church, working with the state, could inaugurate the millennial age.

As a result, Worcester's plan for implementing peace markedly differed from Dodge's. Because he regarded government as an order of creation and therefore viewed it as Christianity's partner in establishing the millennium, Worcester insisted that Romans 13 should balance the Sermon on the Mount, not be overruled by it. Because he trusted the state, he wanted to be sure that it was free to do its God-given work of establishing social order. Whereas Dodge was suspicious of institutions, preferring to speak of redeemed individuals separated from their culture, Worcester was certain that the work of the millennium—and thus the work of peace—would be accomplished with the aid of institutions. Therefore, instead of developing a strategy to achieve peace that focused on the nonresistant individual, he concentrated instead on institutional reforms. He proposed a Congress of Nations to adjudicate disputes between nations.

It was Worcester's moderate temperament that prompted him to define peace reform so differently than did Dodge. Since he did not assume that the world was divided into two groups—those of the Mediator's kingdom and those of the devil's—he felt free to work with anyone who was interested in the cause of peace. Reasoning that the problem of defensive war would never arise if he could persuade people to condemn national aggression, Worcester chose to focus his efforts on that issue. In the years to come, the moderates of the American Peace Society would invoke that strategy repeatedly.

As different as his personality was from Dodge's, Worcester nevertheless shared certain theological assumptions with him. The first was the conviction that both individuals and nations ought to obey the gospel of love, regardless of the consequences of that obedience. From the origin of society, Worcester argued, God had forbidden people to murder one another. The fact that millions of people now inhabited the earth and that they were loyal to different governments did nothing to alter God's original command. Whether they dealt with one another individually or corporately through governments, people were never justified in murdering one another in order to settle their disputes. "For what is modern warfare," he asked, "but a popular, refined and legalized mode of robbery, piracy and murder?" Moreover, Worcester noted, Christians ought not only to avoid murdering others; they ought to imitate Jesus' spirit of love and forbearance as well. "Fortitude to *suffer wrong*, to meet even death itself in the path of obedience to God, rather than to *do wrong*, to *avenge ourselves*, or to *render evil for evil*, is the valor recommended by the precepts and example of the Prince of Peace," he argued. Thus, the gospel bound individuals and their governments to imitate the pacifism of Jesus.[48]

Like Dodge, Worcester had to admit that all of Scripture did not forbid war. The holy wars of the Old Testament were occasions on which God had ordered the faithful to the battlefield, in stark contrast to the example of Jesus, who had died rather than defend himself or attack others. After perusing the Scriptures, Worcester came to the same conclusion that Dodge had offered—in the New Testament a new dispensation had begun in which God no longer commissioned faithful people to go to war. If God should order a nation to battle, it ought to obey, even as ancient Israel did, but under no other circumstances could any nation justify going to war. The fact was, Worcester insisted, that the age of the Mosaic covenant had ended and social conditions had changed. Just as no one considered making all the violations of the Mosaic code that called for death capital offenses, so no one should presume to argue that the holy war tradition continued to be a viable one. God had replaced it by a gospel of love that promised a messianic reign in which the nations would study war no more. Unhampered by depravity and empowered to live the life of the kingdom, Christians could, Worcester was confident, inaugurate the millennium through their own efforts.[49]

As convinced as he was that God expected the state, as well as individual Christians, to obey the gospel of love, Worcester did not agree with Dodge that the Sermon on the Mount was the sole hermeneutical key for interpreting the New Testament. Instead, he argued that Romans 13 must balance Matthew 5–7. By that Worcester meant that Jesus' command not to resist evil with evil should not be interpreted so as to deny the magistrate's responsibility to exercise the police function of the state. Critics of the peace societies had argued that Paul's claim that the magistrate "beareth not the sword in vain" gave the state the right to wage war. Worcester denied that reading of the text, answering that the magistrate's "sword" referred not to the power to wage war but to the state's obligation to punish refractory subjects for evil deeds. In private conduct and public policy, the magistrate was, like all Christians, bound to imitate the Prince of Peace. Under no circumstances could the magistrate initiate a war, but because God had ordained the state to establish order in society, the magistrate could not allow criminals to go unpunished.[50]

Worcester's distinction between the state's power to wage war and its power to preserve law and order within its own borders was significant. Both he and Dodge agreed that the state had no right under the gospel to initiate a war. Worcester's attitude toward the state's police function, however, was far more positive than Dodge's. Because of Romans 13, Dodge had to concede the magistrate's right to punish wrongdoers, but he demanded the abolition of all forms of vindictive punishment. "By vindictive," he said, "I mean what is intended to vindicate the law, as executing strict justice, and prevent offenses only, as taking away life, but which is not designed to promote the individual good of the person concerned." Even in its police function, Dodge wanted the state to adhere as closely as possible to the gospel of love. The state should not serve justice at the cost of mercy nor answer violence with violence. If it had to punish, it should seek to reform wrongdoers, not simply torment them.[51]

Worcester did not advocate the tormenting of criminals either. But neither did he share Dodge's ambivalence about the state's police function. The same Bible that condemned war mongering established the state's obligation to punish wrongdoers, and Worcester was content to leave the matter at that. His temperament was such that he trusted the state to do its work. Dodge, on the other hand, fretted that the state invariably established a temporal order disobedient to the gospel. He wanted more consistency; indeed, he wanted the ethic of love to regulate every social or political setting. As he wrote in his *Anonymous Letter,* "The *precepts of God* to the Church *now* extend not only to the regulation of *spiritual,* but *temporal* concerns. And it is the opinion of this writer, that there is no higher authority, and that the laws of the Church are *sufficient,* and *ought* to regulate all the conduct of its members, not only in *spiritual,* but *temporal* matters."[52]

It was typical of Worcester that his suggestions for reform were less radical than Dodge's. Dodge thought the world was hopelessly trapped in sin, and he directed his efforts for peace reform at those few individuals whom God's grace had regenerated. Worcester, however, thought that the world was basically good. He regarded war not as an expression of a horrible depravity that stained the human character, but as a regrettable custom that people had adopted out of ignorance. He denounced it as uncivilized and pagan, but he did not denounce its practitioners as servants of Satan. "To censure an *opinion* or a *custom* as hostile to Christianity is *one thing,*" he said. "To censure *all* as *ungodly men* who have been its advocates, or who have been deluded by it, is *another.*"[53]

Worcester was convinced that there was nothing about human nature that forced people to exhibit warlike behavior. Rather than attributing war to human sinfulness, he argued that it was the result of bad judgment and education. "Every man, whether good or bad," he noted, "is liable to be influenced by the customs of the age and country in which he receives his education."[54] Refuting Dodge's claim that nonresistance was a product of regeneration, Worcester answered that "the Quakers, Shakers and Moravians are of the same nature with other people. . . . All the difference between them and others results from education and habit." Because Western Christians lived in a culture that had ignored Christ's teachings on war, they had come to assume that war was consistent with the gospel. But, Worcester asserted, they would be quick to denounce war once the advocates of peace had demonstrated its incompatibility with the New Testament. After all, he concluded, "the custom of war *depends entirely on popular opinion;* and it will of course cease when it ceases to be popular."[55] Like the slave trade and excessive drinking, war was a habit that public opinion could abolish whenever it chose.

Worcester therefore viewed peace reform as a process of educating the public to abhor war. The goal of the peace reformer was to shape public opinion according to the gospel. Once people saw what was right, he believed, they would naturally want to do it. The point was to convince them that war was wrong. With that end in mind, he saw no need to get bogged down in debates over defensive wars and self-defense. The Massachusetts Peace Society deliberately established a broad platform, welcoming those who could oppose any aspect of the custom of war.[56]

Whereas Dodge's reform urged regenerated individuals to withdraw from the fallen state in order to lead lives of gospel perfection, Worcester's reform focused on institutions. Unlike Dodge, Worcester did not distrust the state. Nor did he regard the church as hopelessly fallen since the time of Constantine. He regarded the state as an order of creation ordained by God to aid in the development of Christian citizens, and he urged the church to "apply" the gospel specifically to the cause of peace so that the state and its citizens could amend their behavior. Worcester's most famous contribution to pacifist thought was his suggestion for the formation of a Congress and Court of Nations. Reasoning that governments did a good job of maintaining internal order, he argued that an international governing body, with an international court of equity to aid it, could create the same social order among nations that individual governments already provided their own citizens. With no reason to go to war, nations would no longer do so, and the millennial age, "effected by the blessing of God on the benevolent exertions of enlightened men," would draw nigh.[57]

In this plan, Worcester articulated a strategy for peace reform and an appreciation of Christian institutions that became characteristic of the American Peace Society. If Dodge was a distressed outsider encouraging nonresistants to withdraw from the sinful society around them, Worcester was the confident Christian, at home in his culture and optimistic about the human capacity to accomplish good. Both Dodge and Worcester expected nations and individuals to obey the New Testament of love; both agreed that that ethic required people to live in peace with one another; both were laboring to help inaugurate the millennium—but beyond that they agreed on little. Their temperaments were incompatible: one was a sectarian nonresistant, the other a cultural Christian. Their debates in the earliest days of the peace movement foreshadowed later disputes that repeatedly disrupted the movement. Peace reform attracted two distinctly different temperaments, and at no time would they be at peace with each other.

The Formation of the American Peace Society:
The Debate Continues

The earliest publications of the American Peace Society confirm this assertion. The formation of the society in 1828 demonstrated that peace reform continued to attract adherents, but uniting the advocates of peace into a central society did not unite them in opinion. From the first they divided into the two camps that the Dodge–Worcester debate had anticipated.

That the advocates of peace were able to unite at all was due to the untiring efforts of William Ladd. Born in 1778, Ladd graduated from Harvard at age twenty and went on to have a successful career as a sea captain. In 1801 the government of Spain gave him twenty-five acres in Florida for an agricultural experiment. Hoping to undermine the slavery system, Ladd imported free Dutch laborers to raise cotton on his land. The experiment failed—a contemporary complained that the Dutch workers were "sometimes lazy, always stupid"—and Ladd gave it up after five years. He retired from the sea in 1812 and settled on a farm in Minot, Maine. By 1819 he was planning to write for a religious journal on agriculture when he became acquainted with the cause of peace. He was present during the last hours of Rev. Jesse Appleton, president of Bowdoin College. Appleton, he said, "in his joyful anticipations of the growing improvement of the world, and the enumeration of the benevolent societies of the day, . . . gave a prominent place to *Peace Societies;* and this was almost the first time I ever heard of them." After Appleton's death, Ladd read Worcester's *Solemn Review.* From that point on, he claimed, "I felt it a duty, which I owe God and to my fellow-creatures, to do something to hasten the glorious era, when men shall learn war no more."[58]

Ladd took his duty seriously. An energetic man with an unfailing sense of humor, he was soon writing and traveling on behalf of peace. He composed a series of essays on peace for the *Christian Mirror* in 1823–26, wrote articles against the erection of the Bunker Hill monument (on the grounds that it glorified the spirit of war), spoke on innumerable occasions (including the 1825 annual address to the Massachusetts Peace Society), and corresponded with Europeans interested in peace.[59] Of the eleven new peace societies started in 1827, Ladd was the founder of six.[60] Heartened by the success of the London Peace Society in uniting into a central organization the various British peace groups that had started after the Napoleonic wars,[61] by 1827 he was also traveling the country in an effort to create a similar central society in this nation.

The exertions that would have exhausted the average person only exhilarated Ladd. "Conquerors and heroes (as the world calls them)," he wrote to Unitarian pastor Samuel J. May, founder of the active Windham County [Connecticut] Peace Society, "would be sick with envy at the happiness I experience in this cause—but they have no taste for benevolence."[62] In 1828, when the American Peace Society at last came into being, Ladd rejoiced at the success of his efforts and vowed to continue to devote himself to the cause. His health was not good, but he refused to heed friends' advice that he slow down and take care of himself. In 1833 he suffered a stroke. Unable to work for a number of months, he nonetheless overcame his infirmities and returned to the lecture circuit.

In the autumn of 1840, Ladd set out on a long-awaited tour of western Massachusetts and New York. In the course of his lectures, he visited the prison at Auburn, New York, and wept to see "six hundred and seventy human beings, as good by nature as myself, degraded to the condition of automatons." Niagara Falls disappointed him, though he thought that "had I stayed long enough, [the falls] would, perhaps, have equalled my imagination. But my journey here was not on account of any other fall than the fall of man, nor to examine any other rapids than the rapids of human passions, which have, ever since the fall of Adam, been hurrying men into the abyss of misery." The exertions of this tour took such a toll that he was forced at times to lecture sitting down and occasionally from his knees. When he died in March of 1841, a "martyr as well as an apostle" to the cause, the American Peace Society lost the man who had, from the beginning, been its driving force.[63]

In the course of his peace advocacy, Ladd employed a number of strategies, which he shared in an 1827 letter to Samuel J. May. Everything, he claimed, depended on changing public opinion. Ladd recommended newspaper essays as the easiest way to get recognition, since editors would print them for free. The next most efficient thing to do was to start peace societies. Ladd suggested getting an "influential character" for president and then creating as many offices as there were other influential characters to fill them. After forming societies, he noted, public addresses could be arranged; and, if any money had been raised along the way, tracts and periodicals could be published. Like all peace reformers, Ladd stressed that it was "of utmost importance to influence the minds of the rising generation." He hoped, as did many others, to teach children to deplore war rather than find it exciting or romantic. Accordingly he stressed that the task of educating the next generation to love peace fell especially to mothers.[64]

Ladd conceded that the American Peace Society did not appeal to everybody. Jacksonians, for instance, rarely responded favorably. Nor did peace activists think highly of Jacksonians. The Jacksonian party system, with what Lawrence Friedman has called its "secret bribes, coarse self-congratulation, and . . . evasion of fundamental moral problems,"[65] represented godless demagoguery to evangelical reformers. Andrew Jackson's reputation as a slave holder, a duelist, and a military man did nothing to endear him either to peace activists or abolitionists, who by 1830 identified Jacksonianism with racism and antiabolitionism.[66] The presence of Jacksonians among the peace reformers was unusual enough that, in April of 1828, Ladd noted that two of the seventeen new subscribers to the *Harbinger of Peace,* were "democratic Jackson men."[67]

Notwithstanding its limited appeal, the society did hope to garner popular support. In its literature, the society frequently appealed to the "common man," presenting war as an attempt by the elite to profit from the suffering of the average person. Nevertheless, few "common people" joined. Failing there, another strategy was to enroll influential persons in the society in the hopes that others would be impressed by the group's respectability. The American Peace Society also attempted to gain political influence by befriending state and federal officeholders. Its proficiency in enlisting the well educated and the well-to-do always outweighed its success in attracting common folk.[68]

When Ladd assumed leadership of the peace movement in 1828, his understanding of peace reform was compatible with Noah Worcester's. Like Worcester, he believed that the custom of war rested entirely on public opinion. As Christian nations rejected barbaric customs and embraced true Christianity, peace would become the order of the day.[69] Enamored by Worcester's idea of establishing a congress of nations, Ladd wrote an essay on the topic that became the standard in the field. The organization that Ladd helped create was similarly sympathetic to Worcester's brand of pacifism. The American Peace Society's constitution noted that "the object of the Society shall be to diffuse light respecting the evils of war, and the best means for effecting its abolition."[70] An organization with such a broad goal could include members of Dodge's persuasion, but it was not limited to those who denounced all forms of violence. Anybody who wanted to work against any aspect of war could join.

One of Ladd's first acts was to establish a journal for the society. Entitled the *Harbinger of Peace,* the publication reflected from its first issue the members' ambivalence about the appropriate goal of peace reform. The first issue contained a circular letter stating that the goal of the American Peace Society was to create a public disgust for war and a relish for peace. As an organization, the letter explained, the society did not "agitate" the question of defensive war. Though it condemned the "defensive" wars that Napoleon and Tamerlane claimed to have conducted, it was prepared to approve a defensive war carried out on Christian principles. The latter statement was ambiguous enough to mean anything—it could have meant, as Worcester had written, that "*no war can be just or necessary, except it be clearly required by God,* and consistent with the command, 'All things whatsoever ye would that men should do to you, do ye even so to them.' " Or the society might have meant that it accepted as legitimate any defensive war that met the relatively more lenient criteria traditionally asserted by just war theorists. In any case, the American Peace Society welcomed the aid of any who cared to help, hailing "as a brother" every human soul, regardless of color or creed.[71] Ladd noted in his "Prospectus" to the journal that the society had made no official statement on defensive wars and invited people to write articles debating the question.[72]

Under the theory that both radicals and moderates could unite to work against war as long as there was no formal policy to disagree about, the American Peace Society continued to avoid making an official statement about defensive wars. For the next several years, that strategy worked. David Low Dodge presided over the society's first annual meeting in 1829, and the *Harbinger of Peace* ran articles advocating a variety of views of defensive war. American Peace Society members included a number of military men, as well as political officials.[73] In May of 1831, the society changed the name of its journal to the *Calumet*.[74] Once again, the society's journal ran articles expressing varying opinions of defensive wars. And the society's fourth annual report reiterated its deliberately ambiguous stance by noting that, although the society did not officially oppose defensive wars, it would have to *see* a defensive war conducted on Christian principles before it could approve it. Not, the society added, that it was suggesting that such a thing was possible—or impossible.[75]

It was impossible, however, to avoid controversy forever. In the spring of 1831, the relatively radical Windham County Peace Society of Connecticut had distributed a thousand copies of a pamphlet by Jonathan Dymond, a British Quaker, entitled *The Applicability of the Pacific Principles of the New Testament to the Conduct of States*.[76] An absolute nonresistant, Dymond's persuasive prose excited pacifists sympathetic to his radical position. It also converted Thomas Grimke, a South Carolinian who had been a member of the American Peace Society from its inception.[77] Grimke was a Yale graduate, a senator in the South Carolina legislature, and a distinguished plantation owner (not to mention the brother of Angelina and Sarah Grimke, who later became famous in the antislavery movement and the women's movement). He was involved in a number of reform activities, such that historian Gilbert Barnes described him as "one of the most famous of the rulers of the benevolent empire." To celebrate its first anniversary, the Connecticut Peace Society (an American Peace Society affiliate) invited him to deliver an address in New Haven on May 6, 1832. When the audience gathered at Center Church that night, it included numerous members of the Connecticut legislature, as well as other state dignitaries. None was prepared for the bombshell he dropped upon them.[78]

Grimke began his address by contrasting the spirit of Christianity with the warlike ethic of the classical age. He asked why young Christians should be educated through the study of ancient texts that celebrated the cult of militarism when the Bible so clearly taught a different ethic.[79] Anticipating later pacifists who would applaud the virtues of free trade, he pointed to commerce as a practice essentially peaceful since it created bonds of mutual dependence and interest between nations. Finally he stated the unequivocal message that shocked his audience. "War," he said, "in any shape, from any motive, and carried on in any mode, is utterly indefensible on Christian principles and utterly irreconcilable with a Christian spirit."[80] Warming to his task, Grimke declared,

> Let the heathen take arms against each other and even against us, but come what may, Christians never will bear arms against each other or against them . . . Let the heathen rule us . . . Let them insult, persecute, oppress, slay us. Let them confiscate property, slander character. . . . Let them separate husband and wife, parent and child; let them seduce the brother to betray the brother . . . Let them poison the comfort and happiness of private and social life; and heap on us all the enormities and cruelties that malice can suggest and tyranny execute. Still we will bear it all, nor shall the sword ever be employed to deliver, much less to avenge us . . . Cost what it may, we will return good for evil.[81]

Finally, if that were not enough, Grimke ended his address by condemning the American Revolution not only as unchristian, but also as unnecessary, since determined nonviolent resistance could have achieved political independence without the loss of life. From the time of Dodge onward, advocates of peace had known that the touchiest subject of all was the Revolution—Americans regarded it as a sacred battle for liberty.[82] If Grimke had been looking to stir up trouble, he had come to the right place.

And trouble was not long in coming. Grimke was not the first peace reformer to condemn all warfare, but the American Peace Society had been cultivating a noncontroversial image since its inception. Before his May 6th speech, no one had even known that Grimke had converted to radical pacifism. When the distinguished Connecticut audience settled back to listen to its speaker—a Yale man, after all, a successful lawyer and a wealthy slave owner—they did not anticipate such radicalism. Certainly they had no idea that this member of the society of Cincinnati would denounce the Revolution, a war that Grimke himself had praised in a Fourth of July oration in 1809. And not surprisingly many of them did not like what they heard. Most of the society's members were not ready to condemn all war, and the Connecticut state legislature was assuredly not ready to do so. Consequently, Grimke found that the society was divided over his address, while the general public ridiculed it.[83]

Grimke soon came upon more troubles. Eighteen thirty-two was the year of the nullification crisis in South Carolina, and anticipating the possibility of fighting between federal troops and the state militia, Grimke petitioned the South Carolina legislature for an exemption from military service. Since he was forty-seven years old, it was unlikely that he would have been called upon to fight, but Grimke wanted to make a point. "It is the duty of the American family, and their safety and happiness demand it, *that the sword never should be drawn among themselves*," he insisted. "Let them resolve inflexibly, that this shall be the GREAT LAW of their social compact: that the law of violence and blood shall be forever blotted out from the tables of their Law and the Golden Rule of love, the test of a Christian People . . . shall be written there in its stead."[84]

The legislature denied Grimke's request for exemption, and the people of South Carolina turned upon him with disgust. One of the most hated men in the state, he found angry South Carolinians threatening to attack his house.[85] Indeed, Grimke's apparent disloyalty to the Southern cause in the nullification struggle highlighted for many Southerners what they had already suspected: that the peace crusade was tied to Northern interests. From the start of the movement, peace societies had had their greatest success in the Northeast. Peace societies had existed in the West (especially in Ohio) and in the South (particularly in Georgia and North Carolina), but the Southern societies had never flourished. After the Grimke debacle, the South was lost to the advocates of peace.[86]

Southerners were not the only people unhappy with Grimke. After reporting Grimke's speech, the *Calumet* ran articles from subscribers debating the merits of nonresistance, but it was in William Allen, president of Bowdoin College, that the champions of defensive war found a leader. He wrote two articles entitled "Defensive War Vindicated" in the first half of 1834 to refute Grimke. His logic was twofold. First, he denied that Grimke could prove that the early church had in fact been nonresistant. Second, he argued that "I maintain the right of defensive war on the principle, that the magistrate may use the sword against evil doers, and that he is bound to protect the community against the attack of robbers, and armed assaulters and murderers." Of course, he added, individual Christians would be nonresistant in their private lives, but the magistrate's public duty required the maintenance of civil order. Thus, to believe that defensive war was lawful was not opposed to the promotion of universal peace. Besides, Allen asked, if the magistrate could (according to Romans 13) put a murderer to death, why was the magistrate not also required to beat back an invading army? And was Mr. Grimke prepared to surrender Charleston to bloodthirsty pirates should they invade?[87]

By the time the *Calumet* could publish Grimke's reply, he was dead, the victim of an untimely illness. But the answers he had penned to Allen before his death were coherent explications of his position. He began by asserting that the magistrate's responsibility to punish wrongdoers in no way proved that the magistrate had the right to execute murderers. The duty of the magistrate was to reform offenders, not kill them, for "life is not the property of society under the Christian system. It is the property of God." Moreover, the magistrate's responsibility to establish order within the community had no parallel in the international realm. There, no international law existed, nor any social compact among states, so it was pointless to pretend that the magistrate had some kind of mandate to enforce the law against aggressor nations. Finally, Grimke concluded, if a band of pirates invaded Charleston, he would throw open the city's gate and meet them with the clergy and the Sunday School. The city would be theirs for the taking, with only the presence of nonresistant Christian love to dissuade them.[88]

Such an answer typified the differences in temperament and theological interpretation present among the peace reformers from the start. Grimke was doing no more than expanding on the position that Dodge had set out, and, similarly, Allen was reasoning along the lines that Worcester had earlier suggested. For the first time since the formation of the American Peace Society, however, the distinctions between radical and conservative peace reforms were being debated publicly. Grimke's New Haven address and his stance against nullification in South Carolina had ensured that reaction to his views on peace would not be limited to the pages of the *Calumet*. Members of the American Peace Society disagreed among themselves on the Grimke–Allen debate, and reformers outside the society—particularly abolitionists—began to show interest in the society because of the controversy that Grimke had raised. As more people were attracted to the radical position, the moderates retrenched and became more conservative. As a result, dissension increased within the society until it at last split in two in 1838. Though members regretted the schism, no one was surprised, for the grounds of division had been present all along. The descendants of Dodge's sectarian temperament would go one way, while the followers of Worcester's cultural Christianity would go another.

2

SCHISM

By 1837 those opposed to all war came close to capturing the American Peace Society. Tired of the apathy that had greeted the society's work since its formation, William Ladd was ready to advocate a more radical public stance. But he was not prepared to alienate possible sympathizers by wedding unpopular "extraneous" issues to the cause of peace. As he wrote to William Lloyd Garrison in 1838, "I believe that *all* war is contrary to the spirit of the gospel. I also believe that capital punishment should be abolished in civilized and Christian countries. But I do not believe that it is necessary or proper to attach this question to the cause of peace, any more than to the temperance or antislavery question."[1] That Ladd was writing Garrison at all indicated that the constituency of the American Peace Society had changed. From the first editions of Garrison's *Liberator* in 1831, the radical abolitionist had linked the gospel of peace with the gospel of liberty.[2] The *Liberator* abounded with antiwar articles.

The Garrisonians were a different breed from the moderate, respectable persons who had typically joined the society. They blended religious perfectionism with a missionary zeal that demanded that their culture forsake sin and be regenerated. At the same time Ladd was writing conciliatory letters to Garrison, Garrison was sending the following advice to his friends:

> Do not make the American Peace Society and its auxiliaries, your pattern. They are radically defective in principle, and based upon the sand; and, in my opinion, will do as much towards suppressing the spirit of violence among men, as the Colonization Society will do in abolishing prejudice and slavery—that is to say, they are mischievous, instead of being beneficial, because they occupy the ground without being able to effect the object. What a farce it is to see a Peace Society enrolling upon its list of members, not converted, but belligerous commands-in-chief, generals, colonels, majors, corporals, and all! What a wonderful reform may be expected where there are none to be reformed! . . . You have no body to reform, friend Ladd. Be assured that, until you occupy other ground—until your cause is honored with lynch law, a coat of tar and feathers, brickbats and rotten eggs—no radical *reform* can take place, to the ushering in of that period when "swords shall be beaten into ploughshares and spears into pruning-hooks, and men shall not *learn war* any more."[3]

In September of 1838 the nonresistants left the American Peace Society and held a convention to form their own group, the New England Non-Resistant Society. Many American Peace Society members attended the convention, but most walked out in horror after the new organization decided to allow women to join as full members. This violation of "woman's sphere," the custom that assumed women should confine their activities to the home, where they could be most effective in Christianizing their menfolk, was only the first of many radical measures the convention would oversee. Ladd gamely stayed till the end and tried to view the new group in the most favorable light:

> If the American Peace Society are called ultra for adopting the principle that *all* war is contrary to the gospel, the new society must be called ultra beyond ultra. . . . I fully agree with many of their sentiments, and bid them Godspeed so far as they follow Christ. . . . I consider the new society as ultra high; but almost the whole world are ultra low on this subject, and if I must choose between the two ultras, give me the ultra high one; for I have always found it more easy to come down to the truth, than to come up to it.[4]

Garrison, on the other hand, exulted in the convention's outlandishness. He excitedly described its events to his wife:

In the afternoon, a committee of nine was appointed to draw up a Constitution and a Declaration of Sentiments, of which I was chairman. I first wrote the Constitution, radical in all things, and presented it without delay. . . . Yesterday forenoon . . . I [then] absented myself to write the Declaration. In the afternoon, it was reported to the Convention, and never was a more "fanatical" or "disorganizing" instrument penned by man. It swept the whole surface of society, and upturned a deep and lively sensation, and a very long and critical debate; and, to my astonishment, was adopted by those present, by a vote of more than 5 to 1. . . . It will make a tremendous stir, not only in this country, but, in time, throughout the world. . . . By this procedure, your husband will have subjected himself afresh to the scorn, hatred and persecution of an ungodly world; but my trust is in the God of Jacob. I know that the sentiments of the Declaration are of God, and must prevail.[5]

Garrison was hard to work with, even for his friends, and Ladd was not part of his inner circle. Most of the American Peace Society was glad to see him go in 1838, and by 1840, even Ladd had given up on him. Before attending the nonresistant society's convention in 1840, Ladd remarked,

If I were asked if the non-resistant society were more likely to do good than hurt? I should answer, not much of either. . . . I do not think the society will ever produce any great effect. When they began, they thought they were as ultra as possible; but the convention to be called will go beyond them, and they will start off together in a tangent, from this sublunary sphere, and will either explode, or be lost in the limbo of vanity, among gone-by chimeras and abortions, and the odd ends and bits of creation.[6]

Up until 1838 the American Peace Society had been able to accommodate a variety of views, but the nonresistant schism permanently divided the nonresistants from the more moderate reformers. By 1840 Ladd and others loyal to the society regarded the nonresistants as absurdly unrealistic, while the nonresistants characterized the society as stodgy, half-hearted, and timid. The uneasy alliance that dated back to the early days of Dodge and Worcester had at last shattered.

The second half of the 1830s was a chaotic period for the American Peace Society. It was in the thirties for the first time that people outside the group began to take interest in its activities. In 1832 the society introduced the plan of asking ministers to devote the Sunday before or after Christmas to a sermon on war and peace. In 1833 only sixty-seven ministers had pledged to do so, but by 1838 the number had risen to a thousand.[7] Ministerial associations and church conferences were also getting into the act. In 1833 the Conference of Baptist Ministers of Massachusetts declared all war inconsistent with the gospel and urged the formation of a Congress of Nations. The New England Conference of the Methodist Episcopal Church passed a similar resolution that year, and the General Conference of Congregational Churches of Maine recommended a statewide day of prayer for peace.[8]

By 1837 such resolutions had become commonplace, and George Beckwith, the society's general agent, reported that he had easy access to the pulpits and Sunday School classes of nine denominations. Nine out of ten New England congregations, he claimed, regarded the cause of peace as "a distinct department of Christian benevolence," and he believed that the fifty articles he had written the previous year had reached two to three hundred thousand readers.[9] Moreover, in 1837 the Massachusetts state legislature responded to repeated American Peace Society petitions by passing a resolution calling for the formation of a Congress of Nations and the inclusion of a clause requiring arbitration as the basis of every international treaty. The society even managed to send a similar petition, with 1,500 signatures, to Congress.[10]

Despite all this activity, the inner life of the society was anything but settled. Ladd published two issues of the *Calumet* in 1835, only to give voice to Grimke's answer to Allen. After that he retired from editorial work, and the society turned to William Watson of the Connecticut Peace Society, who had started the *American Advocate of Peace* as a rival to the *Calumet* in 1834.[11] Watson moved the society from New York to Hartford. His sudden death in the autumn of 1836 upset everything; the society had to scramble to keep a journal going. Its first edition of the *Advocate of Peace* in June 1837 announced Watson's death and noted that the society had moved its headquarters from Hartford to Boston, "the focus of business, intelligence and religious influence to all that section of our country where the deepest interest has been taken in this cause."[12] The *Advocate's* June 1838 edition later admitted just how pressed the society had been. Without funds, subscribers, or pledged supporters, the society had managed to print two thousand copies of each edition over the year—and was able to distribute them "for the most part" among people who conceded to pay for them.[13]

Nevertheless, moving to a new city and producing a journal that had no subscribers was not the most unsettling event of 1837. Given the Garrisonians' interest in peace and the fallout from Thomas Grimke's relatively radical views, an increasing number of members had become convinced that it was time for the society publicly to renounce all warfare. At the 1837 annual meeting, such a group managed to amend the society's constitution so that it described "all war as contrary to the spirit of the gospel."[14] Unfortunately, that declaration satisfied no one. The nonresistants wanted to condemn self-defense as well, and the conservatives fretted both that Romans 13 had been compromised (because the magistrate was denied the right to defend the nation against attack) and that this new "ultra" constitution would scare away potential friends of the cause. In 1838 the nonresistants left to form the New England Non-Resistance Society, leaving the opponents of defensive war and those who wished only to condemn offensive wars to battle it out for control of the American Peace Society.

As a result, the differences in theology and temperament that had always distinguished the two factions of the American Peace Society at last split the organization. Though both factions agreed that the New Testament presented a gospel of love that nations and individuals were duty-bound to obey, regardless of the consquences, they were unable to reach a consensus about defensive wars, personal nonresistance, and the role of government. William Ladd and the revised constitution of 1837 attempted to devise a mediating position satisfactory to both sides, but this compromise failed. The grounds for schism had been present for twenty years, and though it was regrettable, it could hardly have been surprising when the division finally occurred. By Ladd's death in 1841, the peace movement had permanently divided into two camps: the sectarian radicals of the New England Non-Resistance Society and the champions of Christian civilization of the American Peace Society.

William Ladd and the Failure of Compromise

If anyone could have held the two factions together, it was William Ladd. The radicals liked him. In fact, Ladd had converted Garrison to pacifism in 1826 when Garrison attended one of Ladd's peace talks and was so impressed that he predicted Ladd was destined to be the leading philanthropist of the age.[15] Though Garrison worried that occasionally Ladd's remarks were "too funny, to produce a serious impression" and that his speeches were "more of anecdote than close argumentation," he respected Ladd's work enough to have dedicated a sonnet to him in the first volume of the *Liberator*.[16] And Frederick Holland—who denounced the society's record under George Beckwith, Ladd's successor, as "the period when the envenomed sectarianism of its Secretary consigned it to a slumber which will last with his life"—also had high regard for Ladd. Ladd, said Holland, was "one of whom we were not worthy—one as generous as he was prudent, as fervid as he was wise, as tenderhearted

as he was intrepid, as patient with opposition as he was hopeful, unselfish, enterprising, persistent."[17]

The regulars of the American Peace Society liked Ladd too. At Ladd's
death in 1841, George Beckwith confessed that "the fate of our cause
[has] seemed to rest on him alone. . . . His bosom was full of kindness,
and it was constantly flowing out upon all around him. . . . Not one
man in ten thousand would have prosecuted an enterprise, so little
appreciated, through so long, so unbroken a series of obstacles well nigh
insurmountable; but through them all he held on his way."[18] In spite of
Ladd's popularity, however, he was unable to hold the society together.
Indeed, every new strategy he devised served only to raise more trouble. When he continued to push the society's pet project of a Congress of
Nations, the nonresistants ridiculed him. When he was ready to ask the
society to take a clear stand against defensive wars, the conservatives
revolted against him. And when he tried to tone down the testimony of
the nonresistants so that they did not alienate the less radical friends of
peace, the nonresistants deserted him. Ladd was antiwar but progovernment—a stance that ought to have been attractive to many—but the
American Peace Society was in too much turmoil to rally around any
position.

Typical of Ladd's lot was the response that greeted his work for a
Congress of Nations. The society had from the beginning been committed to institutional peace reform, and the impetus for establishing a
Congress of Nations to adjudicate international disputes went back to
the sainted Worcester. The society sponsored essay contests on a Congress of Nations and corresponded with politicians who might be converted to the cause. When the Massachusetts legislature in 1837 called
for the formation of a Congress of Nations, it was a triumph for the
movement. No one was more active in promoting a Congress of Nations
than Ladd. His *Essay on a Congress of Nations,* which suggested creating a
Congress of Ambassadors to set international law and a Court of Nations
to administer it,[19] became the standard work in the field, and his tireless
lobbying on behalf of the scheme led to audiences with members of
Congress as well as with the president.[20] In 1840 he could even report
that John Quincy Adams had assured him in private conversations that
he expected to see a Congress of Nations established within his own
lifetime.[21]

Nevertheless, the Garrisonians mocked Ladd's work. At best, his
scheme for a Congress of Nations was an "inoffensive hobby . . . [that]
cannot effect much good"; at worst, it was a wrongheaded plan that gave
aid and comfort to the sinful governments that true peace reform ought

to seek to supplant, not strengthen. Besides, the nonresistants believed that social change occurred from the ground up. By making individuals peaceful, there was hope that their societies could become peaceful as well. But a reform that concentrated on the peace of nations, while "leaving *individuals* to hate and devour one another *ad libertum*, unrebuked and uncondemned," was a pitiful expression of the gospel of peace.[22]

At the same time that the nonresistants criticized Ladd for his stance on institutional peace reform, the conservatives were attacking him for his desire to amend the society's constitution so as to indicate opposition to all warfare. Ladd had not originally opposed defensive warfare, but he gradually came to occupy this "high ground." In his opinion, by 1837 the time had come to embrace, in imitation of the temperance movement, the "tee-total principle." Just as temperance societies had originally advocated moderation in drinking, he said, so had the American Peace Society first officially opposed only offensive warfare. In time, however, the temperance movement had chosen to oppose all drinking; so, too, ought the peace society to oppose all warfare.[23] Predictably, William Allen found Ladd's brand of pacifism as objectionable as he had found Thomas Grimke's. Ladd had only to turn to the *Advocate of Peace* to find a new letter from Allen attacking him; for further diversion, he could also leaf through the *Liberator* to find editorials deprecating the society's timidity.

Ironically, many of Allen's objections to the new position declaring all war contrary to the spirit of the gospel focused on his insistence that Ladd had thereby annihilated government. By denying the state the right of self-defense, Allen argued, Ladd had deprived it of the power to govern. External enemies could overrun it and internal criminals could destroy domestic order. Indeed, to follow Ladd's proclivities would meaning turning the American Peace Society into an anti–capital punishment organization.[24]

In actuality, of course, nothing could have been further from the truth. Ladd had no intention of linking opposition to capital punishment with peace reform,[25] and eliminating the police function of the state was unthinkable. Ladd advocated a Congress of Nations because he believed it would, by providing international laws and a regulatory agency, create a "police" and "legislative" force in the community of nations similar to those that already existed within the governments of Western countries. A Congress of Nations would do for the international scene what individual governments already did for their citizens: provide a framework of law and order that outlawed murder and robbery. Rather than annihilating government, such a reform perpetuated it.

Moreover, as the nonresistants knew all too well, Ladd's opposition to war was anything but a blanket approval for the more radical reforms that they were proposing. Ladd was not suggesting the repudiation of all violence or the abolition of capital punishment or withdrawal from the work of government. Indeed, when Henry Clarke Wright, one of Garrison's dearest friends, became an agent for the American Peace Society in 1836, he immediately found himself hampered by Ladd's cautious tactics. In July of that year Ladd wrote to him, saying,

> I have no objection, to your calling war sin against God in the pulpit. . . . What I mean is that you should preach against war generally & and not to specify *defensive* war unless you are asked. . . . Nor do I wish you to mix up with your public exercises the subject of capitol [sic] punishment . . . If you are asked your own private opinion give it, but do not implicate the American Peace Society as though they commissioned you to preach against capitol [sic] punishment or any other punishment.[26]

Ladd was pursuing a moderate reform. As in the case of Grimke before him, his opposition to defensive warfare startled the conservatives, yet they had no reason to fear that either Ladd or Grimke hoped to "annihilate" government. As adamant as Grimke had been in arguing for the inviolability of human life, he had never suggested that government was evil. Nor had he said that it was sinful for Christians to be involved in the work of the state. Rather, Grimke had argued that there was no office that the Christian "was not bound to fill, provided the taking of life be not one of its dutys [sic], or means to be employed."[27]

Ladd's plan for reform was equally respectful of government. If he had not approved of government, he could never have advocated a Congress of Nations. And the 1837 constitutional change did not even mention the issue of self-defense; it merely declared all war to be inconsistent with the gospel. Thus, the "high ground" of 1837 did not lead to a cliff so precipitous as the conservatives in the society feared. Capital punishment and self-defense—the nonresistants' favorite targets—went unmentioned, and the work of peace was confined to an institutional level. The revised constitution affirmed the work of the state at the same time it focused the work of peace on the task of reforming governments. Moreover, the society had no intention of using the revised constitution as a test or pledge for membership; all the friends of peace would continue to be welcome in the peace society, regardless of their stance on defensive wars.[28] Thus, following the path that Grimke had laid, Ladd devised a style of peace advocacy that mediated between the two extremes that had been present in the American Peace Society from the beginning. Like Worcester, Ladd concentrated on institutional reform, and like Dodge he repudiated all forms of war. Unlike Dodge, however, he did not advise Christians to withdraw from the work of government. Instead he urged them to reform the state from within.

Ladd hoped that this mediating position might give the society the note of stringency its conservative members needed at the same time that it tempered the demands of the nonresistants. He set forth an antiwar, progovernment position that admirers would repeatedly revive in the years to come. Yet such was the opposition between nonresistants and conservatives that Ladd's mediating work went for naught. The 1838 schism gave expression to the two distinctly different temperaments that had, for ten years, managed to work together within the society.

The New England Non-Resistance Society: Gadflies of Reform

There had been radical pacifists in the peace movement from the beginning, but there had never been anything quite like the Garrisonians. As historian John Demos remarked, nonresistance was a "prototype of nineteenth-century 'ultraism,' " involving "a kind of . . . either-or mentality" and a "penchant for following out a principle wheresoever it might lead."[29] Like David Low Dodge before them, the nonresistants understood a commitment to peace to be the result of the regenerating effects of God's spirit, and, like him, they believed that Christian nonresistants should refuse to participate in institutions that had not been regenerated. In that sense, they were sectarians. Dodge had hoped that Christian preaching and example would convert people to the cause of peace. The nonresistants shared that hope, but they developed a strategy for reform that aggressively confronted people with their sins and demanded that they change their ways. Dodge had never considered such tactics. In fact, he found them appalling. In 1838, he wrote a letter to the nonresistants, explaining,

> The principles of peace are not confined to withdrawing from the field of battle, or refusing to carry weapons of death: they extend to the thoughts and intents of the heart, are exhibited in private and public by a meek, kind, and benevolent deportment. However correctly we may theorise on this subject, we shall do more harm than good, unless the principles of peace are living and active in our private relations, in society, and especially toward our opponents. . . . Controversy is apt to stir up the spirit and return railing for railing.

Dodge closed his letter with a plea that the nonresistants temper their zeal to remove vice, reminding them that they were not clothed with the same authority as Christ and the apostles.[30]

The nonresistants, however, rejected all pleas for moderation. Reform was successful, they believed, when it confronted people with their errors and forced them to repent. Thus an organization like the American Peace Society, which went to any length to avoid controversy, was certain never to accomplish anything. As Garrison explained in an 1838 letter to William Ladd, the reformer was like a gadfly who buzzed around creating disturbances until finally people were moved to do something about it.

> You do not understand the philosophy of reform. If you would make progress, you must create opposition; if you would promote peace on earth, array the father against the son, and the mother against the daughter; if you would save your reputation, lose it. It is a gospel paradox, but nevertheless true—the more peaceable a man becomes, after the pattern of Christ, the more he is inclined to make a disturbance, to be aggressive, to "turn the world upside down." For the sake of quietude, he will make a noise. In order to induce men, "by the meekness and gentleness of Christ," to love one another, he will "get them by the ears," stir them up to wrath, and create a great tumult among them. It was so with the prophets, with Christ, with the apostles, with Luther and Calvin and Fox.[31]

His goal, Garrison explained, was to reconcile the human race, but because "there can be no peace without purity," he could not be gentle or mild until the American people were righteous before God. That righteousness would come through struggle, not through inoffensiveness or apathy.[32]

One thing was certain: the nonresistants were expert at creating controversy. The only peace reformers who viewed women as men's equals, their commitment to gender equality flowed from the perfectionism basic to nonresistant theology. Those attracted to the cause tended to be free spirits devoted to turning the world upside down. The structure of the New England Non-Resistance Society was remarkably loose, as its members considered nonresistance more a philosophy of life than an organization. Fearful of inhibiting freedom of thought, the nonresistants noted that even the society's Declaration of Sentiments was only an expression of the movement's spirit, not a delineation of its doctrines. Maria Weston Chapman explained in 1840 that the signers of the declaration were free to interpret it in any way they chose. "Forms of organization," Chapman advised, "are but trifles. The spirit is all." Nonresistance, she concluded, was founded upon "a sacred respect for the right of opinion."[33]

Though not all Garrisonians were nonresistants, most nonresistants were abolitionists devoted to Garrison. Lawrence J. Friedman has noted that the Garrisonians were troublemakers by design. Those attracted to

Garrison's cause tended to be "young insurgents" who had come to realize that the American Colonization Society, the original antislavery group, was racist. Rather than seeking to make American society biracial, it hoped to keep America white by shuttling blacks off to Liberia. Disillusioned by the "duplicity" of the colonization society, the young insurgents turned against it, attacking it with fury. In its place, they started their own clique, devoted to holiness and immediate abolition. Recognizing that their commitment to racial equality and their unusual fervor to abolish slavery set them apart from others, these abolitionists rallied around Garrison as their leader and built a close-knit group that served as a substitute for ordinary society.[34]

Important nonresistants included the irrepressible Henry Clarke Wright, who served as the nonresistance society's general agent; Lydia Maria Child, who equated nonresistance with the gospel but attended only one meeting of the society; Boston aristocrat Edmund Quincy, who, with Maria Weston Chapman, edited the first incarnation of the society's journal, the *Non-Resistant;* Stephen S. Foster and Abby Kelley, radical reformers who eventually married; Charles K. Whipple, the first treasurer of the society and one of the movement's notable authors; and Samuel J. May, a gentle Unitarian pastor who attended meetings and wrote articles for the cause yet could never bring himself to join the society.

Together they were a lively bunch. If Garrison was the father who welded them into a family, Maria Chapman was the one who provided the group sanctuary. Extraordinarily involved in abolitionist activities, she nevertheless seldom accepted out-of-town engagements. As a result, she was usually at home, and her house became a daily gathering place for Garrisonians to sip tea and share abolitionist gossip. A proud woman convinced of the righteousness of nonresistant abolitionism, Chapman seemed arrogant to outsiders, who occasionally sneered that Garrison was nothing but her front man. From 1835 onward, she took charge of the annual Boston Anti-Slavery Fair and produced a memorial volume of the *Liberty Bell* for each fair. One of the most successful abolitionist fundraisers, antislavery fairs offered believers the chance to purchase antislavery stationery, handkerchiefs, and even earthenware (in order to "silently preach abolitionism to their guests, and train up their children in sound principles, by the simple process of furnishing their tables").[35]

Lydia Maria Child was one of the most famous women of the antebellum period. A popular novelist who in 1826 began publishing *Juvenile Miscellany,* the first American children's magazine, she married David

Child in 1828. By 1832 the Childs were deeply involved in the abolitionist movement. Maria's 1833 *Appeal in Favor of That Class of Americans Called Africans* was such a biting critique of slavery and racism that it earned her social ostracism. Her book sales plummeted, and in 1836 she and David were forced to sell their Boston house. In 1838, hoping to prove that free labor could produce affordable goods, they moved to a Northampton swamp that doubled as a farm, determined to cultivate sugar beets. By 1841, Maria was sick of the drudgery. Leaving David on the farm, she accepted a job offer from Garrison, moving to New York City to be the editor of the *National Anti-Slavery Standard*. Though she and David lived apart until 1850, she became famous as an expert on domesticity. Uncomfortable with public controversy, Maria never enjoyed abolitionist meetings and preferred to practice nonresistance as a private individual, apart from the Non-Resistance Society.[36]

Stephen Foster and Abby Kelley Foster were an unforgettable pair. Stephen Foster was raised on a New Hampshire farm, and his temperament was evident from the following remark: "I should hate farming in the West; I should hate to put my spade into the ground where it did not hit against a rock." As a student at Dartmouth, he organized an antislavery society, and, in spite of student opposition to women speakers, invited Angelina Grimke to give an address. He was jailed while at Dartmouth for refusing to perform militia service, and he quit Union Theological Seminary in New York when he was denied permission to use a seminary room for antiwar prayer meetings. He served as an antislavery lecturer for a number of years, devising in 1841 a strategy that won him considerable attention. Each Sunday he attended a different church, rose during the service, and began an antislavery oration. Sometimes he was thrown out, and sometimes he was allowed to leave on his own power, but never was he ignored. His 1843 pamphlet, *The Brotherhood of Thieves: or a True Picture of the American Church and Clergy*, revealed his estimate of American Christianity.[37]

When Stephen Foster married in 1845, he joined his future to an equally colorful reformer. Abby Kelley had the distinction of causing stirs at a number of crucial benevolent society meetings. In 1838 she was the woman on the business committee whose call to order prompted George Beckwith and other moderates to walk out of the New England Non-Resistance Society's organizing convention. When she was granted a seat on the business committee of the American Anti-Slavery Society in 1840, Lewis Tappan and other more temperate immediatists left to form the American and Foreign Anti-Slavery Society. At the 1840 World Antislavery Convention in London, she was refused a seat, even though she was a member of the Massachusetts delegation. Great controversy arose, resulting in Garrison leaving his chair to sit in the gallery with the women. A Quaker who wore bloomers, Abby Kelley endured a stream of abuse both from the clergy and from mobs who disrupted the lectures that she dared to address to mixed audiences. Like Maria Chapman she was active in the women's movement as well as in abolitionism and nonresistance. In the first years of their marriage, Stephen stayed home, attending to the farm and to their child, while Abby continued to lecture. Eventually, they decided to lecture together and found much enjoyment in sharing the platform.[38]

One of the most important members of the society was not a member of the Garrisonian clique. Adin Ballou was a Universalist minister who credited the abolitionists with shaking him out of his complacency and lifting the "thick veil of reverent patriotism" that had blinded him to the evils of slavery and violence. Awakened to his social responsibilities by the spring of 1837, Ballou soon founded the Hopedale Community, a nonresistant Christian group dedicated to living the regenerate life in society with one another. In 1849, while he was serving as the "voluntary, unhired agent" of the Non-Resistance Society, Henry Clarke Wright established his headquarters at Hopedale, though he did not stay long. Ballou, however, proved to be the leading theoretician of the nonresistance movement. His *Christian Non-Resistance*—as well as another work entitled *Primitive Christianity and Its Corruptions*—were unrivalled. In addition to being its leading thinker, Ballou was also the nonresistant most committed to keeping nonresistance before the public's scrutiny. He was constantly reviving the society's journal.[39]

Ballou had a more irenic temperament than most. The Garrisonians' antislavery tactics were as upsetting to more moderate immediatists as the Garrisonians' antiwar tactics were to the American Peace Society. Moderate immediatists denounced slavery as a sin just as strongly as Garrison did, but they did not share his alienation from the larger culture. For them, American society was flawed, but not depraved. As Friedman has observed,

> Although all early immediatists shared certain ideas, values, and experiences, attitudinal diversity was detectable from the start. In some measure, at least, these differences derived from variation in missionary temperaments. Insurgents [Garrisonians] craved undefiled piety at all costs; untainted moral associations meant more to them than the camaraderie of Christian fellowship. Despite greater attitudinal variation among them, more temperate immediatists desperately desired the convivial mixing of benevolent missionaries even if this risked "taint" from the less than pious.[40]

Moderate immediatists simply did not share the sectarian instinct that typified the Garrisonians. Nor were they as eccentric. What with the women defying social conventions, the men disrupting churches, and the even more bizarre cases like Charles Calistus Burleigh, who with his unshorn hair, long beard, and flowing robes fancied himself an Old Testament prophet, the Garrisonians were countercultural by any standards. As James Brewer Stewart noted, "by 1838, it appeared to many in the movement and outside it as if abolitionism, extreme though it was, was about to be overrun by dreamers and cranks."[41]

Ultimately, it was the Garrisonians' perfectionism that split the antislavery movement as well as the peace movement. Antislavery immediatists directed their reforming activities through the American Anti-Slavery Society. Formed in 1833, this society was always an uneasy alliance between radicals and moderates. At its organizing convention, the delegates had chosen Arthur Tappan as president. They also located the society's headquarters in New York City, Tappan's home, and appointed his brother Lewis to the executive board. Clearly the Tappanite reformers had the leading hand, though Garrison, along with radical pacifists John Greenleaf Whittier and Samuel J. May, received the task of composing a Declaration of Sentiments. That document, which the convention unanimously voted to accept, pledged the American Anti-Slavery Society "to reject, and to entreat the oppressed to reject, the use of all carnal weapons for deliverance from bondage."[42]

That commitment to nonviolence united the immediatists for the next several years. Nonviolent abolitionism enjoyed its greatest growth in this period, increasing from about five hundred societies in 1835 to 1,350 societies in 1838, with perhaps 250,000 members. Yet behind that success lurked division. There was, for example, no agreement on what nonviolence meant. Many Tappanites did not think that they had given up their right to self-defense. In the 1834 antiabolitionist riot in New York City, Arthur Tappan armed the clerks at his warehouse with guns and told them to shoot proslavery rioters in the legs if they entered the building. Alvan Stewart, a Tappanite lawyer, distributed guns to his friends when an antiabolitionist mob threatened his home in Utica. James Birney acted similarly in 1836 when a proslavery mob threatened his Cincinnati home. None of those men fired their weapons, but Garrisonians thought they were wrong even to brandish them.[43]

That debate came to a head in 1837 when a proslavery mob shot Elijah P. Lovejoy, an abolitionist editor in Alton, Illinois, as he tried to defend his press. A native of Maine, Lovejoy had moved to St. Louis in 1827 hoping to become a journalist. He had been raised in a strict Congregationalist family and was active in benevolent societies in St. Louis. In

1832 he experienced a conversion at a Presbyterian revival and decided to return east for theological studies. After finishing his studies at Princeton, he accepted a position with the American Home Missionary Society in St. Louis, where he established the *Observer*, a newspaper devoted to "Christian politics, the diffusion of religious intelligence, and the salvation of souls." Originally sympathetic to colonization and gradual emancipation, he became radicalized by the hatred that his antislavery stance solicited. At one point, he narrowly escaped being kidnapped after preaching a sermon that denounced slavery.[44]

Lovejoy was eventually forced to leave Missouri for the free state of Illinois, but even there he faced great difficulties. Mobs destroyed his press three times and invaded his house as well. Running out of money and "hunted as a partridge upon the mountains," he arranged to have one more press delivered to him. Lovejoy and his friends were able, under cover of darkness, to unload the press from the boat that delivered it and transport it to a warehouse. But soon they were discovered, and a mob demanded that Lovejoy surrender the press. Lovejoy refused, and shots were exchanged. The mayor of Alton declared that he was unable to control the situation and told Lovejoy that he had the right to defend his property. A crowd of two hundred came to watch the shootout. Finally, the mob sent men with torches to set fire to the roof. Lovejoy came out of the warehouse to fire on them and was shot to death. Once the roof was set aflame, the other defenders surrendered and the mob destroyed the press.[45]

No one doubted that Lovejoy was a martyr, but was he a hero or a traitor to the ideals of abolitionism? The American Anti-Slavery Society issued a statement that did not express regret at Lovejoy's actions. Beriah Green, a Tappanite Presbyterian minister who had headed up the manual labor Oneida Institute, gave an address in which he likened Lovejoy to Stephen, the first Christian martyr.[46] The American Anti-Slavery Society published the address. The Garrisonians, on the other hand, criticized Lovejoy for using violence to defend himself. Samuel J. May pointed out that Stephen had not thrown stones at the crowd that later executed him; and Henry Clarke Wright called upon every abolitionist to "plant his feet on the firm, lofty, everlasting Rock of nonresistance to evil, physical violence."[47] Ominously—though no one could have predicted its significance—at a memorial service for Lovejoy in Hudson, Ohio, a man named John Brown stood up at the end of the meeting and vowed to consecrate his life to the destruction of slavery.[48]

At the 1838 annual meeting of the American Anti-Slavery Society, Samuel J. May presented a resolution declaring Lovejoy's actions inconsistent with the principles of the society. The majority, however, thought it unwise to imply that the antislavery society required nonresistance of its members. Moderate immediatists feared that anarchy would result if they adopted the nonresistants' claim that it was sinful to use force to uphold human laws. Unwilling to sacrifice social order for a nonresistant principle, the moderates balked. The motion failed, leaving May to grieve that the glory of the Christian character had departed from the society.[49]

Other disagreements were in the air as well. Though no issue was more divisive than the debate over nonviolence, the "woman question" and the issue of political abolitionism were also troubling the American Anti-Slavery Society. Garrison had given up hope for the reformation of the political system after the election of 1836, when neither political party would take an antislavery stand.[50] For him, American politics were tainted by the sins of slavery and violence, and he wanted no part of it, any more than he wanted to be part of a culture that refused to afford political rights to women. Moderates, on the other hand, were increasingly interested in establishing an antislavery political party.

It was, finally, the issue of women's equality that split the American Anti-Slavery Society. The Grimke sisters' famous 1837 tour, in which they advocated abolitionism before "promiscuous assemblies" and drew the wrath of the New England clergy, prompted abolitionists to reconsider the role of women. In addition, the society had launched a major legislative petition drive in 1837. Women were particularly active in circulating petitions, and by 1838, 415,000 petitions had been sent to Congress. Women who had played an important role in the petition campaign were no longer content to be unequal partners in the Anti-Slavery Society. The Garrisonians agreed, but more moderate immediatists did not. The idea of welcoming women as their equals struck them as wrongheaded. Moreover, issues like nonresistance and women's rights appeared extraneous to the primary goal of abolishing slavery. With the women and the Garrisonians aligned, however, control of the American Anti-Slavery Society appeared to be in the hands of the radicals. After a couple of years of bickering, the moderate immediatists left the society to the Garrisonians in 1840 and, with the Tappans's support, started the American and Foreign Anti-Slavery Society.[51]

Thus, both the peace movement and the immediatist abolitionist movement suffered schisms over the same issues at about the same time. In many ways, the same people were arguing over the same problems in both movements. And even after the Garrisonians pulled out, the American Peace Society would continue to be torn apart by infighting, for the

Garrisonians left behind them both moderate peace reformers like Ladd and conservative ones like Beckwith. The peace society was home to colonizationists like Leonard Bacon and to immediatists like Gerrit Smith. In the antislavery movement, colonizationists wanted to eliminate slavery but were unwilling to alienate people outside the movement by branding slavery and its supporters sinful. Conservatives in the peace society took the same approach to war—they wanted to eradicate it without implying that its practitioners were sinners. Moderates in both groups disagreed, certain that both war and slavery were sins for which God held the nation responsible. Nevertheless, both the moderates and the conservatives in each movement lacked the sectarian desire to make all things new that typified the Garrisonians. They wanted to reform their culture, not overthrow it. Both felt comfortable using political means to achieve their goals, and neither wanted to establish women as equal members of their societies. Temperamentally, at least to that degree, they belonged together. But their goals were not the same, and the partnership in the peace society would not be smooth.

The Garrisonians were another story. Garrison argued that God had instituted government after the Fall in order to control sin. He was willing to concede that government served a useful purpose, but he still regarded it as sinful, since it was based upon coercion.[52] The only answer to the current sinful social order, Garrison concluded, was regeneration—people had to become perfect (and thus nonresistant), even as Christ had been perfect. Garrison knew, of course, that there was little likelihood that the American people would spontaneously embrace immediate emancipation or nonresistance. Garrison's demand for a nonresistant social order functioned in the same way as his insistence on immediate and unconditional emancipation. Such a decision was possible only for individuals as they were liberated from sin to live according to the perfection of the gospel. Sinful persons simply did not have the mind of Christ, nor were they inclined to imitate Christ. Nevertheless, because Garrison designated slavery and violence as sins, he was obliged to demand that persons renounce them immediately. The only way to overcome sin was to renounce it, and having renounced it, the only ethic to put in its place was the gospel ethic of love.[53]

In his work as an abolitionist and in his efforts as an advocate of peace, Garrison assumed that the reformer was to be an agitator who stirred people up until they rejected the sinful status quo and embraced the gospel. That his antislavery tactics—and those of his followers—were identical to his antiwar tactics was hardly surprising. Both causes sprang from a theological mindset that deplored sin at the same time that it insisted that regeneration enabled persons to lead lives of Christian perfection.

In Distress for Christ's Sake: Exemplary Martyrs or Exultant Victors?

Though Garrison and the nonresistants offered a model of reform far more confrontational and aggressive than Dodge's, their theology followed the lines that he had set out a quarter of a century earlier. Like Dodge, they regarded the Sermon on the Mount as the hermeneutical key to Scripture. They advocated an ethic of love that remained faithful to that sermon regardless of the consequences, and they assumed that regeneration made such behavior a present possibility. Aiming at personal conversion rather than institutional reform, they insisted on absolute nonresistance to all acts of violence and encouraged Christians to withdraw from institutions that were unready to conform to such behavior. In short, they were, like Dodge, sectarian reformers, but their zeal for instituting the kingdom of God on earth made them missionaries of nonresistance with a fervor that even Dodge had not known.

Nonresistance began with the resolve to obey Jesus' commands in the Sermon on the Mount. Indeed, the masthead of the *Non-Resistant*, the society's journal from 1839 to 1842, ran as its motto "Resist not evil—Jesus Christ." The nonresistants had no patience with those who wanted to use Romans 13 to soften the Sermon on the Mount's radicalism. They were willing to concede that Romans 13 admonished Christians to submit to the state, but they denied that it encouraged Christians to be active in politics.[54] Nor did the nonresistants worry that strict obedience to the Sermon on the Mount would destroy the police function of the state. Since they opposed vindictive punishment as well as self-defense, the police function of the state was hardly their first concern. Adin Ballou and Charles K. Whipple managed to preserve modified forms of the state's police function,[55] but the nonresistants spent far more time fretting that the members of the American Peace Society were using Romans 13 as an excuse to avoid applying the gospel to the work of the state than they did worrying that Romans 13 was being neglected. Garrison groused about excessive reliance on Romans 13, that "frowning Gibralter, inaccessible by sea and land, filled with troops and all warlike instruments," and warned that those who relied on Romans 13 instead of the Sermon on the Mount had misinterpreted the gospel. "He who pertinaciously clings to a particular passage of scripture to uphold a favorite theory, and is always dwelling upon it, and refuses to compare scripture with scripture, so that what is 'hard to be understood,' or is of doubtful interpretation, may be clearly apprehended, does virtually acknowledge that the mass of evidence is against him," he said.[56]

For the nonresistants, the Sermon on the Mount laid out the rules of Christian behavior, and the life of Jesus incarnated them. "Were it not for the illustration of the spirit of non-resistance given us in the life of Jesus," Samuel J. May explained, "it might be difficult to determine the precise meaning of his precepts." Given the concrete example of Jesus' life, however, nonresistants could fulfill the precepts of Christianity by behaving as Jesus had.[57] Nonresistant literature was full of *imitatio Christi* language. "If the Son of God could suffer himself to be led as a lamb to the slaughter, and to be nailed unresistingly to the accursed cross," Garrison commented, "surely we are bound to imitate his example even unto death, and by so doing we shall be eternally victorious."[58] The constitution of the New England Non-Resistance Society proclaimed that God had given Jesus to the world as an example of how to practice nonresistance.[59] And Adin Ballou explained that Jesus had replaced the Old Testament ethic of justice with the New Testament ethic of love.[60] The task of the Christian, he said, was to be conformed to the example of Christ, to "everlastingly insist on the principles and practices of Jesus Christ." Indeed, when Ballou organized the Hopedale Community in 1840, he described it as a "systematic attempt to establish an order of Human Society based upon the sublime ideas of the Fatherhood of God and the Brotherhood of Man, as taught and illustrated in the Gospel of Jesus Christ."[61]

Imitating Christ had a number of implications for the nonresistants. In the first place, it entailed being obedient to God even as Jesus had been, regardless of the consequences. Jesus' behavior and the rules that he outlined in the Sermon on the Mount set up an ethic of love. Christians should not worry about the morrow; rather, trusting in God to work all things for good, they should live in love for all people. Moreover, institutions were as bound by this ethic of love as were individuals. Just like Dodge and other radical pacifists before them, the nonresistants refused to allow governments to follow an ethic different from that appropriate to individuals. "WHAT IS SIN IN AN INDIVIDUAL IS SIN IN A NATION," Henry Clarke Wright insisted.[62] For the nonresistants, every human relationship—whether between individuals, nations, or between citizens and their governments—owed obedience to the gospel of love as it was exemplified in the life of Jesus.[63]

Finally, imitating Christ meant being willing to accept his cross. Particularly in the early days of the movement, nonresistance literature teemed with references to martyrdom and the crucifixion. A willingness to suffer death rather than to resist evil with violence, of course, had traditionally been a component of the nonresistant ethic, but in the 1830s there were other reasons for abolitionist pacifists to have the cross on their minds. In 1835 Garrison had been mobbed in Boston and led through the streets by a rope. Although he accepted the aid of law enforcement officials in extricating himself, he had warned his friends that he wanted no one to use violence to protect him.[64] Other abolitionists also faced angry mobs. And there was no forgetting the fate that had met Elijah Lovejoy. The nonresistants did not excuse him for abandoning the faith, but neither was his death far from their minds.

On one level, the nonresistants appeared to welcome martyrdom. "Most assuredly," Garrison wrote James G. Birney, "he is not a Christian, who does not 'take pleasure in infirmities, in reproaches, in necessities, in persecutions, in distresses *for Christ's sake'*—who does not know, experimentally, that blessed are they who are persecuted for righteousness' sake."[65] The *Non-Resistant* ran articles proclaiming, "It is a privilege to be a martyr to the truth. . . . Let us preach our Savior's peace, even if it brings us to our Savior's cross." And Henry C. Wright wrote such articles as "To Die Is Gain," in which he argued that only those who were "ready to suffer and die with Christ in reality" were true nonresistants.[66]

As prepared as they might have been to die for the cause, however, there was a note of ambivalence in the nonresistants' discussion of martyrdom.[67] At the same time that American pacifists had for thirty years championed an ethic of love that sought to imitate Christ regardless of the consequences, they had also developed a tradition that regarded pacifism as "efficacious" in preventing wars and personal injury. From the start, peace literature had abounded with this argument. In its least ambitious sense, such a view meant only that nonresistance worked as well as or better than other strategies did. Refusing to return evil for evil might not succeed in every instance, but it could hardly be more disastrous than the average "victorious" war. In addition, there was always the happy example of the Quakers' harmonious relationship with the Native Americans in Pennsylvania, as well as innumerable anecdotes of hardened criminals repenting from evil intentions when met by a kindly nonresistant, to demonstrate that nonresistance often worked better than the "war spirit."

When its proponents said that nonresistance was efficacious, however, they often meant more than that it was as good a strategy as any other. They also meant that nonresistance would ultimately conquer the world. Adin Ballou argued that nonresistance would not only cause far less human suffering than its opposite temperament would, but also that it would make the "wicked world" so much better that ultimately all aggression would disappear. Nonresistance, he contended, was founded upon perfect love, and it accepted "the essential efficacy of good, as the counteracting force with which to resist evil." Only good, Ballou contended, could defeat evil: Jesus, "the great self-sacrificing Non-Resistant . . . declares that good is the only antagonist of evil, which can conquer the deadly foe." Because nonresistance *was* good, it could be certain of victory, and the nonresistants who dared to lay their lives on the line could be certain that they did not act in vain. "Faith," Ballou said, "in the inherent superiority of good over evil, truth over error, right over wrong, love over hatred, is the immediate moral basis of our doctrine."[68]

In reality, the nonresistants were asserting two different things. On the one hand, they were arguing that Christians should imitate Jesus, even though following in his footsteps could easily entail suffering and death. In this understanding, it was not the *results* of following Jesus that made the endeavor worthwhile; instead, it was being *like* Jesus and being *obedient* to his example and precepts that were meritorious. On that level, suffering martyrdom could be a joyous event. On the other hand, however, the nonresistants were also asserting that nonresistance was a good strategy because it produced felicitous results. That conclusion depended on consequential reasoning, a style of moral discourse that their ethic of love precluded.

It was at best confusing to say at one and the same time that Christians should imitate the crucified Jesus and that they should be nonresistant because that was the best way to succeed in the world. In this early period of the movement, the nonresistants indeed appear to have been confused. They liked to think of themselves as social outcasts, people who had given up everything for the cause. They also liked to believe that their sacrifices were achieving great results. In 1838 Garrison described the American Peace Society as a group of men "high in station and strong in influence" who for years had "fruitlessly endeavored to awaken an interest in peace." In contrast, Garrison characterized the nonresistants as "a few obscure, moneyless, unpretending men and women—ridiculed as fools and fanatics and despised for the lowliness of their station," who had, in a matter of weeks, broken the calm of public indifference and arrested attention "as if by magic." This success, Garrison believed, proved "the potency of principle."[69] By being true to the cross—a symbol of failure that the rest of the world rejected—the nonresistants had in fact tasted victory.

That confusion surfaced in other places too. The fifth edition of the *Non-Resistant* provided a notable example. The second page of the paper carried two articles describing the efficacy of nonresistance. The first, entitled "Safety of the Non-Resistant Pledge," argued that nonresistants need not fear aggressors, for no aggressor would dare attack them. "The aggressor of a nonresistant," the article contended, "will be placed in the wrong; he will be condemned by himself, by byestanders [sic], by the public. The public will take the side of the oppressed. Even warriors will fight for him." Following that article was a letter from Charles Marriott of New York, who was convinced that the cause would make great strides when Christians realized that God would allow no harm to befall a nonresistant. "The cause of Non-Resistance can make little progress, *unless the mind become settled in its confidence in Divine protection,* and in the belief that to seek to redress its wrongs by crimes, would justly forfeit that shield." On page three, directly across from those two articles, was one by Henry Clarke Wright entitled "Clerical Opposition." Describing difficulties he had encountered in converting a minister to nonresistance, Wright noted that "I told him that our fundamental principle was, we claimed it as our *right* and *duty* to suffer and die ourselves, rather than be the occasion of suffering or death to our enemies."[70]

Though Wright's expectation of martyrdom on page three was directly opposite the sentiments regarding divine protection expressed in the articles on page two, the editors of the *Non-Resistant* made no effort to reconcile the two. Perhaps they saw no contradiction. At this point in the movement's history, few people were aware of the conflict. Maria Child did raise the question. After attending the first New England Non-Resistance Society conference in 1838, she wrote, "I was sorry so much was said about the 'meek's *inheriting* the earth'. Unquestionably, there is an exceeding great reward *in* doing the will of God; but it should follow, as the shadow follows the substance; not be presented as a *motive*. It is a very refined form of selfishness, still it seems to me it is selfish."[71]

A related issue that the nonresistants did recognize and debate was whether it was appropriate—since they refused to vote or hold office—to petition the state to enact legislation that they favored. Ballou thought such petitioning was wrong and refused, on that account, to sign the society's Declaration of Sentiments. Edmund Quincy, however, insisted that petitioning the government did not entail an acknowledgment that the state had a right to substitute its rule for God's; it merely asked governments to exercise their power to do what was right. On those grounds, the Garrisonians approved petitions.[72]

In any case, nonresistants were activists who expected to make things happen, either by the power of their example or by the force of their criticism. It was their commitment to the gospel, in their opinion, that was the source of both their suffering and their success. A disobedient world rejected and despised them because they preached the foolishness of the cross, yet it was that very gospel that converted others to the cause.

There was validity to that argument. Historians now contend that one of the abolitionists' most effective strategies in the 1830s stemmed from their willingness to suffer violence. Abolitionists were regularly assaulted in the North, and in the South, vigilante committees routinely interrogated Yankee travelers and examined their baggage. It was illegal to own or distribute antislavery material in the South, and Southern papers openly dared abolitionists to cross the Mason-Dixon line. After the massive antislavery petition drive of 1837–38, Congress instituted a gag rule that prohibited open congressional debate over slavery. Such developments frightened Northerners who would not otherwise have been sympathetic to the antislavery appeal, for they feared that the slave South was conspiring to deny them their civil rights. By presenting themselves as victims of a demonic "slaveocracy" that threatened free institutions throughout the North, abolitionists thus began to court popular support.[73] It was only later, when the nonresistants despaired that the daily martyrdom suffered by the Southern slaves would ever end, that they grew impatient with their theology of the cross. Though they never abandoned that theology, they did turn their attention away from patient suffering toward means that would liberate the slaves more expeditiously. In the late 1830s and early 1840s, however, the nonresistants were content to ignore the latent tension between their ethic of love, which upheld Jesus the martyr as the example for faithful Christians to imitate, and their assumption that faithfulness to the gospel would ensure the success of their efforts.

One of the reasons the nonresistants were initially confident of success was due to their peculiar eschatological views. The nonresistants believed that human efforts would bring about the full realization of the kingdom of God on earth. This was true because Jesus had already initiated the kingdom at his second coming; the task remaining to Christians was simply to live in the millennial reality that Jesus had inaugurated. Peace workers of all stripes in the American Peace Society commonly argued that the millennial age would not come about until peace reigned throughout the world. They stressed that it was possible even now for people to live in peace, as they would in the kingdom. Among peace workers the belief that the second coming had already occurred, however, was peculiar to the nonresistants. The conviction that they were living in the millennial age only accented the nonresistants' natural tendency toward perfectionism.

The Garrisonians borrowed this eschatological interpretation from John Humphrey Noyes, the founder of the Oneida Community. Adin Ballou developed a theory that varied somewhat from Noyes's. Both argued that Christ had returned to earth at the dispersion of the Jews in 70 A.D. According to Ballou, a general resurrection then occurred; Noyes disagreed, arguing instead that only a resurrection of the Jews and the faithful disciples of the early church took place at that time. Ballou contended that Christ had established the primitive church as a regenerated group to "stand morally at the front of the procession of humanity . . . to salt it with divine principles, to show it 'a still more excellent way', and so gradually convert it to pure Christianity, and thereby bring in the kingdom of God."[74] When they deserted the purity of the gospel and allowed Christianity to become the state religion, the early Christians failed in their mission; but the regenerating power of Christ set loose upon the earth in his life, death, resurrection, and return was still available, and the kingdom, when God would be "all in all" still awaited their efforts.[75]

According to Noyes, at Christ's return in the year 70, faithful Jews were resurrected, and those Christians who were watching for Jesus were taken up into heaven with him. The Christians who remained on earth were apostates who had not believed Christ when he promised to return to earth. The subsequent history of the church was a story of disbelief and bondage to sin. Yet the time had come, after centuries of maturation, for the "Gentile crop" to be harvested. In preparation for that general resurrection, God had opened the "second generation of true Christian regeneration." The age of apostasy had passed, and now rebirth into Christ's perfection was a possibility for those who sought it.[76] Noyes believed that God's regenerating spirit would pass rapidly over the earth, and he advised Christians to commit themselves to achieving perfect holiness. He urged them to declare their independence from the governments of this world and to seek obedience instead to what he called God's "eternal government"—that condition of closeness to the Almighty which lifted individuals out of sin and allowed them to act in perfect concert with the will of God.[77]

However they explained the details of the parousia, the practical effect was the same for Ballou and Noyes. They believed that Christ had returned to earth in power and that his regenerating spirit was available to sanctify individuals and to extend the kingdom of God. Given those assumptions, it was not surprising that the nonresistants were confident of success. Though they celebrated the example of a crucified Savior, they had already begun to live in the age of the church triumphant.

Whenever they discussed the characteristics of that age, the nonresistants invariably described it in terms of individualism and perfectionism. By individualism they meant that regeneration began in individuals, not in institutions. The nonresistants had argued all along that the way to reform society was to change individuals and wait for them to change institutions rather than to seek (as the American Peace Society did) to achieve reforms by convincing institutions to change their policies. Commitment to reform by converting individuals, however, was more than just a strategy for the nonresistants. It was a theological affirmation that God had created persons to live in relationship with God and to be governed directly by God. Rejecting the idea of the state as an order of creation, the nonresistants insisted that the state was an order of preservation, an institution that God had established only because the Fall had interrupted the direct relationship that existed between God and humanity at creation. Since the nonresistants believed that the kingdom had come, and thus the original order of creation had been restored in the redeemed, they were eager to explore the implications of regenerate individualism.

Their discussions of individualism included both an antipathy toward institutions and a conviction that it was solitary individuals, faithful to the gospel, who would bring about social change. Henry Clarke Wright explained their celebration of the individual in an 1841 letter to the *Liberator:* "Thousands are beginning here to see that MAN is something nobler than a social organization in Church and State—that men are responsible as *individuals*—not as corporations—that Christianity is not an ORGANIZATION, but an INDIVIDUALITY. As soon as this is seen and felt, men dare to look at non-resistance and embrace it."[78] Ballou, too, explained in an 1840 article for the *Practical Christian* his conviction that true Christianity began with the individual:

> With us, at present, perfect individuality is a fundamental idea of the true man. We believe that by setting the individual right with his Creator, we shall set social relationships right. We therefore go for unabridged independence of mind, conscience, duty, and responsibility; for direct divine government over the human soul; and, of course, for as little *human* government as possible. We wish to know whether there is any such thing as man's being and doing right from the law of God written on his heart, without the aid of external bonds and restraints. We believe this is possible, and that it is every man's privilege, by the grace of God, to attain to such a

state. And more than this, we believe that men in the flesh will yet by thousands actually arrive at that blissful state.[79]

Ballou had often spoken of the leavening effect that the regenerate individual produced in society. Others also liked that metaphor. "The conviction returns upon me and daily gains strength," Maria Child wrote in 1838, "that if but *one* human being earnestly and perseveringly sought to reach perfect holiness, the emanation from him would purify the world."[80] Noyes's insistence that perfect holiness was a present possibility for Christians also impressed the Garrisonians. "I believe in an indwelling Christ, and in his righteousness alone," said Garrison. " 'He that is born of God doth not commit sin'. . . . If Christ cannot cleanse me from all sin here, he cannot do it anywhere."[81]

Because freedom from sin was a present possibility, it was also each individual's responsibility to cultivate that freedom. Apart from re-generation, people were helpless to obey God. As Ballou noted, without "a prior radical regeneration of human opinions, feelings, custom, and institutions," it was absurd to call upon them to act from sinless motives.[82] Once regenerated, however, all things were possible; the Christian perfection of the nonresistants would serve as leaven throughout humanity and usher in the kingdom of God in its pristine purity. Indeed, individuals who were already regenerated were even now dwelling in that kingdom.

Convinced that God was willing to make all things new, the nonresis-tants had no patience for those who wished to dwell in the old dispensa-tion. They had no tolerance for institutions that were imperfect. Consequently, the Garrisonians joined the "come-outer" movement, leaving the church and the government because they were unregenerate. Though they would not participate in a fallen church or a fallen govern-ment, they intended, through their reform activities, to spur those institutions on to perfection. Other perfectionists, such as Ballou and Noyes, were not so enamored with political agitation. Instead, they founded alternative communities to demonstrate to the fallen world that it was possible for Christians to live in peace with one another according to the gospel. Whether through reform agitation or alternative commu-nities, the goal of withdrawal was the same: to convince American society to abandon its unregenerate ways and turn instead to the perfec-tion of the gospel.

Once Christians had been made perfect, the nonresistants believed, they would no longer need government. Each individual's immediate obedience to the will of God would make the state superfluous. Thus, as

Ballou explained, "it is the object of this Society neither to purify nor to subvert human governments, but to advance in the earth that kingdom of peace and righteousness, which supersedes all such government."[83] Critics characterized this as the "no-government" view; the nonresistants called it the "government of God" or "divine government" position. The nonresistants conceded to their critics that those floundering in sin needed some kind of government, but they deprecated human governments for substituting their own rule in place of the laws of God. "God creates men to be ruled by himself, and be subject to his dominion," the society's document on "National Organizations" explained. "Men form nations to dethrone the Deity, and subject men to the dominion of man."[84]

The nonresistants' objection to civil government generally took two forms. It was always easy to denounce national laws or customs that fell below the perfection of the gospel. Here all the usual arguments against the penal code, capital punishment, and war came into play. An even more fundamental objection, however, was that government usurped God's role as humanity's ruler. Whereas God had created humankind to be obedient to the divine rule, human governments rushed to establish themselves as alternative authorities. They paid no heed to the divine rule, but established their own fiefdoms in defiance of God.

Nothing angered the nonresistants more than the spectacle of earthly governments attempting to usurp God as lord of creation. Only God was humanity's true governor, and only the laws God laid down were to guide human behavior. At the heart of those laws was the Sermon on the Mount, with its admonition to love one's enemies and to return no one evil for evil. As Garrison explained,

> The more I look into the subject, the deeper is my conviction that the principles of the Non-Resistance Society are immutably true; that whoever feels unable or unwilling to forgive all manner of injuries, and the worst of enemies, has no right to rank himself among the followers of Christ; that the attempt of men to govern themselves by external rules and physical penalties is and ever must be futile; and that from the assumption, that man has a right to exercise oppression over his brother, has proceeded every form of injustice and oppression with which the earth has been afflicted."[85]

David Low Dodge had suggested, long before, that prior to the Fall there had been no government, since humanity was in its created state naturally obedient to God's rule. The nonresistants were arguing that the time had come to reinstitute the reign of God on earth, and any law, custom, or institution that attempted to interfere with the individual's sacred obligation to be directly responsive and obedient to God was sinful.

The assumption that God demanded immediate obedience to the divine laws articulated in the gospel was the basis of every reform that the nonresistants attempted to achieve. One of the results, as revealed in the constitution of the New England Non-Resistant Society, was that it repudiated not only international war, but also every form of violence, vengeance, or coercion:

> No one who professes to have the spirit of Christ, can consistently sue a man at law for redress of injuries, or thrust any evil-doer into prison, or fill any office in which he would come under obligation to execute penal enactments—or take any part in military service—or acknowledge allegiance to any human government—or justify any man in fighting in defence of property, liberty, life or religion; that he cannot engage in countenance any plot or effort to revolutionize, or change, by physical violence, any government, however corrupt or oppressive; that he will obey "the powers that be," except in those cases in which they violate his conscience—and then, rather than to resist, he will meekly submit to the penalty of disobedience.[86]

That same reasoning impelled them to denounce slavery as a form of violence. The first annual meeting of the Non-Resistance Society resolved "That the abolition of slavery is involved in the doctrine of non-resistance, as the unity is included within the aggregate: for if a slaveholder become a non-resistant, he never again could *strike* a slave; never *compel* him to labor; never reclaim him, if he chose to leave him; in a word, never resort to that law of violence, in which the relation of master and slave originated, and by which it must be continually sustained."[87] By making the Sermon on the Mount normative for Christian behavior and insisting that human institutions and relationships not usurp the direct "government of God," the nonresistants managed to repudiate lawsuits, military service, self-defense, participation in government, and slavery. It was no wonder that Garrison exulted at the "disorganizing" tendencies of the nonresistance movement.

The decision, moreover, to define slavery as a form of coercion, as well as a usurpation of God's government, revealed much about immediatist psychology. Eighteenth-century objections to slavery had focused on its cruelty, stressing the suffering that the slaves endured. Immediatists, however, had chosen to highlight the issue of power. Because the master usurped the place of God in assuming domination of the slave, the master was guilty of the original sin of presumption. And the slave, in losing personal autonomy, was both deprived of his or her moral agency and rendered incapable of obeying the government of God. For both the Garrisonians and the moderate immediatists, slavery was sinful because it robbed the slave of the opportunity to achieve self-mastery in obedience before God at the same time that it exalted the master to the place of God.[88]

The issues of control and self-mastery were personally important to immediatists. Raised as children to think that uncontrollable passions would overtake them if they could not achieve an iron will dedicated to self-control and holiness, the immediatists saw in the Southern slaveholders an almost mythic instance of passion run wild. Ronald Walters has observed that "in antislavery propaganda the plantation was less a real place than an imaginary one where the repressed came out of hiding." While abolitionists were curbing their own passions by manual labor, bland food, cold water, and circumscribed sexual expression, they looked South to see, in Walters' words, "a society in which eroticism had no checks put on it."[89] Kentuckian James A. Thome set the theme in the famous Lane Seminary slavery debate of 1834 when he warned his classmates of the licentious consequences of slavery: "Pollution, pollution! Young men of talents and respectability, fathers, professors of religion, ministers, all classes! Overwhelming pollution!"[90]

It was an easy step to connect sexual debauchery with violence, as both were the result of unrestrained passion. Immediatist abolitionist literature abounded with graphic tales of brutal beatings, shameful rapes, and horrible drunken rages. As Theodore Dwight Weld noted in his introduction to *Slavery As It Is*, he intended to show that slaves

> are frequently flogged with terrible severity, have red pepper rubbed into their lacerated flesh, and hot brine, spirits of turpentine, &c., poured over the gashes to increase their torture; that they are often stripped naked, their backs and limbs cut with knives, bruised and mangled by scores and hundreds of blows with the paddle, and terribly torn by the claws of cats, drawn over them by their tormentors; . . . that their ears are often cut off, their eyes knocked out, their bones broken, their flesh branded with red hot irons; that they are maimed, mutilated and burned to death over slow fires. All these things, and more, and worse, we shall *prove*. Reader, we know whereof we affirm, we have weighed it well; *more and worse* WE WILL PROVE.[91]

The Garrisonians were no less detailed in their own accounts. The *Liberator* was full of explicit descriptions of Southern atrocities, and in her *Appeal in Favor of That Class of Americans Called Africans*, Maria Child wrote of a master dismembering a slave, bit by bit, from the feet up, and throwing his flesh in the fire while the other slaves watched in terrified silence.[92]

For the abolitionists, the South was Sodom revisited, encompassing, in Garrison's words, "one vast system of crime and blood, and all imaginable lewdness and villany [sic]."[93] The nonresistants in particular saw the Southern "slaveocracy" as the evil counterimage of the government of God that they championed. Richard Hughes and Leonard Allen have noted that antebellum Americans often identified their group or nation with idealized epochs. From Mormons to the "Christian" movement, American groups chose some primordial age of significance and claimed to have recaptured it in their own day. In espousing an eschatology that allowed them to think that complete regeneration was a present possibility, the nonresistants presented the government of God as a return to the pre-Fall perfection of creation. Released from the shackles of all domination, individuals could reverse the flow of human history and live in perfect freedom and obedience before God.

Southerners, as Lewis Perry has persuasively argued, offered a vision of the good society that was precisely reversed.[94] Convinced that God intended the social order to be a hierarchy in which each person had duties and responsibilities corresponding to her or his station, Southerners saw the nonresistants' government of God as sheer anarchy. James Henley Thornwell, a noted South Carolina minister, wrote that "the fundamental mistake of those who affirm slavery to be essentially sinful, is that the duties of all men are specifically the same. . . . The argument, fully and legitimately carried out, would condemn every arrangement of society, which did not secure to all its members an absolute equality of position; it is the very spirit of socialism and communism."[95]

In place of the egalitarian order the nonresistants proposed, Southern Christians suggested a kindly patriarchy, where cultured slaveowners would discipline and provide religious guidance to the childlike slaves for whom they were responsible. Ironically, evangelical theology prompted Northerners to espouse free institutions, but it inspired Southerners to defend slavery as a Christian vocation. "The gift which white evangelicals decided to give blacks," Donald Mathews observed, "was moral order instead of freedom, and slaves were judged Christian and certified as acceptable to whites in so far as they behaved themselves."[96] Seeking to achieve Christian order, Southerners invoked primordial visions of their own. Hughes and Allen noted that Southerners claimed the South—not the North—to be the true heir of ancient Israel, the early church, and the Puritan founders. Southerners also pointed to a primordium that the North had not thought to claim. In Noah, the "New Adam," they found the primordial patriarch. "Father" of the human race, Noah had founded the original plantation. In relegating Noah's son Ham (representative of the black race) as a slave to his brother Japheth (the white race) and ordering the third son, Shem (the red race), to allow Japheth to dwell within his tents, God had established racial hierarchy as part of the divine will for society. Thus, New Orleans Presbyterian minister Benjamin Palmer concluded that "the abolitionist spirit is undeniably atheistic. . . . [It] blasphemously invades the prerogatives of God, and rebukes the Most High for the errors of his administration."[97] In defining the ideal society, nonresistants and Southern Christians thus provided answers that were precise opposites.

What the nonresistants had done, of course, was define violence so broadly that their other causes became subsets of violence. War, slavery, voting—and all the other activities they denounced—were sinful because they flowed from that spirit of violence that was antithetical to the gospel of love. To condemn one was to condemn them all, since all had the same root. In place of the current culture of violence and coercion, the nonresistants offered the government of God. For regenerate Christians, human laws were superfluous, since those born into Christ needed no external coercion to make them behave. The notion of the government of God frightened the nonresistants' opponents; it threatened every institution and seemed to invite chaos and anarchy. The nonresistants, however, saw the government of God as the only means to do away with false authorities and establish God's reign on earth. "Surely," said Garrison, "if all mankind would embrace these views, there would no more blood be shed, the use of all carnal weapons would cease, every man would sit under his own vine and fig-tree, and there would be none to molest or make afraid. How insane, therefore, are they who say that non-resistance will lead to anarchy and bloodshed!"[98]

In thus arguing for the government of God, the nonresistants had come a long way from the moderate peace advocates of the American Peace Society. Their missionary zeal for reform, their intolerance of imperfection, and their insistence upon linking other reforms—such as those concerning slavery, capital punishment, and self-defense—with the cause of peace all made them improbable allies of the American Peace Society. Their theory of the reformer as agitator differentiated them even from David Low Dodge, but in other ways they merely extended the work that he had begun. Like him, they assumed that nations and individuals were bound to obey the Sermon on the Mount. They insisted, as he did, that a true peace witness was possible only through regeneration and that reform would come through individual conversions, not institutional ones. They urged Christians to withdraw from government and to live according to the perfection of Christ. The nonresistants continued the tradition of sectarian reform that Dodge had begun. Their schism from the American Peace Society could hardly have surprised him.

George Beckwith and the American Peace Society: Champions of Christian Civilization

While Garrison and the nonresistants were busy destroying the institutions of Western culture, the American Peace Society was suffering a thousand deaths at their antics. The members of the society were prepared to accept ridicule for their peace advocacy; they were accustomed to being regarded as well intentioned yet naive. But they were not ready to accept the epithets being tossed at the nonresistants. The Haverhill *Gazette*, referring to the nonresistants' "wild and impractical hallucinations," concluded that "to talk of living in the world *as it is*, without government . . . is an idea more suited to the McLane Asylum for the insane, than for Marlboro Chapel" (where the nonresistants had gathered to meet). The New York *Journal of Commerce* condemned nonresistance as "part of the system of universal ultraism, extravagance and folly, which has been precipitated upon our country, like a blighting mildew"; even abolitionist James Birney dismissed nonresistance as "but a new growth of . . . fungi."[99]

These characterizations were all the more painful in that George Beckwith, Ladd's chosen successor as secretary of the society and editor of the *Advocate*, was determined to show that working for peace was a sensible thing for American Christians to do. Beckwith was a New York Congregationalist who attended Andover Seminary at the same time as Henry Clarke Wright. After his graduation, Beckwith served as a pastor in Lowell, Massachusetts, and then as a professor both at Andover and at Lane Seminary in Cincinnati.[100] He was serving as pastor in Portland, Maine, before taking employment at the American Peace Society. In the years to come, he would exercise increasing control over the society, and his instincts were always to steer it in a conservative direction. Though his *Book of Peace* (1845) and *Peace Manual* (1847) were solid additions to the peace literature of the age, his efforts received little recognition. Moderates in the society came to regard him as power hungry, as well as far too cautious in his peace advocacy, and plots to overthrow him would abound in the years to come. His reputation has fared no better in recent scholarship. He has yet to find a biographer, much less a sympathetic one.

Given his desire to present the cause of peace as respectable, Beckwith found the nonresistants horrifying in more ways than one. He considered their government of God theory—or "no government" position, as he insisted on calling it—blasphemous. Since Scripture showed that government was ordained of God, Beckwith thought that government ought to be honored, not disregarded. He also thought, in accordance with the standards of the day, that women ought to stay in their own spheres. The night before the New England Non-Resistant Society opened its organizing convention, Beckwith held a private meeting of less radical peace activists. The group made plans to take control of the new society, but it was outmaneuvered the next day when Garrison asked that those in attendance sign "his or her name" to the membership role. Women were then appointed to various committees. Beckwith stayed until the afternoon, when Abby Kelley of the business committee called him to order. Suspicious of the proceedings to begin with and now pushed beyond endurance, Beckwith and other "women-contemners" (as Garrison labeled them) removed their names from the roll.[101]

Even more irritating to Beckwith than the nonresistants' theological errors was the horrible public image that they gave to the cause of peace. From the first edition of the *Advocate of Peace*, Beckwith printed every possible disclaimer to dissociate the American Peace Society from the nonresistants. When the society adopted the constitutional changes of 1837, he explained that the group came to condemn all war "*not* through the ultraism of the age, or blind visionary enthusiasm, but a calm, prayerful examination of the gospel." He insisted repeatedly that the society's only goal was to change public opinion so that Christian nations would cease to go to war. And he stressed that the society advocated a "conservative reform" that sought to work with, not against, Christian institutions. Following the nonresistants' first convention, the *Advocate of Peace* printed an official disclaimer, characterizing the principles and aims of the nonresistant society as "entirely foreign to the cause of peace."[102]

More than anything else, Beckwith sought consensus among the friends of peace and respectability for their cause. He did not find controversy helpful in attaining either goal. When William Allen resigned over the 1837 constitutional change, Beckwith led a group who attempted, in 1838, to reword the constitution once again so that it would be vague enough not to offend those who wished only to condemn offensive wars.[103] Beckwith's proposals, however, met with defeat at the annual meeting of May 1838, and so for the time being he had to be content with the 1837 constitution. Nevertheless, Beckwith was set upon returning the American Peace Society to a more conservative stance that would allow all the friends of peace to work together without controversy.

When the nonresistants left to form their own organization, Beckwith saw his opportunity. Without the nonresistants as a constant source of embarrassment and internal controversy, it might be possible to reunite the remaining members of the American Peace Society and restore the group's respectability. To do the former, Beckwith returned to the theological assumptions that the members had always shared, regardless of their positions on issues like defensive wars or capital punishment. To accomplish the latter task of presenting the society as a socially respectable reform group, Beckwith answered the nonresistant model of sectarian reformer with his own vision of the peace reformer as the champion of Christian civilization. He proposed institutional peace reforms, calling on Christian nations and churches to take the first step toward the millennium by creating a Congress of Nations.

In his desire to differentiate the American Peace Society from the New England Non-Resistance Society, however, Beckwith went beyond the pioneering work of Worcester and Ladd by insisting that Romans 13 was an exception to the Sermon on the Mount. Thus, he ensured that the police function of the state—which the nonresistants had virtually discarded—overruled Jesus' command not to resist evil with evil. The Worcester/Ladd branch of the society had always been sympathetic to government and institutional peace reform; now, Beckwith endeavored to wed the support of government to the cause of peace. In that way, he hoped to lead the American Peace Society out of the confusion of 1837 into a conservative, socially respectable consensus that allowed the society to function as a champion of Christian civilization.

The peace society was aided by Thomas C. Upham, professor of moral philosophy of Bowdoin College, who published *The Manual of Peace* in 1836. A Congregational minister originally from New Hampshire, Upham was a graduate of Dartmouth and Andover Seminary, active in the colonization and temperance movements and notable as well for being the first man to attend Sarah and Phoebe Palmer's Tuesday Night Meeting for the Promotion of Holiness. A reputable scholar, Upham lent both visibility and distinction to the cause of peace. The American Peace Society published its own edition of Upham's work in 1842, and Upham wrote a number of articles for the *Advocate of Peace* at this time. In his

Manual, Upham called for peace societies in which members would pledge not "to submit to any military requisitions whatever, and not to contribute any thing, either directly or indirectly, either of their personal efforts or their money, in furtherance of military measures." He insisted on the absolute inviolability of human life, and while he went beyond the peace society in asking Christians to refuse to be a part of military affairs, he joined with the society in urging that a Congress of Nations be established.[104]

Even more important than Upham's support were developments in moral philosophy. One of the staples of the society's prescription for peace was the by now familiar rubric that both individuals and nations were bound to obey the gospel without regard for the consequences. That conviction had been characteristic of the society from the beginning, but now the society was fortunate enough to find educators throughout the nation agreeing. For years colleges and universities had used William Paley's work on moral philosophy as the standard text for their senior course in ethics. Paley had based his ethics on utilitarian reasoning, arguing that "Actions are to be estimated by their tendency to promote happiness.—Whatever is expedient, is right.—It is the utility of any moral rule alone which constitutes the obligation of it." He had also denied that the rules of personal behavior were necessarily obligatory upon nations, had asserted that Scripture did not condemn just wars, and had argued in favor of personal self-defense.[105] For years Paley's ethics ruled the field. By 1830, however, Paley's utilitarianism, with its assumption that private happiness was the only motivation for virtue, no longer seemed particularly moral. Educators were looking for a replacement.[106]

The friends of peace, of course, had implicitly rejected Paley all along. Eventually they refuted Paley specifically. The American Peace Society published a number of Jonathan Dymond's works, and the British Quaker rejected Paley point by point, replacing his utilitarianism with an ethic of love required of individuals and nations alike. The Windham County Peace Society noted as early as 1832 that it had distributed copies of Dymond in the spring of that year. The society praised Dymond for refuting Paley's doctrine of expediency and urged that Paley's textbook be dropped.[107] When William Allen, in his debate with Ladd, was foolish enough to cite Paley, Ladd was quick to inform him that he found Paley's method of reasoning repugnant.[108]

But the greatest breakthrough was the publication of Francis Wayland's *Elements of Moral Science.* First issued in 1835 and then endlessly revised and reissued, Wayland's work became the standard moral philosophy textbook in America. Though Wayland did not rule out the police function of the state, he did reject Paley's utilitarianism. In its place, he insisted upon an ethic of love for individuals and nations that condemned all war as "contrary to the revealed will of God."[109]

That meant that Wayland had, by the 1836 edition of his *Elements*, already argued the position that the American Peace Society would adopt when it amended its constitution in 1837. In fact he had not simply argued the position; he had given it national exposure. Wayland did not credit any peace organization with helping him develop his views on war; rather, he claimed to have arrived at his conclusions through the study of Scripture. Moreover, though he was a vice-president of the American Peace Society as early as 1838 and served as president from 1859 to 1861, he was never particularly active in the peace movement. Nevertheless, the fact that the most revered moral philosopher of the era had used reasoning similar to that of the American Peace Society's could only have helped lend respectability to an organization that had suffered from its association with the wild-eyed radicals of the New England Non-Resistance Society.

Certainly the peace society took comfort in Wayland's determination to preserve the police function of the state. In his *Elements* Wayland described three possible types of injurious relationships: those committed by an individual upon another individual, those committed by a society upon another society, and those committed by an individual upon a society. In the first two instances, he claimed, the party receiving the injury ought never return evil for evil. Here the Sermon on the Mount applied both to nations and to individuals. In the third instance, however, society was bound, as an institution of God, to do what was necessary to see that the state was not destroyed. For that reason, government could punish criminals, both to preserve the social order and to attempt to reform the offender. Wayland conceded that even capital punishment was at times justifiable.[110] By that analysis, he managed to bind nations and individuals to the nonresistance of the Sermon on the Mount at the same time he reserved to the state the right to punish criminals.

Members of the American Peace Society had already used that line of reasoning. Implicitly they acknowledged that the police function of the state was an exception to the Sermon on the Mount,[111] but no one had bothered to develop that idea as a positive doctrine. Occasionally advocates of peace had mentioned that it was impossible for the state to abide by the Sermon on the Mount when it strove to enforce the law. William Ellery Channing, for example, warned that "the precept 'Resist not evil', if practiced to the letter would annihilate all government in the family and state; for it is the great work of government to resist evil passions and evil deeds."[112] But usually (as in the case with Worcester), the members of the society were content to support both the Sermon on the Mount and the police function of the state without explaining how it was possible to advocate both simultaneously. It was Beckwith who finally conceded the obvious: the police function of the state violated the Sermon on the Mount. By that admission he changed the character of the society's doctrine. As long as Beckwith's views held—and they prevailed through 1865—the members of the American Peace Society were told that obedience to Scripture at times entailed disobeying the Sermon on the Mount. God, according to Beckwith, valued civil order even more highly than nonresistant love. At times, an ethic of coercion held precedence over Jesus' ethic of love.

Beckwith reached that position by using Wayland's distinctions regarding the relations of individuals and society.[113] As articulated in an 1839 article in the Boston *Recorder,* Beckwith's argument was fourfold. First, he appealed to the Sermon on the Mount to prove his personal opinion that all wars were contrary to gospel. In this way, he agreed with Wayland that, when threatened, individuals and societies should respond with love. Second, he asked whether the public was correct in fearing that peace advocacy subverted the work of government. Beckwith answered by stating that he wished to take a stand not only for government, but for "*strong* government." When God ordained government, Beckwith contended, God designed it to be a "temporary substitute for his government." Armed with the sword, government went forth as "a revenger, to execute wrath upon him that doeth evil." Beckwith concurred with what the nonresistants had argued all along— when it corrected wrongdoers, government did not forgive them, as Jesus might; instead, it punished them. Beckwith admitted that this coercion was opposed to the nonresistant love that Jesus had urged upon his followers. "All penal acts," he said, "are in direct, palpable contradiction of the precepts found in the sermon on the mount, and can be justified only on the ground of exception by the same authority that enjoined the former."

Third, Beckwith addressed the obvious question of why God allowed governments to punish or even execute criminals when God denied governments the power to punish foreign aggressors. For this question, Beckwith admitted, there was no obvious solution. True, there were Old Testament precedents—such as the Mosaic legal code, which, in contradiction to the Sixth Commandment, inflicted the death penalty for some crimes. Nevertheless, why God would permit the taking of life in the case of criminals, but not in the case of war, remained a mystery. Beckwith suggested that Christians had no right to ask God's reasons. Finally, Beckwith concluded, it was important to note that the state's right to govern was not an issue in the cause of peace. Neither, in his view, was the cause committed to "either side of the vexed question of defensive war." The only goal that the friends of peace sought was to abolish the practice by which nations attempted to settle disputes by force.[114] All other issues were extraneous to the cause of peace.

In that fashion, Beckwith argued for an ethic of love that followed Jesus regardless of the consequences and for a strong government that preserved internal order by punishing criminals in the only way that it was possible to advocate both: by admitting that the internal workings of government violated the gospel ethic of love. Beckwith was honest enough to admit the contradiction. By doing so he hoped to reassure potential allies that the American Peace Society did not threaten social order. He also hoped that, by setting aside divisive questions like capital punishment, slavery, the role of women, and the police function of the state, the cause of peace could focus on practical questions. The society continued to believe that a "determined application" of the gospel[115] would bring about an age of peace that would usher in the millennium. Nevertheless, the focus of the society's work was on substantive issues— how to set up mechanisms that would allow nations to settle disputes without resorting to violence.

This institutional focus differentiated the American Peace Society from the New England Non-Resistance Society. Garrison had assumed that individual regeneration necessarily preceded social change, and so the nonresistants concentrated on convincing individuals to withdraw from the fallen culture around them in order to live in obedience to the government of God. The American Peace Society, with its confidence in "Christian civilization," simply did not believe that Christians or their societies were depraved. Clinging to the notion that education—leading to shifts in public opinion—was all that was necessary to create a climate of peace, the society was free to concentrate on institutional reforms. Restricting its efforts to "Christendom," where the gospel had already prepared people to respond sympathetically, the society appealed to social institutions to help it establish peace.[116] It begged churches and ministers to preach on peace; it applauded commerce and industry for making nations so dependent upon one another that they were reluctant to go to war;[117] and it tirelessly petitioned Congress to create a Congress of Nations and to include stipulated arbitration in its international treaties.

In short, the American Peace Society concentrated on decorous, sober reforms. In November of 1838, Ladd wrote to Garrison, warning him that "there is such a thing as going beyond the millennium." Ladd worried that the nonresistants spent their "time and energies in exploring far distant and unknown regions of speculation." If, he warned "we do not use the light we have to some *practical* purpose, it will be taken from us, and we shall be left to grope in error." Let us act according to *duty*, Ladd urged, and not speculations. Let us work to abolish international war rather than getting bogged down in fanciful notions about a world that needs no government.[118]

In actuality, however, Ladd and the American Peace Society had the same confusion over "duty" that the Non-Resistance Society did. The nonresistants claimed to abide by an ethic of love that was unconcerned about results, when in fact they assumed that, by dutifully practicing nonresistant love, they would achieve the goals toward which they worked. The American Peace Society followed the same pattern. Admitting freely that the Sermon on the Mount was to be obeyed regardless of the consequences, members nevertheless peppered their journal with articles about the "efficacy" of peace. Authors spoke of the "wonderful efficacy" of pacific principles, the "practical efficacy" of the principles of peace, and the "safety of pacific principles."[119] Like the nonresistants, the American Peace Society saw no tension between eschewing consequential reasoning at the same time that it argued that its ethic of love would achieve remarkable results. In the case of the state's police function, the society had willingly made an exception to its ethic of love. What it failed to realize was that its assumption that doing its duty would lead to success was also potentially compromising to an ethic that claimed to obey the Sermon on the Mount without regard for the consequences.[120]

In time both the American Peace Society and the New England Non-Resistance Society would face the hard fact that those who obediently did their duty did not necessarily accomplish their goals. By Ladd's death in 1841, however, that unwelcome reality had not yet confronted them. What did confront them was a schism in the body of peace workers. On the one side, the sectarian reformers of the nonresistant society seceded from the American Peace Society in order to convert individuals to the regenerate life of obedience under the government of

God. On the other side, the champions of Christian civilization of the American Peace Society asserted more clearly than ever their support for strong government. Affirming the complementary nature of strong government and international peace, they concentrated on institutional reforms that might achieve practical effects: an end to international armed disputes.

Such a schism had perhaps been inevitable from the start; certainly the American Peace Society had united reformers of two radically different temperaments. For ten years they had managed to work together in a semblance of harmony. Once the two groups divided, however, and there was no longer any incentive to sooth injured feelings, the gap between the two would widen. To the nonresistants, the moderate members of the American Peace Society seemed timid and slow, unwilling to make a full commitment to the cause of peace. To the American Peace Society, the nonresistants were uncontrollable fanatics who could be trusted only to throw themselves into ever more outlandish and impractical projects. Never again would the two work together in a common organization. Nevertheless, in the coming decade the New England Non-Resistance Society and the American Peace Society would find a cause that united them in righteous indignation: the American invasion of Mexico and the ensuing Mexican War. For all their bickering, each group hated wars of conquest with a passion.

3

THE
GAP
WIDENS

In 1810, in New Britain, Connecticut, a remarkable son, Elihu, was born to Elihu and Elizabeth Burritt. The Burritts would raise ten children on their small farm. Money was always scarce, and opportunities for education slim. When his father died and left the family in poverty, the younger Elihu apprenticed himself to the village blacksmith. While working at the forge, he studied classical languages. In 1837 he moved to Worcester, Massachusetts, to be close to the library at the Antiquarian Society there. Still laboring as a blacksmith, he soon composed a letter in Celto–Breton that the Royal Antiquarian Society in France declared to be capably written. In time, Burritt would master fifty languages and gain widespread recognition as the "learned blacksmith."[1]

Though he turned down an opportunity to study at Harvard—preferring, he said, to "stand in the ranks of the working-men of New England"[2]—Burritt accepted invitations to lecture on a variety of subjects.

It was while studying geography that he suddenly realized that the earth's vast array of climates and crops produced a natural interdependence that tied one nation to another. At that moment, without ever having studied the subject formally, Burritt became a convert to the cause of peace.[3]

The movement had enlisted devoted workers before, but never had someone so energetic and charismatic as Burritt become immersed in the cause. Burritt's achievements were phenomenal. From 1844 to 1846, he held a series of peace conventions in Massachusetts designed to appeal to those pacifists who wished to oppose defensive wars as well as offensive ones. He started *The Christian Citizen*, a weekly newspaper that for a time became the most influential peace publication in the land. He helped found the Worcester County Peace Society and sent out a thousand "Olive Leaves"—short articles on peace—a week. Two hundred newspapers routinely inserted them into their texts, and countless of his other publications found their way into railway cars, where passengers found them hard to ignore. For a time Burritt even became editor of the *Advocate of Peace*. He also threw himself into his "Ocean Penny Postage" project in the hopes that cheap intercontinental mail might cement the bonds of peace throughout the world.[4]

Nor was that all. Burritt's work on behalf of peace in Europe was astounding. In 1846 he traveled to England and began the League of Universal Brotherhood. Prospective members were required to sign a pledge never to support or sanction the preparation for or prosecution of any war. By 1850 tens of thousands on both sides of the Atlantic had signed the pledge. When the dispute over the Oregon territory strained relations between the U.S. and Great Britain, Burritt organized the "Friendly Address" movement, in which he paired cities from each country. The cities wrote letters to one another, pledging to respect the bonds of peace that lay between them, regardless of the way their governments behaved. In 1846 and 1852, during times of political tension, Burritt arranged Friendly Addresses between towns in England and France. Burritt also published the *Bond of Brotherhood*, an international peace journal. He arranged for Olive Leaves to be published in French, German, Spanish, Danish, and Russian newspapers and founded over 150 Olive Leaf Circles—discussion groups for women—in the British Isles.[5] And if that were not enough, he became a leader in organizing International Peace Congresses in Europe in 1848 (Brussels), 1849 (Paris), 1850 (Frankfort), and 1851 (London).[6]

Despite all his efforts, however, by 1850 both the American Peace Society and the New England Non-Resistance Society had rejected Burritt's leadership. Burritt's pacifism was in the tradition of Grimke and Ladd; he held human life inviolable and opposed all war. He was not, however, opposed to participation in government. In fact, he even consented to run for the state senate in New York on the Liberty party ticket in 1844. In addition, though he was passionately committed to abolitionism and the free labor movement, he was a proponent of compensated emancipation. The Garrisonians could forgive neither his attitude toward government nor his plan for emancipation. Nathaniel Rogers, editor of the abolitionist paper *Herald of Freedom*, sniffed that Burritt's *Christian Citizen* was an incongruous title—one could be either a citizen or a Christian, but not both. The *Liberator* wondered at the "marvelous inconsistency" that allowed Burritt to run for an office that would require him to swear allegiance to a state constitution that gave the governor the power to "kill, slay, and destroy if necessary." And Edmund Quincy was merciless in evaluating the League of Universal Brotherhood: "We never joined it ourselves," he noted, "simply because of the fatuity it bore in its countenance, and the absurdity that was written in its very face. We thought it an honest humbug, well devised to enable gentlemen to think they were doing a great deal when they were doing nothing."[7]

George Beckwith was not much kinder. "As a practical measure," he said, referring to Burritt's league, "or a system of instrumentalities for the promotion of peace, or any other single object, I hardly know what it means. It is a fine conception, but altogether too vague and broad for any specific purpose."[8] Though Burritt and other pacifists who wanted to stress the inviolability of human life and the sinfulness of all types of warfare managed to capture the *Advocate of Peace* for a year, Beckwith soon regained control. He was determined to base the American Peace Society on the broadest possible platform, and there was no room at the top for an "extremist" like Burritt. Too moderate for the nonresistants, Burritt was too radical for the American Peace Society.

By 1850 there was no room in either society for the mediating position—even if its leading advocate was the most dynamic peace reformer on two continents. Poor Burritt found that few of his other causes fared much better. Down to his few last dollars in 1857 yet busily organizing still another convention on behalf of compensated emancipation, Burritt sighed, "All the enterprises which I have launched before this have broken down. The League of Brotherhood is dead. I gave it ten of the best years of my life; but it could not live, while I was absent from England. The Christian Citizen died because of my absence from America. The Ocean Penny Postage movement is suspended. The Free Labor undertaking has miscarried."[9] Like so many other voices of moderation, Burritt found by the late 1850s that he was speaking to deaf ears.

The decade of the 1840s was a curious time for the cause of peace. Both the American Peace Society and the New England Non-Resistance Society encountered organizational difficulties. The arguments that rocked the American Peace Society were continuations of the old debate between those who condemned only offensive war and those who opposed all war. This time, the conservatives won. Extraneous concerns were forever banished from the cause of peace, and the moderate faction lost any hope of controlling the society. From 1847 onwards the society steered away from the relatively radical stance of 1837 and concentrated instead on preventing offensive wars.

The nonresistants experienced organizational problems of a different kind. Owing to Adin Ballou's unflagging devotion, the Non-Resistance Society continued to conduct annual meetings,[10] but interest in maintaining the society waned. By 1844 even Garrison admitted that the society was defunct. Nevertheless, though enthusiasm for the organizational existence of nonresistance had died, its adherents continued to practice the nonresistant way of life. Nonresistance was such an extreme position that few people—even among the abolitionists—ever adopted it. Among those who did, however, lively debates continued to rage. And nonresistant theology continued to inform its adherents' daily decisions.[11]

The peace reformers' rejection of Burritt illustrated increasing polarization between the American Peace Society and the nonresistants. Burritt and the moderate advocates of peace who gathered around him were the legitimate heirs of William Ladd, yet they would receive no honor from the leaders of the fight for peace. Garrison and the nonresistants had always respected Ladd, even when they thought his pacifism was insufficiently radical. Beckwith had adored the man. Yet neither the Garrisonians nor Beckwith had sympathy for Burritt. The American Peace Society dedicated itself to a conservative reform that excluded Burritt's position from its platform, while the Garrisonians toyed with an interpretation of nonresistance that excluded the Old Testament—not to mention Elihu Burritt—from the fold. There was simply no place for Burritt's brand of peace advocacy.

At the same time the groups grew further polarized, however, both were in accord on one issue: each regarded the 1846 Mexican War as a war of American aggression. Despite all the disagreements that divided them, both the American Peace Society and the nonresistants vigorously opposed American involvement in the war. Though they had quarreled about many things, neither group had ever relinquished the commitment to the ethic of love that was basic to their pacifism. Thus, it was never right, either for nations or for individuals, to do evil that good might come of it. Regardless of the consequences, both individuals and nations were obliged to follow the model of Jesus, who, when confronted by enemies, steadfastly refused to strike a blow. Appalled at their government's actions, both the nonresistants and the members of the American Peace Society condemned the war as immoral and demanded that it end.

Thus, despite reorganization within the two groups and an increasing alienation between them, the American Peace Society and the nonresistants came to a consensus when confronted by the Mexican War. According to their theological analyses, the war was wrong. In light of that understanding, they condemned it unequivocally and publicly agitated for a cessation to the fighting. Temperamentally and institutionally the nonresistants and the members of the American Peace Society were growing ever further apart, but each of them had the courage to dissent from a war they deemed immoral.

The American Peace Society: The Reform Party Flounders

As Ladd's handpicked successor to edit the society's journal and serve as its secretary, George Beckwith was in a strong position at Ladd's death in 1841. Beckwith's power, however, was not absolute. Samuel E. Coues, who became president of the society in 1841, was also a force to be reckoned with. Coues hoped to make the society's opposition to all war abundantly clear. Convinced of the inviolability of human life, he was also active in opposing capital punishment. Along with others such as Amasa Walker and Joshua P. Blanchard, Coues was ready to continue the battle for the "high ground" that Ladd in his later years had occupied. He did not share Beckwith's fears about alienating more conservative members from the cause of peace. When Elihu Burritt became involved in peace activities, Coues and others sympathetic to his antiwar, progovernment position rallied around him.

Coues and Blanchard were New England merchants. Blanchard's financial generosity—particularly needed after Ladd's death eliminated the cause's most faithful giver—helped keep the American Peace Society afloat.[12] Coues was active in several reform movements in New Hampshire. He labored hard to establish an asylum for the insane and was a voluble opponent of capital punishment. In addition, he contributed numerous articles to the cause of peace. Henry Clarke Wright applauded Coues for respecting the law of love to such a degree that he refused to employ lawyers to collect outstanding bills or to buy an insurance policy to cover his losses. In 1839 Wright reported that Coues and his partner engaged in business costs that annually ran over several hundred thousand dollars. Yet on the average they paid less than eight dollars a year to lawyers. Marveling on the efficacy of the gospel, Wright remarked, "What a comment on the law of love in collecting debts!"[13]

Amasa Walker was a banker and politician who in 1851 would become the secretary of state of Massachusetts. Still later he would serve as a member of Congress. His influence in the peace movement became noteworthy in 1836, when he agreed to chair the board of directors and the executive committee of the American Peace Society. In the 1840s he lectured on political economy at Oberlin College, an activity that was also significant to the cause of peace. With Charles Finney as president, Oberlin had emerged as the western leader of evangelical reform. In his tour as a faculty member, Walker promoted peace societies on campus; he traveled to Europe as a delegate to the International Peace Congresses of 1844 and 1849.[14] It was, moreover, through Walker's influence in the West that Burritt was able—as Ladd had always ached to do—personally to bring the cause of peace to the provinces.[15]

The 1840s was a time in which the American Peace Society was especially active in missionary efforts. In addition to Burritt's peripatetic endeavors, other strategies were put into play. Sylvester Judd, a Maine Unitarian minister who belonged to the peace society, made a stir in his home state by preaching a sermon on the evils of the Revolutionary War while the state legislature was in session. The legislature responded by dismissing him from his position as honorary chaplain. Judd then published his sermon, and the peace society, consistent with its long established opposition to the Revolution, promoted Judd's work.[16] The society once more concentrated on sending speakers to denominational gatherings, and church groups once again began passing resolutions in favor of peace. In 1844 Beckwith distributed peace literature to the ministers who attended the April Triennial Convention of Baptist Ministers in Philadelphia and the May meeting of the Methodist General Conference. In that way, he reckoned, one half of the ministers in the country had directly received publications on peace.[17]

In December of 1844 the society hired Rev. E. W. Jackson to act as the society's agent to the Methodists.[18] Within a year he had toured western New York, obtaining resolutions commending the society from the Baltimore Conference, the Philadelphia Conference, and the Oneida Conference as well.[19] In 1847, encouraged by the interest achieved at Oberlin, the society decided to concentrate on the West, hoping to send a copy of *The Peace Manual* to each Sunday school and every minister in the region.[20] In 1848 Rev. H. B. Pierpont and Rev. W. H. Dalrymple both began traveling in Michigan on behalf of the society, and donations, as well as ecclesiastical resolutions, soon followed.[21]

Despite these signs of vitality, the American Peace Society was a deeply troubled organization. In his later years, William Ladd had come to believe that the society faced no bigger obstacle than the public's apathy to the cause of peace.[22] Ladd resolved to advocate more controversial positions in order to breathe life into the movement. The reform party that followed in his tradition agreed with that strategy. In his "History of the Peace-Cause," Frederick Holland remembered that, once the nonresistants separated from the society, there was nothing left to argue about. "Everybody," he said, "even generals and kings, professed to condemn wars of *offence*. For the purpose of avoiding opposition and obloquy, the motive power was destroyed."[23] The reform group wanted to condemn all war, and, though they did not wish to join the nonresistants, they were willing to work with them in the crusade against war. Amasa Walker declared at the first annual meeting of the New England Non-Resistance Society that he applauded the "glorious truth" that it was never right to fight for any cause. The Massachusetts Peace Society, he said, had been so mild in its peace witness that it had accomplished nothing;[24] it was only once the American Peace Society declared all war wrong that progress had become possible. Though he belonged to the American Peace Society, Walker noted, he was a friend to the nonresistants.[25]

George Beckwith did not consider the nonresistants his friends. Nor was he enthralled with the tactics Ladd had adopted in his last years. He wanted, Beckwith explained, the *moderate* friends of peace—as were Noah Worcester and William Ladd (at first) and William Ellery Channing—to feel free to work with the society. Rather than alienate the "moderates" (most people called them conservatives) with outlandish claims, Beckwith urged that the friends of peace concentrate on the things they could agree upon. As he stated in his introduction to Upham's *Manual of Peace:*

> We wish the cause of Peace to be distinctly understood. It seeks only the abolition of a specific, well-defined custom,—the practice of international war,—and has nothing to do with anything else. All the relations among men consist either in the relation of individuals to one another, in the relations of individuals to society or government, or the relation of one society or government to another; and the cause of Peace is restricted solely to this last class of relations, and aims solely at *such an application of the GOSPEL to the intercourse of nations, as shall put an end to the practice of settling their disputes by the sword.* This view of our cause relieves it from a variety of extraneous questions. If our only province is the intercourse of nations and

our sole object the abolition of war between them, then have we nothing to do with capital punishments, or the strict inviolability of human life, or the question of whether the gospel allows the application of physical force to the government of states, schools, and families. . . . The cause of peace is not encumbered with such causes, but confines itself to the single purpose of abolishing war.[26]

For Beckwith it only made sense to concentrate on a single reform that all the advocates of peace could agree upon: eliminating international wars. "When this shall have been accomplished," he admitted, "a vast deal more will doubtless remain to be done; but the associated friends of peace will then have fulfilled their specific function."[27]

The reform group wanted to do more. They were tired of restating the same old arguments against defensive wars that Noah Worcester had popularized in 1815. They were ready to take a more radical stance. When Elihu Burritt, with his boundless enthusiasm and energy, threw himself into the cause of peace, he was the catalyst for those who wished to proclaim human life inviolable. The reform group as a whole chaffed at Beckwith's timidity, and Burritt in particular, according to Holland, "felt hampered by Mr. Beckwith's narrowness of scope & dictatorial spirit."[28] After the annual meeting of the American Peace Society on May 26, 1845, the reform group, including Burritt, Coues, Walker, Blanchard, Sylvester Judd, and E. W. Jackson, gathered for a strategy session.[29]

It is not easy to reconstruct the points at issue. Few if any signs of dissension trickled into the *Advocate*, and the notes of the society's subsequent executive committee meetings were sketchy. The partnership between conservatives and moderates, of course, had always been shaky. The moderates were far more disposed to denounce social problems as sins in need of repentance than were the conservatives, who valued respectability and unity above supposed purity. For years, an uneasy truce had united both parties, but with Ladd dead and Beckwith pushing a conservative platform, the moderates felt they were being squeezed out. They resented Beckwith, and they suspected that his frequent complaints of overwork were just a front to mask a plot to monopolize the society. Holland, as a Unitarian pastor, was certain that Beckwith, a Congregationalist, regarded the Unitarians and the Methodists—whom Jackson had recently recruited—as threats to orthodox hegemony in the society.[30] To the members of the reform group, Beckwith's policies were faint-hearted, while his personality was dictatorial. Deciding to do something about it, they turned to the executive committee, where they wielded significant clout.

They started with his salary. In October of 1841 the executive committee had granted Beckwith a salary of a thousand dollars with an additional two hundred to be added when the funds became available. At an
executive committee meeting on May 27, 1845—the day after the reform
group had met in private session—Amasa Walker moved that Elihu
Burritt replace Beckwith as editor of the *Advocate* and that no officer or
agent receive a salary of more than six hundred dollars, plus expenses.
Considerable discussion followed, subcommittees were formed, and the
group adjourned. When it reconvened the next day, a motion was made
to pay the corresponding secretary (Beckwith), the treasurer, and the
traveling agent (Jackson) an annual salary of six hundred dollars each. It
was also moved that Walker and Burritt join Beckwith as editors of the
Advocate. Walker and Burritt declined the partnership, seeing the impos-
sibility of achieving a harmonious working relationship, and another
subcommittee was appointed to study the problem.[31]

The next meeting, on June 23, 1845, determined that Elihu Burritt
alone would edit the *Advocate*. Later meetings worked out the details:
Burritt would assume financial and editorial responsibility beginning
January 1, 1846, at a salary of two hundred dollars. The low salary was a
matter of conscience for Burritt. Accustomed to poverty, he had viewed
Beckwith's financial demands on the society as unconscionable, complaining in his diary that Beckwith

> somehow manages to absorb all the means of the society, and all its
> incidental revenue in his own salary . . . so the whole enterprise is associ-
> ated with the salary of a single individual whose cry on his missions is
> money! money! For the last few nos. of the Advocate, he has had scarcely a
> page of original matter. I told Blanchard if the Society were as rich as
> Croesus, my conscience would not permit me to take more than $200 for
> editing the work.[32]

Burritt promptly changed the society's journal name to the *Advocate of
Peace and Universal Brotherhood*. His flowery prose spiced up the predictably dull *Advocate*, and letters from the Friendly Address Movement also
added a note of vigor. Jackson's work among the Methodists continued
to produce new members who supported the reform group "heart and
soul,"[33] and prospects appeared bright. At the same time the society's
journal was urging people to sign the pledge and join the League of
Universal Brotherhood, however, Beckwith was working behind the
scenes to regain control. By the annual meeting on May 25, 1846, he had
gathered his forces and was ready to strike.

Prior to the meeting Beckwith issued an appeal "to all men of moderate peace views," asking the peace society to return to a broad platform and to make its position on extraneous reforms clear. Beckwith's Congregational friends turned out in large numbers at the meeting. The reform group had anticipated that kind of maneuver and had brought allies of its own. Even William Lloyd Garrison and Stephen Foster of the New England Non-Resistance Society joined the American Peace Society for the occasion to help the reform group stem the conservative tide.[34] The atmosphere was tense—"something like a riot," Merle Curti has said—as the proceedings commenced. After delegates submitted resolutions, Amasa Walker rose to begin discussion. Calling upon the society to rebuke the Mexican War and all war, he declared, "We peace men can make no distinction; we are not traitors to our country . . . but we go against *all* war, for whatever purpose or under whatever pretext."[35]

Elihu Burritt followed him, urging, "It may be imputed to fanaticism and ultraism, but it has come to this: that if the gospel forbids all war, then there never was, and never will be, a period when its demands were more imperative than now. . . . O! stupendous delusions are these defensive wars!" Holland and Walter Channing, two more members of the reform group, added their support, and Stephen Foster rose to urge the society to condemn all wars. Discussion continued, but the delegates adjourned for the evening without taking a vote. Sensing that the conservatives were in the majority, Beckwith met with his allies over the course of the evening to finalize the resolutions that he planned to introduce the next day.[36]

When the meeting resumed the following morning, Beckwith seized control. At his urging, the society passed a series of resolutions insisting that its work be confined to the single goal of eliminating international war; that the basis of cooperation in the cause was the platform of the First General Peace Convention of London in 1843, which stated that war was inconsistent with Christianity and the true interests of humanity; and that all persons were welcome to unite with the society, which would be sure to conduct its affairs without conflicting with "principles, interests, or institutions which the Christian community hold dear and sacred." The reform group managed to exonerate itself of Beckwith's charge that it had mingled extraneous reforms with the cause of peace. In everything else, however, Beckwith emerged triumphant.[37]

Though he continued to edit the *Advocate*, Burritt resigned his position on the society's executive committee on June 5, 1846. Five days later, a committee report recommended revising the constitution to omit the clause stating the society was "founded on the principle that all war is contrary to the spirit of the gospel."[38] No matter how much enthusiasm

Burritt might have generated and regardless of the tens of thousands who would sign the pledge to join the League of Universal Brotherhood, he had not succeeded in capturing the machinery of the American Peace Society. There George Beckwith, determined to steer a cautious course, reigned supreme. Though the board of directors protested in December of 1846, the members of the reform group—Coues (the society's president), Blanchard (its treasurer), Walker (a vice-president), Jackson, and Walter Channing—resigned their positions on the executive committee. Burritt gave the *Advocate* back to Beckwith, and the Peace Society was once again firmly in the hands of the conservatives.

Burritt did not leave without a parting shot. The December 1846 *Advocate* accused the society of choosing the path "that bends to merge with the easy highway of the multitude." Burritt explained that he had no doubt that Beckwith's policy would add numbers to the society, since few in the civilized world—including soldiers with dripping bayonets— would be excluded. "We could not 'keep rank' for a moment," he explained, "with *peace advocates* of defensive wars, which advocates are to be accommodated by cutting down the constitution of the society to their low level of faith." The question, he concluded, was not whether Christianity tolerated war, but whether the American Peace Society did. "Good," Burritt noted in one last barb, "can never come from disobedience to the Prince of Peace."[39] In his history of the society, Frederick Holland railed at Beckwith. "A man of any sort of selfsacrifice [sic]," he complained, "would have asked himself if he alone was worth more to the cause he professed to love than such a world honored philanthropist as Elihu Burritt, such an energetic peaceman as Joshua P. Blanchard, such a philosophical reformer as Amasa Walker," to say nothing of the others who left with them.[40]

And so Beckwith had his victory. At Blanchard's resignation as treasurer, he assumed that position too, and complaints soon surfaced regarding his handling of the finances. No one thought he was embezzling money, but many people were frustrated that Beckwith's reports were so sketchy that it was hard to tell how he was handling it. Controversies would arise until 1851, when Beckwith would squelch the last of them. Yet through it all, he managed to achieve the exact policy that he had sought. Though the members of the reform party resigned from the executive committee in 1846, they did not leave the society. Burritt would spend the next few years in England, but the rest of the reformers stuck with the American Peace Society. Unwelcome in the nonresistant camp, there was nowhere else for them to go.

The reform group did have one consolation: the threatened amendment of the 1837 constitution never occurred. Of course, the stipulations that the 1846 annual meeting laid down for interpreting the constitution deprived it of much of its rigor, but the oft-debated amendment of 1837 survived intact. And Beckwith genuinely seemed to want the reformers to remain in the society. Indeed, Beckwith explained, he was merely creating the kind of atmosphere that the majority of the members desired. When in 1846 he had circulated a petition asking whether the constitution should be altered so as to exclude conservatives, only one person said yes. All that he had done, he insisted, was to resist the reform party's desire to radicalize the society. Instead, he asserted, the society would follow the path originally laid down by Worcester and Channing and the early Ladd—all persons would be welcome within the organization, and the society would focus upon a single goal: abolishing international war.[41]

If anything, Beckwith had recreated the tone of the early years of the American Peace Society when it refused to take a position on defensive wars. In those days it had been impossible to tell exactly what the society's attitude toward defensive war was—some members favored it, others opposed it, and articles in the *Harbinger* and the *Calumet* were likely to argue either case. Beckwith intended to carry on in that tradition. He continued to run excerpts in the *Advocate* from writers who opposed all wars, and on the one occasion, when the speaker at the society's anniversary meeting defended just wars, Beckwith was careful to add a note explaining that the society did not sanction any kind of war, though it did allow for a diversity of opinions among its members.[42] In adopting the language of the 1843 London Convention that declared all war inconsistent with Christianity and with humanity's true interests, Beckwith softened the 1837 constitution so that the society's position could mean almost anything:

> We grant that this language is indefinite, allowing a pretty free play of the pendulum; but this is just what we want in order to meet the diversity of opinion among the friends of peace. We can *make* it express the belief of *all* wars unchristian; but it *pledges* us only to a condemnation of the custom. To this principle there can be no objection from anyone willing to labor for the abolition of war. . . . We should spread our sails for every breeze that may waft us sooner into the port of universal and permanent peace.[43]

In setting his sights on peace, Beckwith had turned back the clock to 1828, a time when immediatists and colonizationists could still work together in the antislavery movement. That alliance had long since dissolved among antislavery workers, among whom there were sufficient numbers and interest to support conservative, moderate, and radical groups. In the less popular peace movement, however, the Garrisonians dominated the radical fringe, leaving conservatives and moderates to struggle among themselves for control of the only other viable peace organization. Under Beckwith's leadership, the conservatives gained dominance. From 1847 onwards, despite the efforts of a dissenting minority, the American Peace Society would be as conservative in temperament as the nonresistants were radical.

The Nonresistants: Disunionism and Changing Views of Scripture

And the nonresistants *were* radical. Though they lost enthusiasm for keeping the New England Non-Resistance Society going, particularly after Henry Clarke Wright went to England as an agent of the society in the early 1840s, they continued to practice the nonresistant ethic in their personal lives. Garrison explained the state of affairs in an 1844 letter to Wright:

> The Society, I regret to say, has had only a nominal existence during the past year—and, indeed, ever since your departure. It is without an organ, without funds, without publications. Yet, I rejoice to add, on the other hand, that the cause of non-resistance is gaining new adherents continually, through the radical character of the anti-slavery movement. At present, that movement is first in the order of progress and reform on this soil, in which every non-resistant is most deeply interested, and which absorbs nearly all our time and means; and this is the reason why our Non-Resistance Society, as such, gets so little attention.[44]

Garrison was not jesting when he described the antislavery reformers as radical. It was during this period that he began to push disunionism as an abolitionist policy. For those abolitionists who were also nonresistants, this tactic intensified the antigovernment sentiments that came naturally to them.

Thus, while the American Peace Society was insisting in a hundred different ways that peace advocacy was consistent with the institution of government, the nonresistants were arguing that the Constitution of the United States was a sinful document and that the Union ought to be dissolved. In addition, some of the nonresistants were having doubts about the authority of Scripture, particularly about the inspiration of the Old Testament. In positing a law of love that was superior to Scripture and that invariably determined divine actions, these nonresistants again moved further to the left of the American Peace Society. Indeed, the entire decade of the forties could be characterized as a time of polarization—a time when the American Peace Society became more conservative and the nonresistants more radical.

The campaign to champion disunionism illustrated the sweeping nature of the nonresistants' reform. As abolitionists the nonresistants faced two dilemmas in the 1840s. In the first place, unlike the Garrisonians, Tappanites and other immediatist abolitionists did not shun political involvement. They were willing to participate in the legislative process in order to dissolve slavery. Some even formed antislavery political organizations, such as the Liberty party, to achieve that end. If the nonresistants wished to continue to oppose political abolitionism, they needed to establish a compelling alternative policy. Second, they had to concede that the organizational life of nonresistance had reached a dead end. The nonresistance society was not growing, and, with the exception of the ever faithful Ballou, even the most devout members were absorbed in the antislavery cause. No one was proposing that nonresistance be abandoned, but everyone could see that they needed to adopt a new strategy if they were to keep the principles of nonresistance before the public eye.

Disunionism proved to be the answer to both dilemmas. Since they believed that governments based upon force were immoral and that reforms that changed institutions rather than individuals were ineffectual, the Garrisonians could not support political abolitionism.[45] Disunionism provided an alternative to political abolitionism by convincing people that, in the words of the Massachusetts Anti-Slavery Society, "THE COMPACT WHICH EXISTS BETWEEN THE NORTH AND SOUTH IS A 'COVENANT WITH DEATH, AND AN AGREEMENT WITH HELL,'—INVOLVING BOTH PARTIES IN ATROCIOUS CRIMINALITY,—AND SHOULD BE IMMEDIATELY ANNULLED."[46] The logic of disunionism was simple: the Constitution was a proslavery document; by adhering to the Constitution, the North protected the "rights" of Southern slaveholders; therefore, the first order of business was to make "the REPEAL OF THE UNION between the North and the South, the grand rallying point until it be accomplished, or slavery cease to pollute our soil."[47] Garrison first proposed this strategy in 1842. The American Anti-Slavery Society officially adopted it in 1844.[48] As Aileen Kraditor has noted, the effect of the demand for disunionism was the same as earlier abolitionist demands for immediate emancipation or individual perfectionism. Disunionism was a moral imperative that compelled each individual to define slavery as sinful and to refuse to be an accessory to the government that sanctioned it. Disunionism did not ask for the North to separate from the South, but for individuals in every section of the nation to renounce the sin of slavery and the sinful government that protected it. Disunionism, Garrison claimed, was not a threat but a moral obligation. It was the citizen's appeal, without the specter of bloodshed, that slavery cease or that the Union that gave it life be dissolved.[49]

As a strategy for reform, disunionism emphasized the antigovernment sentiments natural to nonresistance at the same time it explicated a separatism based on less stringent conditions than those that nonresistants had earlier suggested. From the start, nonresistants had rejected participation in government on the grounds that the state necessarily relied upon coercion to maintain power and enforce its edicts. The constitution of the nonresistance society had prohibited all participation in government for that reason. Later nonresistant writings reinforced that decision. At the second annual meeting, for example, the society passed a resolution declaring that "all existing human governments are based on the life-taking, war-making power, as essential to their existence; and they are therefore wrong, and no person believing in the inviolability of human life, and the sinfulness of war, can be identified with them as electors, or office-holders, without guilt."[50] From the beginning, either by founding alternative communities or simply by refusing to participate in the workings of the state, the nonresistants had been practicing a kind of disunionism.

In advocating a disunionism based upon the assumption that the Constitution was a proslavery document, however, the Garrisonians were presenting a doctrine that had wider appeal than the earlier claims of the nonresistance society, which had opposed the constitution as a proviolence document. Thus abolitionists who were not nonresistants could support disunionism. Yet nonresistants need not believe that they had compromised the faith. Since slavery in their eyes was the prime example of the law of violence in action, they were happy to denounce slavery as a sin and the Constitution as a proslavery text. When they wrote their father's biography, Wendell Phillips Garrison and Francis Jackson Garrison argued that the nonresistance society had by this time reached the limit of its organized growth, thereby obliging the nonresistants to search for another way to fulfill the millennial expectations of their Declaration of Sentiments. They soon decided that "the most appropriate peace measure in America was clearly the abolition of slavery."[51] In fighting the nation's most blatant form of coercion through moral means that eschewed violence, the nonresistant abolitionists could feel confident that they had betrayed neither cause.

In that manner disunionism provided an alternative to political abolitionism at the same time that it allowed the Garrisonians to throw themselves into the fight against slavery without abandoning their devotion to nonresistance. Disunionism was a paradoxical strategy. Though it was not as radical as nonresistance, its antigovernmental emphasis stirred abolitionists who were not members of the nonresistance society into renouncing their support for a government founded upon sin. And the constant antigovernment refrains—no union with slaveholders; the Union is a covenant with death and an agreement with Hell—that peppered radical abolitionist literature and speeches reinforced the nonresistants' tendency to hold government in disdain. Though disunionism was not as sweeping a reform as nonresistance, it nevertheless made abolitionists (nonresistant and otherwise) more opposed to government than ever.[52]

Given their scorn for the Union, it is easy to see why the nonresistants rejected as enthusiastic an advocate of peace as Elihu Burritt. As much as they admired his insistence on the inviolability of human life, the nonresistants could not abide Burritt's views on government. Burritt was devoted to the Union and could refer to it as "the concentrating nucleus of the hopes and interests of the future ages of humanity." In an 1845 speech at the Liberty party convention in Cincinnati, Burritt described the possibility of the dissolution of the Union as a "Satanic" idea that should be "banished from every American heart."[53]

Garrison was so angry that he ran Burritt's remarks under the *Liberator's* "Refuge of Oppression" column—a section traditionally devoted to printing opponents' outrageous or absurd comments. Garrison ridiculed Burritt for regarding the Union "as if it were 'the New Jerusalem, coming down from God out of heaven.'" Denouncing such rhetoric as blasphemous, Garrison insisted that the Union was just another name for the Constitution, and that the repeal or abrogation of the Constitution would be the dissolution of the Union. Rather than envisioning the Union as the work of heaven, Garrison concluded, "I hear the voice of God saying, 'Your covenant with death shall be annulled, and your agreement with hell shall not stand: when the overflowing scourge shall pass through, then shall ye be trodden down by it. Judgment also will I lay to the line, and righteousness to the plummet; and the hail shall sweep away the refuge of lies, and water shall overflow the hiding place.' My soul exclaims—'THE WILL OF GOD BE DONE.[']"[54]

Clearly, Burritt's views on government meant that he could not cast his lot with the Garrisonians. As uncomfortable as the fit was, he and his followers belonged more with the American Peace Society than with the nonresistants. The nonresistants' disenchantment with the Union was as appalling to the members of the peace society as their own insistence that the cause of peace was consistent with the institution of government was abhorrent to the nonresistants. Equally disturbing to the American Peace Society were the new interpretations of Scripture that the non-resistants suggested in the 1840s.

Garrison and the others had begun their journey to nonresistance with the assumption that it was eminently scriptural. "I need not say to you," Garrison wrote Elizabeth Pease in 1841, "that my religious views are of the most elevated, the most spiritual character; that I esteem the holy scriptures above all other books in the universe and always appeal to the 'law and the testimony' to prove all my peculiar doctrines."[55] Like the other advocates of peace, the nonresistants had resolved the embarrassment of the holy war tradition by arguing that the New Testament replaced that dispensation with Jesus' ethic of love. By the mid-1840s, however, that explanation was growing less and less attractive. Though some, most notably Ballou, continued to abide by the dispensation theory, others found it easier to deny that God had ever sanctioned war. Rather than make excuses for God's seemingly immoral behavior in the Old Testament, these nonresistants chose instead to deny that the Old Testament was divinely inspired.

Garrison's biographer, John Thomas, has argued that it was Theodore Parker, the celebrated Unitarian clergyman and Garrison's pastor, who first prompted Garrison to rethink his views on biblical inspiration.[56] In 1841 Parker helped introduce German biblical criticism to New England by preaching a sermon in which he distinguished between the eternal truths of Christianity and its transient forms. Doctrines like the infallibility of Scripture or the authority of Jesus, Parker said, were simply human inventions. The heart of Christianity was a set of eternal truths that were both immutable and accessible to individuals through intuitive reason. Thus, even if Jesus had never lived or the Bible had never been written, the great truths of Christianity would stand. Conservative Christians were outraged at Parker's notions, and even the liberal Boston Association of Unitarian Ministers asked him to resign. Parker was such a powerful preacher, however, that his place was secure. In 1845 he began preaching at a Boston theater called the Melodian, and when that proved too small, he moved to Music Hall, which seated 3,000 congregants.[57]

Garrison was intrigued by the notion that the authority of the Bible lay in its teachings, not in the church's claim that it was divinely inspired. In 1845 he received a copy of the theological works of Thomas Paine, the eighteenth-century Deist. He had earlier dismissed Paine as a "monster of iniquity," but now he found himself admiring Paine's daring in throwing off church tradition to discover religious truth for himself. Paine had trusted his intellect to reveal to him divine truth, and Garrison shared Paine's confidence in the individual's ability to know and obey God directly. He had posited his notion of the government of God on just such a presupposition. The moral philosophers of the day, moreover, with their assumption that conscience provided each person with immediate access to God, also bolstered Garrison's predilection to place religious authority in the individual. As Francis Wayland had argued in his *Elements*, God had placed a "moral principle . . . in the bosom of every man." In assuming that each person could intuit God's will and was responsible before God to obey it, antebellum moral philosophers had grounded religious knowledge in the subjective perception of the individual.[58]

Wayland, of course, had no idea that Garrison would turn God's moral government of the individual into an attack on revealed religion. In Garrison's hands, however, the argument for intuition freed individuals from the "thralldom of tradition and authority." "Truth," Garrison insisted, "is older than any parchment. . . . To discard a portion of scripture is not necessarily to reject the truth, but may be the highest evidence that one can give of his love of truth."[59] Nevertheless, in claiming the authority to sit in judgment upon Scripture and in citing Thomas Paine—whom the public remembered as an enemy of Christianity and as a supporter of the bloody, atheistic French Revolution—Garrison and his followers appeared more fanatical than people had previously suspected. People had already suspected plenty. Henry Wright had written in 1839, " 'Wm. Lloyd Garrison and H. C. Wright are infidels!' This I hear in every place—from ministers and laymen." By 1846 Edmund Quincy complained that the public seemed to think that "we are in the habit of meeting at midnight with dark lanthorns and slouched hats, like so many Guy Fauxes, to gloat over the future explosion of the mine which we are running underneath the foundations of human society, and which is to blow it 'sky high, sir, sky high!' "[60]

To Southerners, the most suspicious of all their critics, the Garrisonians' theories of biblical interpretation proved anew that abolitionism was of Satan. As Hughes and Allen have discussed, Southerners in the antebellum period had grown disenchanted with the natural rights tradition that had inspired Enlightenment thinkers like Paine and Thomas Jefferson to argue that all persons had an inalienable right to liberty. Most Americans had assumed that natural rights and revealed religious truths were compatible with one another. As abolitionists used the natural rights tradition to attack slavery, however, Southerners identified "Nature and Nature's God" with abolitionist infidelity and turned to the Bible for aid. No one stated the Southern strategy more clearly than Robert Lewis Dabney, Presbyterian theologian at Hampden Sydney College in Virginia: "Here is our policy, then, to push the Bible continually, to drive Abolitionism to the wall, to compel it to assume an anti-Christian position." Southern ministers maligned the Declaration of Independence as godless, arguing that the only equality people shared at birth was a spiritual one: universal sinfulness. Holding up patriarchal Israel as the model for a godly society, they exhorted their followers to remember that God had given to them "the high and holy keeping, above all other conservators, of the Bible, the whole Bible, and nothing but the Bible; and of that liberty of conscience free from the doctrines and commandments of men. . . . Upon this rock let the South build her house, and the gates of hell shall not prevail against it."[61]

The Garrisonians were prepared to concede the Bible to the South. As early as 1841 some had argued at nonresistance meetings that the gospel was true, not because Jesus uttered it, but because it gave voice to principles that were eternally true.[62] Garrison and Wright saw that a universal moral law, independent of and superior to Scripture, allowed for a radical critique of the proslavery God the South had discovered in Scripture. Garrison contended that the Bible was not "an inspired book, in the popular sense" and that any passage that suggested God had acted in a way repugnant to the eternal moral law simply could not be true. Is it believable, he asked,

> that God is changeable in his moral attributes; that he rules arbitrarily and capriciously, without any fixed law; that it is his prerogative now to sanction war, and then to enjoin peace, as a moral duty—now to command lying and deceiving, and then to speak the truth and deal honestly with all men—now to indulge in licentiousness and then to enforce purity? If so, then a lie may be as good as the truth, and wrong is equal to right under certain circumstances! Why should it not be examined, criticized, and decided upon like any other book—according to its own intrinsic merits? All that is really good in it we should prize, and it will assuredly remain; whatever we discover in it to be either obsolete, erroneous, visionary, or contradicted by fact and experience, let us treat it accordingly. But to take it as from God, credulously and to be in the fashion—is neither to honor God nor exalt the book.[63]

For Garrison, the old dispensational theory of interpreting Scripture had to be jettisoned since it conceded that God had, in the past, acted in a way contrary to Jesus' ethic of love. Since the nonresistants accepted that ethic as normative, they had to reject the Old Testament God of war. As one nonresistant explained, "I do not see how God, *in Jesus*, could be a meek, peaceful human being, and, out of Christ, a wrathful, man-slaying God. . . . *It is making Jesus to be a great deal better than God*, to hold the common idea in regard to God's taking life."[64]

Henry Clarke Wright was quick to join in the new hermeneutics, writing articles like "The Bible a Self-Evident Falsehood, if Opposed to Self-Evident Truth" and "Is God Unjust and Changeable, or Men, the Writers of the Old Testament, in Some Things Mistaken?"[65] In a book published in 1850 called *Anthropology: or, The Science of Man: In Its Bearing on War and Slavery* he argued that the doctrine of "arbitrary" revelation was a delusion and that "God communicates with man, *only* through the nature he has given him." According to Wright, each individual instinctively sensed the "fixed laws" through which God worked in the world. The first of those laws was the sacredness of human life. Thus, if people only relied upon the knowledge of God innate to them, they would realize that God never inflicted death upon anyone. Using "God in the soul" to judge "God in the Bible," they would reject those parts of the Bible—such as the Old Testament penal code and the holy war tradition—that were inconsistent with God's character. Celebrating the divine presence in each human being, Wright asserted that it was time to quit worshiping a God who dwelt apart from human affairs and start worshipping the God who dwelt within humanity. "Henceforth," he claimed, "anthropology shall be my theology. The science of man is the science of God."[66]

Not all the nonresistants believed that private opinion—or personal intuition of the laws of the universe—was superior to Scripture. Adin Ballou continued to hold to the old dispensational reading of the Bible. Unlike Wright and Garrison, he did not think that God and humanity were bound by the same ethic of behavior. It is one thing, he said, for God to inflict pain or to kill a human being but another thing for us to do so. "We have no power to produce restorative, reparatory, or sanctifying results in another state of being, nor even here beyond certain boundaries," Ballou explained, but "eternity as well as time is His field of activity." Ballou distinguished Christian nonresistance from the "philosophical" nonresistance that arose from the "light of nature," insisting that philosophical nonresistance, while noteworthy, was an inferior human alternative to Christianity.[67]

For Ballou, true Christian nonresistance "came down from heaven. It was born, not of *human* nature, but of the *divine* nature." Insisting that the Bible culminated in Jesus, whose authority as a teacher determined and established the absolute religion of the Bible, Ballou was adamant in maintaining that Jesus was an infallible teacher and that the New Testament was the definitive revelation of Jesus. He was irked that at one moment Garrison would call Jesus fallible, when, in the next breath, he would claim that human nature or human reason were infallible guides to truth. By denying the authority of Jesus, Ballou noted, Garrison had destroyed normative religious truth and had offered in its place the babble of individual opinions.[68]

Wright preferred to say that Garrison had based nonresistance on the "rock of self-evident truth." Yet regardless of what Ballou or the timid reformers in the American Peace Society might think, the proponents of war and slavery had always used the Bible to support their position. And they were continuing to do so. They were also going to the Constitution for aid and comfort. Since there was abundant material in both documents for their enemies to use, Wright and Garrison decided to cut their losses, cede the Bible and the Constitution to their enemies, and find a higher authority upon which to ground nonresistance. Neither document was worth keeping if it allowed God to act immorally. As Wright wrote to Garrison in 1853,

> Your only course was, to deny that the Bible, or any book, has power to sanction war or slavery; and to affirm that nothing is true because it is in a book, nothing false because it is condemned in a book. . . . What sort of reformer had you been, had you admitted that *man's right to life and liberty depended on the construction and authority of a book written two and three thousand years ago?* . . . In behalf of the victims of slavery and war, I bless you that you based your advocacy of humanity on the rock of *self-evident* truth, and not on the interpretations of Bibles and Constitutions. Not an hour could you have stood on any other foundation. . . . I have taken long, deep and earnest counsel of the 'inward monitor'; and the 'spirit of God' had assured me that a God of justice and love never required a slave to obey his master, or men to obey every ordinance of man for the Lord's sake . . . that he never instigated human beings to revengeful, aggressive, and exterminating wars. . . . To God in *my* soul, and in nothing else, will I give heed.[69]

For the Garrisonians, if not for Ballou, the Bible had to be sacrificed to make way for the truth of God.

In developing such a radical view of Scripture, the nonresistants were not in complete accord among themselves. They did agree, however, that the Constitution was expendable and that disunionism was an appropriate strategy for nonresistants as well as for abolitionists. In their attitudes toward the state and toward Scripture, they had moved far to the left of the more conservative members of the American Peace Society.

Nevertheless, despite tendencies for each group to pull away from the other, both the American Peace Society and the nonresistants were at one in condemning the Mexican War.

The Mexican War: A Common Enemy

Both groups could oppose the Mexican War for a simple reason: it violated the ethic of love to which each had adhered from the start. Of course, neither group's ethic was so pure as its members imagined. In the beginning, the ethic of love had presumed two things: first, that both individuals and groups were bound by the gospel of love, and, second, that that gospel ought to be obeyed without regard for the consequences. By 1846 and the start of the Mexican War, both the American Peace Society and the nonresistants had modified their original understandings of that ethic. The American Peace Society had argued that the police function of the state was a God-ordained exception to the gospel of love. In addition, out of fear of scaring away its conservative members, the society refused to apply the ethic of love to relationships between individuals or to defensive wars. The society did not deny that the ethic of love was applicable to those situations, but chose to concentrate solely on the problem of offensive wars.

Though the nonresistants had not admitted any exceptions to the ethic of love, they had acknowledged that most Americans did not adhere to it. The nonresistants did not want to be like those Americans, but they did want to influence them politically. Most nonresistants had no qualms about petitioning the government for reforms that they favored or about advising people who did vote to vote for antislavery candidates. Thus, even though the nonresistants refused to take a hand in running the government, they did want to tell the people who *would* lower themselves to do so what ought to be done. Moreover, the nonresistants—along with the American Peace Society—found it convenient to believe that those who followed the gospel of love would come to a good end. In spite of the martyr imagery that the nonresistants employed, they believed that obedience to Jesus' commands would bring with it prosperity. So did the American Peace Society. Neither group had faced the dark day when the path of duty led only to defeat. For the time being, each of them happily assumed that success was the reward—if not the motive—of obedience.

The Mexican War was a propitious war for both groups. Neither felt ambivalent about condemning it. The Garrisonians immediately branded it a "war for slavery,"[70] as did the American Peace Society. If the

Garrisonians felt any ambivalence, it was only to the degree that they could not help hoping that the "injured Mexicans" would defeat the "lawless" American invaders.[71]

Other Northerners shared the peace activists' assessment of the war. Sectional conflict between the free North and the slave South had been building for years over the territorial expansion of slavery. When Texas won its independence from Mexico in 1836, abolitionists began petitioning against the annexation of Texas, fearing that the addition of a large slave state would guarantee the triumph of the Southern slaveocracy. In the early 1840s, John Quincy Adams and nineteen other Congressmen warned that annexing Texas was grounds for the dissolution of the Union. At times, it appeared to Southerners as if their Northern colleagues thought about nothing other than Texas. An 1842 article in the *Southern Quarterly Review,* for example, complained that William Ellery Channing was so accustomed to connecting Texas with slavery and slavery with crime that he seemed to think "that Texas and sin are identical—that Texas is only another name for the Author of all evil."[72]

The presidential election of 1844 proved to be pivotal. The Democrats nominated James Polk and adopted a platform that promised to annex Texas for the slave states and Oregon for free Northern laborers. The Liberty party and James Birney countered with a campaign that stressed the perfidy of the scheming Southern slave power. Northern politicians in both the Democratic and the Whig parties, fearing that the Liberty party might rob them of votes, hastened to stress that they too were anti-Southern. Henry Clay, the Whig nominee, vacillated so much on the slavery issue that a number of disillusioned Northern Whigs voted for Birney. The crossover vote in New York was enough to throw the state— and the election—to Polk.[73]

With Polk as president, the United States annexed Texas in 1845, prompting Judge William Jay, a moderate peace activist and abolitionist, to urge Northerners to dissolve the Union. By 1846 the worst fears of Northern antislavery activists proved true: annexing Texas provoked a war with Mexico. It was common knowledge among abolitionists that the war was nothing but a fight to extend slavery, and increasingly other Americans in the Northeast agreed. In Congress, Northern Democrats introduced—though they were unable to pass—the Wilmot Proviso, which proposed to prohibit slavery in territory acquired in war with Mexico. Northern "Conscience Whigs," such as Charles Sumner of Massachusetts, began plotting strategy with antislavery politicians in the Democratic and Liberty parties.[74]

It is hard to overemphasize the mistrust and hatred that festered between the North and South. Bertram Wyatt-Brown has shown convincingly that Southerners felt dishonored by Northern implications that Southern culture was so vile it must not be permitted to spread. In response to the Wilmot Proviso, Robert Toombs of Georgia snapped that Southern whites "would be degraded, and unworthy of the name of American freemen, could they consent to remain, for a day or an hour, in a Union where they must stand on the ground of inferiority, and be denied the rights and privileges which were extended to all others."[75] Yankee antislavery activity was, for Southern whites, nothing less than an attack on their characters as well as their civil rights.

Northerners, on the other hand, saw Southern territorial ambitions as a plot to steal the Western frontier from Northern settlers. As James Stewart has observed, Northern rhetoric increasingly depicted the territorial question as a contest between the honest republican farmer and the slaveholding planter. Both the Free Soil party, which emerged in 1848, and the Republican party in the 1850s presented themselves as the champions of free white labor. That sort of antislavery activism was a mixed blessing for abolitionists. Though it popularized anti-Southern and antislavery sentiments, it gave no assistance to the abolitionists' desire to create a biracial egalitarian society. Admittedly, the abolitionists themselves could not claim to be free of racism. White abolitionists in particular did not always succeed in their relationships with blacks, in ridding themselves of racial prejudice. White abolitionists could be patronizing; they could preach when they ought to listen; they could, from their positions of privilege, fail to appreciate the enormity of the caste oppression that even free blacks routinely experienced. But they never lost sight of the goal of racial equality, and in the years to come, the abolitionists would find that antislavery politics designed to safeguard the economic interests of Northern whites fell far short of the millennial splendor they had set as their original aim.[76]

In any case, the prospects of a "war for slavery" created in the Northeast a popular interest in the cause of peace that was exhilarating to its advocates. In 1845 Charles Sumner's Fourth of July address, *The True Grandeur of Nations*, thrilled the American Peace Society with its proclamation that "IN OUR AGE THERE CAN BE NO PEACE THAT IS NOT HONORABLE; THERE CAN BE NO WAR THAT IS NOT DISHONORABLE."[77] The prospect of having a United States senator join the cause of peace was infinitely pleasurable. The peace society published Sumner's address and had the satisfaction of seeing it run in rapid succession through six American editions and five British ones.[78] In addition, once the war with Mexico started, many distinguished persons not normally associated with peace advocacy rallied to the cause. Thoreau went to jail rather than pay war taxes, and Theodore Parker, who made it clear that he was condemning only this war, not all wars, boldly proclaimed to raucous crowds that

> Men, needed to hew wool and honestly serve society, are marching about your streets; they are learning to kill men, men who never harmed us, nor them; learning to kill their brothers. It is a mean and infamous war we are fighting. It is a great boy fighting a little one, and that little one feeble and sick. What makes it worse is, the little boy is in the right, and the big boy is in the wrong, and tells solemn lies to make his side seem right. . . . This is a war for slavery, a mean and infamous war; an aristrocratic war, a war against the best interests of mankind. If God please, we will die a thousand times, but never draw a blade in this wicked war.[79]

Here at last was a well-known, nonpacifist abolitionist apparently converting to the crusade for peace.

Other notables joined in the hue and cry. Francis Wayland preached a dramatic series of sermons in Brown chapel on "The Duty of Obedience to the Civil Magistrate." Wayland argued that the Mexican War was a war of indiscriminate slaughter and that it could not be justified on Christian principles.[80] Indeed, "revolutionary" and "treasonable" speeches by Parker and Channing so excited Garrison that he wrote to Henry Clarke Wright:

> Never before have such meetings been held in this Commonwealth, or in this country. The pillars of government are shaking—Church and State are tottering to their overthrow. Multitudes are lifting up their voices for a new union and a new government, in which nothing oppressive or unchristian shall enter. The times are stirring and eventful indeed. We are living years in days. Every moment is big with a sublime event.[81]

Admittedly many Americans supported the war, but for advocates of peace who lived in New England, where war opposition was fiercest, the days of the Mexican War were eventful indeed.

For the American Peace Society in particular, these days were the headiest of times. Though the society's innate cautiousness deterred it from holding public meetings against the war—as the executive committee at one point considered doing[82]—there were still many ways to protest the criminality of the American invasion of Mexico. The annual report of 1846 declared that the war had been provoked by American troops.[83] Articles in the *Advocate* characterized the war as an act of "unprincipled depravity" and "unmitigated sin,"[84] described atrocities committed by American troops in gruesome detail,[85] and endlessly urged Americans to petition Congress and the president to stop the war.[86] The society offered a five hundred dollar prize for the best essay reviewing the war and published an account by William Jay that argued that President Polk had deliberately lured Mexico into war to strengthen the political power of the slave states.[87] The 1847 annual report included resolutions that damned the Mexican War as wickedness and folly, declaring that the popular motto "our country, right or wrong" was subversive of God's moral character.[88]

Other groups were also protesting the war. Presbyterian synods, Congregational associations, and Methodist conferences passed resolutions condemning it, and the Unitarians petitioned both houses of Congress to end the fighting.[89] Though at no time did opponents of the war unite to form a working coalition, still the cumulative effect of all the protests was anything but negligible. Historian Charles DeBenedetti has argued that the antiwar fervor reached such a pitch by the end of 1847 that President Polk was forced to accept a limited conquest of Mexico and end the war sooner than he wished.[90] At the May 1848 annual meeting of the American Peace Society, the largest crowd ever to attend the anniversary celebration overflowed Boston's Winter Street Church.[91] The days of the Mexican War were the high point of the society's organizational existence. The cause of peace, united with Northern sectional interests, was at last a popular one, and the campaign to end war forever seemed to be making headway.

The advocates of peace were comfortable linking their cause with Northern interests, for they had always viewed the Northeast as an enlightened land called to missionize the rest of the country. At its formation the American Peace Society had divided the nation into two parts: the Northeast (where the society expected success) and everything else, with the implication that everything south and west of New York City was a howling wilderness. The passing of time did little to alter that perception. In 1840 Amasa Walker remarked that the "war-principle" was so rampant in the South and the West that "murders and assassinations are of such frequency . . . as to attract litle attention." In 1844 the society congratulated itself on exhibiting sufficient intelligence, virtue, and piety to stifle the war spirit that surged so strongly in the South and West that it "might have continued till doomsday without rolling back the deluge of liquid fire that was sweeping over our land." During the Mexican War the society insisted that, had the cause of peace had sufficient time to work its civilizing influence on the West, the war could have been avoided. An article in the *Advocate* in 1848 observed that every section of the nation had managed to send antiwar petitions to

Congress except for the extreme Southwest, "that great moral sink and sewer of the nation."[92]

The nonresistants were even more parochial. The South represented to them the "sum of all villainy," while New England was, in Garrison's words, "that paradise of our fallen world."[93] For all their scorn for the Southern slaveocracy, however, the nonresistants had hopes of remaking it in New England's image. As Ronald Walters has pointed out, disunionism was posited upon a nationalistic desire to bring Americans together into a community freed from shame and sin. Disunionism revealed, Walters asserted, "a deeply concealed feeling—a precondition as much as a feeling—that there were noble aspects to America and that the United States had a common fate, for better or for worse." As long as slavery existed, the nonresistants would feel complicitous, for as Garrison said,

> the guilt of slavery is national, its danger is national, and the obligation to remove it is national. I affirm that Pennsylvania is as really a slave-holding State as Georgia—that the free States are as criminal as the slave-holding States—and that the latter are merely the agents of the former. Hence, the people of the United States (not of one portion of territory merely) are wholly responsible, and altogether inexcusable, for the present existence of slavery. . . .

Until they could free the Union of "the most atrocious villainy ever exhibited on earth," Garrison concluded, they could only regard their citizenship "with feelings of shame and indignation."[94]

Both the American Peace Society and the nonresistants hoped, in Bertram Wyatt-Brown's words, "to create new Yankeedoms in places of darkness, firmly convinced that their common culture could be exported."[95] That regional pride blinded them to aspects of their own culture that cried out for reform. Certain, for example, that the slavery system was an inefficient means of production, each group took pride in industrial developments in the North without bothering to critique the abuses of the factory system. Satisfied that capitalism worked for good, both the American Peace Society and the nonresistants elevated free trade to a theological virtue. Henry Clarke Wright announced that free trade would "render international wars impossible," while the *Advocate* hailed free trade as "the Commercial Harbinger of the Millennium."[96] Throwing in their lot with Northern sectionalism, the advocates of peace could at times confuse Northern customs with God's.

In the decades after the war, however, both the American Peace Society and the nonresistants would find that campaigning for peace was not so clearcut as it had seemed during the Mexican War. In the 1850s the groups that had temporarily united with them in opposition to the Mexican War would go their own way, leaving the advocates of peace alone once again. Though the American Peace Society and the nonresistants had grown further apart from each other theologically in the 1840s, they had both clung to the ethic of love foundational to their pacifism. Even that bedrock would be shaken in the decade to come. The issues that confronted them in the fifties—what to do about the increasing incidents of violence in the antislavery movement, how to interpret the slaughter committed by civilized Christian nations in the Crimean War— would challenge to the utmost their understanding of and adherence to the ethic of love. They had tacitly admitted exceptions to that ethic already; in the next ten years, they would have to decide how to respond to the fact that the ethic of love did not, after all, guarantee success to those who did what was right without regard for the consequences.

4

THE
TRAUMA
OF
THE
1850s

Of all the nonresistants, no one was more committed to the cause than Charles Stearns. While Garrison and the other male nonresistants were paying fines to avoid militia duty, Stearns went to prison in 1840 rather than compromise his principles. Later in the decade, while some nonresistants were discussing the possibilities of using "noninjurious physical force" in extreme cases to restrain violent individuals, Stearns flatly denied that it was ever justifiable to use force. One of the leaders in the new interpretations of Scripture developed in the 1840s, Stearns urged his fellow nonresistants to become more radical. Set aside the Old Testament, he told them, for it is the progenitor of war. The God of Jesus never punishes vindictively, nor does God take away life. Never ascribe acts to God that would be sinful in human beings, for if "it is wrong for man to do it, it is not right for God to do."[1] In the mid 1850s, Stearns embarked upon a journey that changed his life forever. Determined to make a witness for peace and for freedom, he left his New England home and moved to "bloody Kansas," where proslavery and antislavery settlers were battling to see who would determine the future of the territory. At first, his new surroundings discouraged Stearns. "I have been much disappointed in the character of the emigrants here," he wrote. "I have almost wished that I had never left my New England home, so great is the difference between the best here and those with whom I have been in the habit of associating." In a few months, however, his spirits had revived, and his belief in the efficacy of nonresistance was as strong as ever. "If anything can save us from utter extermination in the event of the shedding of blood by a few Hotspurs on our side, it will be our steadfast refusal to fight, for principle's sake," he declared. "If you know of a few good men who are willing to do that, pray send them along; but for God's sake, do not send any more California mob-leaders, or fighters of any sort, except those who use the 'sword of the Spirit.' "[2]

Stearns remained sanguine for several months. In September of 1855 he wrote that he was sure he would have been struck, perhaps even mobbed, because of his antislavery principles, if he had not been a nonresistant. "It is always practicable," he concluded, "to be a nonresistant, and to refuse to obey the devil." By December of 1855, however, Stearns was once again wavering. "I take no part in the warlike preparations," he explained, "and yet I am fearful that if a fight should occur, I should not be able to stand by, and see our men shot without seizing a rifle and pulling its trigger." By January of 1856 he had crossed the Rubicon. He had become convinced that abolitionism would triumph only through violence, and after days of prayer he had armed himself with a rifle and a pistol to take on wicked proslavery foes. He wrote to Garrison:

My non-resistance has at length yielded. For ten days I have kept calm, and withstood all solicitations to enter the ranks; but the cold-blooded murder, last night, of one of our best citizens, has decided me. I am sorry to deny the principles of Jesus Christ, after contending for them for so long, but it is not for myself that I am going to fight. It is *for God* and *the slaves. Down with American Slavery!* will be my watchword. . . . I told you that I had given up my non-resistance. I was mistaken; non-resistance simply forbids the taking of the life of a human being. God never made these fiends—they are devils' spawn, and are to be killed as you would shoot lions and tigers. I have always said I would shoot a wild beast. If I shoot these infernal Missourians, it will be on the same principle. . . . If it were an ordinary foe, I should not do it. But these men are not men; they are wild beasts. . . . I love all men as ever, but fools and knaves united, and drunk in the bargain, are not men.[3]

Garrison was having none of it. His reply must have galled Stearns:

> It is evident that our impulsive friend Stearns has got thoroughly frightened
> out of his peace principles, as Peter denied his Lord to save himself from
> impending danger. We compassionate his weakness, and feel no disposi-
> tion to utter a reproachful word; only we hope that he may be enabled to
> imitate the example of Peter, who subsequently lamented his apostasy, and
> brought forth fruits meet for repentance. "Fear not them who can kill the
> body."[4]

"I do not blame you for your harsh language towards me," Stearns
answered, "for I doubtless should have felt in the same way towards
you, if you had come to Kansas and gone to fighting the Missouri wild
beasts, while I had remained behind amid the refined scenes of New
England life, 'with none to molest or make me afraid.' " Nevertheless, he
asserted, he believed that he had continued to show the same courage
that once had prompted him to go to jail in Hartford rather than serve in
the militia. In the past, he explained, he had always turned the other
cheek, but now he lived in a land where there was no law, where
drunken Missourians who were orangutans, not human beings, killed
those who did not defend themselves. He reminded Garrison that the
Missourians had captured an abolitionist and hatcheted him to death.
"Now Mr. Garrison," he added, "tell me if Christ wishes us to submit to
be torn in pieces in this way. For my part, if non-resistance is not a safe
principle, I think it cannot be a true one. . . . I hated to give up a
doctrine so dear to me as Christian non-resistance; but I always wish,
yea I am determined, always to obey the light as fast as it dawns on
me."[5]

For many advocates of peace, the 1850s shed an unwelcome, harsh
light on problems that for years they had been able to ignore. Until that
decade the ambiguities in their ideologies had caused only theoretical
confusions, not practical difficulties. In the 1850s, however, both the
American Peace Society and the nonresistants faced situations that ex-
posed the weaknesses of their thought in painful ways. Both had to
admit that peace was not, as they had assumed, necessarily efficacious in
producing the results they desired. The American Peace Society discovered, to its horror, that the most civilized, Christian nations of Europe—the very countries where the cause of peace had progressed
most—eagerly ravaged each other in bloody combat in the Crimea. And
the nonresistants had to admit that peaceful agitation had not achieved
liberation for the slaves. Some within the fold decided, with Stearns, to

abandon peaceful means when they proved unfruitful. Even those who kept the faith could not help but hope that those who sought to end slavery by violent means would be successful.

It was, all in all, a disturbing decade. By the end, the peace activists' thinking had undergone significant shifts. While it recovered from the shock of the Crimean War, the American Peace Society reacted to native rebellions in India by stressing ever more strongly the necessity for the police function of the state to overrule the gospel of love. By the time of the Civil War, the state's police function was more than an exception to the ethic of love; it was an independent ethic of coercion. The peace society had ceased to believe that all persons and institutions were bound by the gospel of love, and its pacifism was accordingly limited in scope. The gospel that had once insisted that every individual and institution be unconditionally loving, without regard for the consequences, was now tempered by an ethic of coercion, which violently compelled citizens to obey their government.

The nonresistants were also changing. Some of them simply abandoned parts of the nonresistant creed. They could not resist voting for antislavery candidates or helping runaway slaves escape in defiance of the law of the land. And even those who resisted the temptation to vote or to use violence to further their cause often argued that it was the duty of those who were not nonresistants to use violent means to bring about the slaves' liberation. Though most nonresistants never relinquished their devotion to the Sermon on the Mount, their appeals to those who could vote and fight to end slavery revealed an implicit abandonment of the ethic of love that had been foundational to their theology. The nonresistants talked so much about the obligation of those who lived in the world to act according to the best lights available to them—to honor the equality of all human beings as articulated in the Declaration of Independence and to respect the value of liberty as upheld in the American Revolution—that in practice (if not in theory) they too gave legitimacy to an ethic of coercion. One ethic—that of the Sermon on the Mount—was appropriate for the redeemed individual, while an ethic of coercion applied to the unredeemed.

In this manner both the American Peace Society and the nonresistants dealt with ambiguities in their theology by moving away from the ethic of love that had heretofore been the cornerstone of their pacifism. From the beginning both groups had implicitly allowed exceptions to that ethic, but up until the 1850s circumstances had permitted them to avoid resolving the confusions inherent in their thought. In the decade of the fifties most members of each group sought to resolve that confusion by tempering the ethic of love with an ethic of coercion. Ends rather than means—results rather than simple obedience—became increasingly important to their peace advocacy. Though they continued to be pacifists within the appropriate sphere of their ethics, the scope to which the Sermon on the Mount might be applied undoubtedly shrank. The full implications of that shift, however, would not be apparent until the Civil War. It was enough, for the time being, for the advocates of peace to cope with the challenges of the turbulent fifties.

The American Peace Society: The Agony Of Crimea and India

The early years of the 1850s were busy ones for the American Peace Society. The annual meeting of 1851 was the most exciting ever, as the reform party attempted, one last time, to overturn George Beckwith. Led by E. W. Jackson, whose denunciations of Beckwith evoked so much consternation that the meeting degenerated into "a scene of wild confusion and uproar,"[6] the reform group sought to install Jackson as the society's secretary and to gain control of the executive committee. Amid the hubbub, however, Beckwith retained his grip on the society, and business continued as usual.

In keeping with its missionary efforts in the 1840s, the peace society maintained its interest in acquiring converts in the West. By 1853 the society had local representatives in Ohio, Indiana, Kentucky, Missouri, Iowa, Illinois, Wisconsin, and Michigan, plus a few traveling agents who labored for the cause in a full-time capacity.[7] In many ways, the message of the society remained unaltered. Just as it had for the past twenty years, the American Peace Society stressed the relationship between peace and the millennium, insisting that the kingdom would come once peace had been established. Nothing but ignorance and habit, the society argued, prevented humanity from appropriating the gospel of peace. The society was also cheered that the public and the press appeared to be developing ever more positive attitudes toward the cause of peace. Advocates of peace had always recognized that gaining popular support was essential to success, and in the 1850s they believed that signs of progress were evident. "Public opinion on this subject," one article in the *Advocate* declared, "is confessedly very different now from what it was at the commencement of our efforts more than one third of a century ago."[8] A poet looked forward to the time when "The PRESS, at last, will usher in/The bright millennial day."[9] In seeing peace as a necessary precondition for the millennium and describing public opinion as an essential element in establishing peace, the American Peace Society was reiterating themes that went all the way back to Noah Worcester.

Yet some things were new about the society in this period. Since the popular uprisings in Europe in 1848 and the international peace congresses held from 1849 to 1851, the society's attention had increasingly been drawn to European affairs.[10] The activities of the London Peace Society held a particular attraction for the American Peace Society, and the pages of the *Advocate* were dotted with articles and quotations from the London society. Stipulated arbitration—the inclusion in international treaties of mandatory arbitration procedures for the adjudication of disputes—also received increased attention during this period. In the past the society's enthusiasm for a Congress of Nations had overshadowed the appeal of arbitration. Now, however, realizing that stipulated arbitration was a goal more easily attained than the establishment of a Congress of Nations, the society endlessly urged its members to petition Congress to include stipulated arbitration in future international treaties.

It was a great day for the movement in 1853 when a Senate committee reported to the president that future treaties should include stipulated arbitration whenever possible. Because Southern senators had treated them courteously in their lobbying efforts, the members of the peace society dared to hope that the cause of peace might find allies even in the South. "Our Society had done next to nothing in the South, though a few copies of our periodical are circulated there," the *Advocate* noted, "but we have many reasons for believing, that there are, all over our Southern States, what physicians would call 'sporadic cases' of intelligent, warm-hearted interest in our cause. . . . We think the South much riper for this enterprise than most persons expect, or will readily believe. On this point, our own views, we confess, have undergone a change in the light of facts, that we could neither gainsay nor resist." Heartened by his conversation with Senator Foote of Mississippi, Beckwith declared that "the omens of hope are thickening all around us."[11]

In the mid 1850s, however, an event of catastrophic dimensions put an end—at least momentarily—to optimism and business as usual. When England and Russia went to war in the Crimea, that conflict called into question some of the society's basic theological assumptions. In the first place, the cultural Christians of the American Peace Society had believed all along that Christianity and civilization went hand in hand. Where Christianity reigned, there existed "Christian" nations with "Christian governments" and "Christian citizens." From the beginning, the society had stressed that it directed its efforts only at Christian civilizations, for only there, where the gospel had prepared the way, were people ready to take up the cause. It was, then, enormously galling when, as society president William Jay noted, two of the world's most civilized and refined nations had resorted in the Crimea to a custom so barbaric.[12] It had, after all, not been long ago that Beckwith had declared that "the world is becoming too wise and too good to tolerate much longer a custom so foolish and so wicked."[13]

As discouraging as it was to see these two nations locked in mortal combat, it was even more upsetting to realize that the citizens of each state supported the war effort. The American Peace Society had decided, all the way back in the days of William Ladd, that governments would never be leaders in the campaign for peace. "We cannot expect much from politicians," Ladd had asserted, "until we get the people."[14] Writers for the society had assumed that politicians fought wars for their own personal gain, while the common people shouldered the suffering and sacrifice that accompanied the wars. If the cause of peace were to triumph, the society believed, it would do so only because the public had pressured the state into reform. To discover, then, that the war in the Crimea was popular among Russian and English citizens was more than a little disconcerting. According to William Jay, "Most melancholy and disheartening is the fact, that, especially in England, this horrible exchange was made, not to gratify the personal ambition and selfishness of rulers, but in obedience to popular clamor."[15] To add to the gloom, the annual report of 1855 noted that the war in the Crimea had awakened the war demon throughout Europe, putting to naught the work of the past thirty years and creating a state of mind "exceedingly unfavorable to our efforts." It would be hard to crusade for peace among people whose minds had been "well-nigh paganized."[16]

For some members of the American Peace Society, Crimea was not merely discouraging. It was devastating. In his 1814 *Solemn Review of War,* Noah Worcester had argued that the world was, in modern times, less barbaric than formerly. For that reason he thought that the world was ready for the cause of peace. The society had for years assumed the same thing. Yet, as the author of "Demoralization Inseparable from War" noted in the August–September 1855 issue of the *Advocate,* the daily revelations of the Crimea proved that war was as fiendish and tigerlike as ever. Nothing had changed from the barbaric days of old.[17] Humanity had not progressed beyond wanton slaughter. In October of 1855 George Beckwith fell seriously ill, and in December of that year the executive committee appointed Joshua P. Blanchard as editor of the *Advocate* for the duration of Beckwith's illness.[18] Articles published in the *Advocate* during Blanchard's tenure revealed the depths to which some members had fallen.

A December 1855 article set the tone by asserting that the Crimean War had "overwhelmed us with astonishment and grief" by revealing the ineffectiveness of the cause of peace. The Mexican War, the author explained, had been startling, but not dismaying, since it "had not the sympathy of our moral and respected citizens and derived its chief support from a portion of our land into which the demonstrations of the friends of peace had not penetrated." On the other hand, he explained, the Crimean conflict was horrible in every way, since it was "a war waged by the most enlightened part of the most civilized nations of Europe; sustained by popular applause, in all the horrors of former barbarian chivalry." Examining the case with honesty forced the author to draw a painful conclusion:

> From this event we have learned a solemn lesson: the war spirit is not to be exorcised by the methods we have tried. Irresistible demonstrations of the evils and sins of war have been spread through the million pages of the press, over every land in Christendom; and martial history, and poetry and the fleeting journals of the day yet soar above them in malignant triumph: crowded popular assemblies and Conventions of the learned and talented of the age have resolved against war in every form; but these voices have died away in the breeze of popular excitement, or are unheard in the din of conflicting powers: pacific appeals to Sovereigns and rulers, have been received with encouraging courtesy; but not a single arrogant demand on a foreign power has been mitigated in conformity to them; then danger to peace, to liberty, to safety, to morality, or military force, has been fully pointed out; and Europe still throngs with innumerable armies.

The only hope, the author concluded, was in Christianity, "vigorously applied." The state with its "nominally Christian hierarchy" must be converted, and the church itself must preach the gospel of love, not the abrogated Old Testament ethic of war. "Purify the Church from the adulteration of the war spirit," the author concluded, "and the world will follow with joy in the path of peace."[19]

The idea of purifying the church resurfaced repeatedly in the months ahead. The peace society's relationship to organized Christianity had always been ambiguous. On the one hand, the society had consistently contrasted the pacifism of the early church with the "war spirit" of modern Christians. On the other hand, the society had invariably defended the churches of its day against the attacks of the nonresistants and had depended on ministers to spread the cause of peace. Rather than rejecting the churches of America as fallen, since most did not concentrate on the gospel of peace, the society had urged each congregation to become a local peace society. It was hard to be too critical of the churches or of the Christian society that supported them since the peace society assumed that, for the most part, the churches were doing their jobs. All that was required to initiate the age of peace was for the churches to "apply" the gospel of peace more vigorously—to focus specifically on the necessity for all to heed Jesus' words in the Sermon on the Mount. Thereby educated and motivated, the Christian citizens of the land would freely choose to become loving individuals, and the millennial age would begin.

In the first half of 1856 not everyone in the American Peace Society found that scenario convincing. "B" of Castleton, Vermont, wrote two articles calling for a change in the "public religion of Christendom." The churches, he charged, had given their blessing to the Crimean War and had clothed government with a divine sanction so as to suppress individual responsibility. While he conceded that Christians ought to revere government, he insisted that the churches ought also to remind believers that they were obliged to follow their consciences. They must not go blithely off to war in defiance of God's oracles. Instead, he said, the church must remind believers that "our political and all our acts pertaining to state affairs must be regarded as subject to the same law of responsibility to God as our other acts." If necessary, Christians must disobey the state rather than rush off to war.[20]

Other articles also argued that individuals should disobey their governments and refuse to join the war effort. One author praised the London Peace Society for teaching British soldiers that it was wrong to enlist and urged the American Peace Society to establish similar efforts in the United States. Another article announced that, in the future, the society not only should aim at suppressing the martial spirit, but should also begin to teach that every Christian had a solemn duty—and not simply a right—to disobey a government endeavoring to embark upon the crime of a national war.[21]

Others went even further, calling for worldwide disarmament. In the past, one author explained, peace methods had managed to modify public sentiment, but that had done nothing essential in preventing war. Rather,

> The various appeals made by peace societies to rulers, churches and people, to preclude the occurrence of war, by petitions, congresses, negotiations, pledges of arbitrations, etc., are ineffectual, because they presuppose a sincere desire in all parties to settle their disputes pacifically, which is but seldom the case. There is nothing to induce unprincipled

governments to refrain from hostile aggressions but the want of power; take away that power in their armies, and we ensure the reign of peace.

If war were to be abolished, the author concluded, the advocates of peace must insist that not only the conduct of war, but also preparations for it, were "absolutely sinful." To prepare to commit a crime, he asserted, was as criminal as actually committing it. Thus all those involved in the war system—the soldier who accepted enlistment, the officer who directed him, the ruler who governed military establishments, the legislator who appropriated money for them, and the manufacturer who produced the weapons of war—were equally guilty of sinning against God.[22] Another author agreed, arguing that reliance on military preparations was nothing less than faithlessness in the promises of Christ, who had commanded his followers to love one another.[23]

From their willingness to criticize the cultural Christianity of the day and to call military preparations sinful, it was clear that the war had shaken some members of the American Peace Society severely. Since Blanchard, who belonged to the reform party, was controlling the *Advocate* when many of the most critical articles were published, it is not unreasonable to ask if those articles were representative of the society as a whole or whether they were the opinions of the reform party only. One wonders if those articles would have seen the light of day if Beckwith had been editing the *Advocate*. Most of the articles—as was typical for the *Advocate*—were unsigned, so it is impossible to know if their authors were members of the reform party or if they belonged to the wider constituency of the society. Several things, however, are certain. First, Beckwith had never made the *Advocate* into a journal that denounced only offensive wars. Though he wanted the society's official stance to be limited to a condemnation of offensive wars, it was his policy to insert articles of a variety of views. Therefore, there is no reason to assume that he would have censored the articles in question if he had been the editor.[24] Second, as already discussed, the annual report of 1855—prepared before Beckwith's illness—revealed a deep disillusionment over the war in the Crimea. So did President William Jay's address to the annual meeting in 1855. Therefore, despite Beckwith's absence as editor in the first half of 1856, it is not unfair to conclude that the society as a whole was hit hard by the Crimean War. The war called some of its most fundamental assumptions into question.

Nevertheless, once the war ended the American Peace Society gradually returned to its optimism. As the annual report of 1856 declared, "The last two years have been a severe trial to our cause; but through it all we can see decisive indications of progress."[25] The friends of peace took particular hope from the negotiations that ended the Crimean War. The London Peace Society had pressed British representatives to include stipulated arbitration in the peace treaty concluding the war. Though that bid failed, the British negotiators did push through a resolution urging nations to resort to mediation before rushing to arms.[26] The American Peace Society found that achievement heartening.

The annual report also applauded the role that public opinion had played in the war. The war demonstrated, it said, "on the part of even despotic rulers, *an unusual degree of deference to public opinion. . . .* It began, and has closed, with this deference to public opinion as the real law-giver of the civilized world, the grand tribunal before which rulers themselves must ultimately bow." For the American Peace Society, it was progress when rulers paid attention to the public. And, while the peace society had to admit that paying heed to public clamor was one of the things that had prompted rulers to pursue the war, still the society was certain that public opinion had come a long way from the warlike days of 1815. If public opinion had been what it was in 1815, the annual report argued, the war in the Crimea would have started a year earlier and lasted ten to fifteen years longer. Thus the relative brevity of the war was a testament to the success of the cause of peace.[27]

Once the war in the Crimea had ended, the society's attention turned to other pressing problems. All over the world, it seemed, political disturbances threatened domestic order. In the United States the struggle between proslavery and antislavery forces threatened to tear Kansas apart. In India indigenous revolts against British rulers had led to frightful acts of violence. And then, to top it all off, in October of 1859, John Brown launched his own holy war at Harper's Ferry.

Committed as it was to orderly government, the peace society found those developments frightening. Only once had the society ever wavered in that commitment. During the popular European uprisings of 1848 the society had not been certain that the cause of peace ought to concern itself with internal political disturbances. An article in the *Advocate* following the ouster of Louis Phillipe in France could not help but remark that the promise of a French republic was marvelous. The author conceded that Scripture did not support armed revolution but added that, in any case, "the cause of peace . . . does not concern itself with any such questions of internal policy."[28] Happy about the developments in France and hopeful that democracy was about to take hold, the American Peace Society was not about to get into sticky questions regarding the legitimacy of revolutions.

Never again, however, did the society give even passing approval to revolution. Indeed, the society was increasingly unwilling to allow domestic disturbances it did not find hopeful to pass by without comment. In the riotous conditions in Kansas in the second half of 1856, an *Advocate* article entitled "A Word to Peace Men Just Now: Their Duty in the Present Crisis of Our Country" observed once again that maintaining internal peace was not one of the society's goals. Nevertheless, the article continued, forsaking the rule of law at such a time would spell death for the republic. Though the article professed not to judge Christians who chose to bear the sword, it urged everyone to effect lawful changes through the ballot box, not by rifles.[29]

By 1858 and the uprisings in India, the American Peace Society was ready to do more than simply encourage people to be lawful. Though one article in the *Advocate* suggested that the troubles in India were divine retributions for the immoral way that England had acquired India,[30] at no point did any member of the society profess not to judge the Indians for turning to violence. An article in the *Advocate* noted—as always—that the cause of peace was not concerned with questions outside its own reform, but added that obedience to the gospel precluded the kind of fighting that the Indians had initiated. In response to the vicious retributions the British had exacted, the article contended that the whole issue depended upon whether or not England had a right to rule in India. If the British had no such right, then their acts were villainous. But if they did have a right to rule, then they were obliged to quash the rebellion. "If she [England] has such a right," the article noted, "then she may and must force it against banded rebels as well as all other wrong-doers; and such enforcement would not be so much an act of war, as of justice, by restraining and punishing wrong." Indeed, the article concluded, even if England were governing India illegitimately, at this point the British were obliged not to "let go" but to govern the Indians for their own welfare.[31]

That the American Peace Society would assume such an unbending stance regarding England's "obligation" to enforce the law was especially noteworthy in light of the London Peace Society's reaction to the Indian rebellion. Rather than appealing to the police function of the state to justify British actions as its American counterpart did, the London Peace Society concentrated upon England's sins against India, denouncing England's "unbounded cupidity and ambition" and its "shameless aggressions." The lesson the Anglo-Saxon interlopers had learned, the society insisted, was that "we must relinquish the attempt to govern India by the sword." Either England should rule India in righteousness and mercy and quit treating Indian citizens with contempt, or it should get out of India. "If our prestige can be maintained only by the degradation of 150 millions of people," the society declared, "we may say let it fall."[32] Asserting that "brute force is no safe basis for empire" and defining England's efforts in India as "the cause of wholesale usurpation," the London society concluded that the Archbishop of Canterbury, instead of thanking God that "Thou has maintained our cause" or asking that God teach the Indians "to prize the benefits which they have long enjoyed through the supremacy of this Christian nation," should tell the church of Christ to weep bitterly over the depravity of the race, and pray to God that wars might cease.[33]

The London Peace Society thus had no difficulty calling the troubles in India a war, and it had no reservations about condemning its government's actions. But the American Peace Society insisted that the Indian revolt was a criminal act, not a war, and that England was obliged to govern, even if it had gained power illegitimately. At no point did the American Peace Society question British tactics—which included torture—against the Indians. Instead, the society concentrated on Britain's obligation to enforce the law. This tendency to insist above all else on the state's obligation to govern had been present at least since Beckwith's replies to the nonresistants in the early 1840s, but the society had not invoked that principle in the European revolutions of 1848. It was only later, when events in their own country seemed to be leading to anarchy, that the members of the peace society insisted upon defining large-scale revolutions not as wars, but as criminal activities. An *Advocate* article from the May–June edition of 1859 completed the logic of this line of thinking. Enforcing the law against criminals, the author argued, was not the same as war. And the number of people who were involved in a particular crime could not change the nature of law enforcement. Thus, if thousands of people had died in Shay's rebellion in the previous century, still that rebellion would have been a criminal act, not a war. The state had to protect its citizens and maintain the supremacy of the law, whether threatened by a single criminal or by thousands.[34]

It was not surprising that the author appealed to the supremacy of law. In the 1850s, a number of articles in the *Advocate* suggested that war was wrong because it ignored the rule of law and thus operated outside the realm of justice. Frederick D. Huntingdon, a Unitarian minister and editor of the *Monthly Religious Magazine*, argued that point in his address to the society's annual meeting in 1852,[35] and in 1857, several authors reiterated the view. "B" of Castleton declared that peace principles were based not upon the rejection of penal law, the inviolability of life, or nonresistance, but upon civil law. Because war abandoned all law, he claimed, it was immoral, and the goal of peace activities was to replace the rule of force with the rule of law in the international realm.[36]

An 1858 article repeated that argument, explaining that to favor peace was not to oppose government. On the contrary, the article contended, it was war and government that were antagonistic, since government sought to establish justice, while war operated outside the rule of law. Though the state in its operations might occasionally resort to force, in no way was that use of force similar to the lawless violence typical of war. "True," the author conceded, "there is force [in government], and a threat of violence and punishment; but in neither of these is there of necessity any war, or any essential element of war."[37] Finally, an 1859 article once again made the case for peace as the rule of law by explaining that "here is the substance of our plan in a few words—*war superseded by a better means of international justice and safety.*"[38]

The final event pushing the society to identify the cause of peace with law and order came with John Brown's abortive attempt to capture Harper's Ferry. Before his raid in Virgina, Brown had won notoriety in Kansas. A fierce man who had raised his children with iron discipline, Brown had failed at several business ventures before moving with five sons to the Kansas frontier in 1855. Years earlier, at the death of Elijah Lovejoy, Brown had vowed before God to devote his life to the abolition of slavery. Taking upon himself the authority and demeanor of an Old Testament prophet, he found much to keep him busy in the strife-torn Kansas plains. In May of 1856 he and a small group of men whom he called his "Northern Army" rode to the homes of proslavery settlers, abducted five men, and hacked them to death with broadswords. Later, in August of that year, Brown was wounded in the "Battle of Osawatomie," a shootout between proslavery and antislavery forces.[39]

By January of 1857, Brown had traveled to Boston, hoping to persuade antislavery sympathizers to bankroll his scheme of starting a war of slave liberation in the South. He met Garrison at a social gathering, and the two had an interesting debate on nonviolence, with Garrison quoting the New Testament and Brown citing the Old. Brown knew better than to share his plans with Garrison, but he did secretly obtain financial support from six prominent reformers: Samuel Gridley Howe (a physician and the husband of Julia Ward Howe), Thomas Wentworth Higginson (a Unitarian minister), Franklin B. Sanborn (a Concord schoolteacher), Theodore Parker, Gerrit Smith (Liberty party activist and member of the American Peace Society), and George Luther Stearns (a humanitarian who chaired the Massachusetts Kansas Committee that had aided Brown's work in Kansas).[40]

By the time Brown launched his raid in autumn of 1859, at least eighty

Northerners knew something of his plans. But no one in Harper's Ferry, Virginia, suspected anything the night of October 16th, when Brown and his twenty-one raiders freed a few local slaves and seized the federal armory. Brown had hoped that, as word spread, slaves from Maryland and Virginia would rush to Harper's Ferry to join the fight. Instead, he and his men were trapped in the armory, and after a thirty-six hour siege, federal forces under the command of Robert E. Lee stormed their position. Brown's war of liberation was over, leaving seventeen dead—including two of Brown's sons—and Brown himself severely injured. The army turned Brown and the other survivors over to Virginia authorities for prosecution, while Brown's Northern conspirators were panic-stricken that they, too, would be imprisoned. Gerrit Smith was so distraught that his friends confined him to a mental institution, and except for Higginson the other conspirators either destroyed all documentation linking them with Brown, left the country, or both.[41]

Brown's raid horrified many Americans, none more so than the members of the American Peace Society. The society found all domestic acts of violence appalling, but John Brown's raid was the limit. "We have, under the gospel, no right to attempt the cure of such evils by such means," the *Advocate* insisted. "It is a process subversive of all order, and must, if pushed to its legitimate results, end in utter anarchy."[42] Whereas the Crimean War had shaken the society's confidence that the cause of peace was progressively converting Christendom, the political disturbances of the 1850s threatened to throw the God-ordained Christian societies that the society held dear into anarchy. That was a possibility too horrible to consider for pacifists who had always regarded the Christian culture around them as the means through which the cause of peace would work. The members of the American Peace Society had always stressed that the state ruled by authority from God, and, after Beckwith's clash with the nonresistants in the late 1830s, they had even insisted that God's desire for social order overruled the ethic of love delineated in the Sermon on the Mount. Faced with rebellions against the British in India and virtual warfare in Kansas over the slavery issue, the peace society focused more and more on issues of law and order. By 1860 it was identifying the cause of peace with the cause of law and order. It repudiated war because war violated the rule of law and insisted that the state must, at any cost in human lives, enforce the civil laws.

In short, the American Peace Society had tempered its ethic of love, which had argued that both nations and individuals must in purity of heart obey the gospel of love, regardless of the consequences, with an ethic of coercion. The police function of the state—the necessity that the state maintain order and punish criminals—had become an ethic entirely separate from the ethic of love Jesus had enjoined in the Sermon on the Mount. In general, the society argued, God willed that people live in love for one another, refusing to return evil for evil. In the social realm, however, God authorized the state to use any measures necessary to control and punish evildoers. For without the rule of law there was only chaos, and where chaos reigned, the cause of peace was helpless. In the world of the late 1850s, when factions warred against each other in bloody Kansas and a madman named John Brown had inaugurated his own holy war in Virginia, the American Peace Society could not allow the Christian culture of America to be destroyed.

Allowing for an ethic of coercion did not mean that the members of the society ceased to work for peace. It did mean, however, that they circumscribed their peace activism to a narrow sphere. The peace reformer as a law-abiding Christian who created social order had become an even stronger metaphor than that of the peace advocate as the dutiful servant who followed Jesus' bleeding footsteps without thought for the morrow. The goal of the peace movement had become far more modest than formerly: law and order rather than the peaceable millennial kingdom became the society's principal preoccupation. And even more important, the members of the American Peace Society had lost their earlier emphasis on means rather than ends. From the beginning, of course, they had propounded an ethic of love that, at the same time it eschewed concern about results, also paradoxically expected to achieve success. The advocates of peace had always planned on changing the world, even as they protested that they sought merely to be faithful to a redeemer who gave his life rather than compromise his principles. At last they had run into a situation where they could not obey the Sermon on the Mount *and* achieve their political goals. Something had to give. But the society was unable to see that, in turning away from the Sermon on the Mount, it had come to value success over love, at least in domestic politics. Peaceful obedience had taken a back seat to violent achievement.

Nevertheless, the American Peace Society continued to condemn offensive wars, and those members who had also opposed defensive wars continued to do so. What was new was the fervor with which the society increasingly came to contend that matters of law and order were governed by an ethic other than the gospel of love. The group had suggested that for years, but never before had its members insisted so strongly on the necessity for the state to use force to control criminals. Also new was the argument that no civil disturbance, no matter how many people it involved, could ever be anything other than a criminal action. Though the society had traditionally denied that the American Revolution was a just war, it had never argued that the revolution was not a war at all but a criminal disturbance. By 1860, however, that was exactly the logic the society was pursuing, for the group had defined war so precisely—as a conflict of arms between nations—that no rebellion against an established government could be understood as anything but a criminal act.

Given the circumstances of the day, combined with the society's natural predilection to see governmental authority as ordained by God, it was hardly surprising that the group should have come to such a conclusion. Nevertheless, nothing in the logic of its original position necessitated that the American Peace Society define all internal disturbances as criminal acts. It would have been possible to define armed rebellions, for example, as offensive wars and thus to condemn them on that basis instead of denying that they were wars at all. In addition, the society could have moderated its unqualified support for the state by insisting the state had an obligation not simply to establish law and order, but also to create just social conditions. In that way, the society would have given redress to those oppressed by the state, rather than suggesting—as in India—that government, whether just or not, was to be obeyed at all costs.

In defining civil war out of existence the peace society left little room to maneuver for those who believed their government was oppressive. By 1860 the advocates of peace were distressed at world events, fearful that their own nation was falling into anarchy, and in no mood to tolerate those who were critical of the state's right to enforce the laws against criminals. That was an ominous mood to be in as the group prepared to face the challenge of the 1860s.

The Nonresistants: The Temptations of the 1850s

The American Peace Society was not the only group to struggle through the decade. For the nonresistants, these were years fraught with temptations—temptations all the more enticing because they seemed to offer hope that slavery might at last be abolished. Between the troubles in Kansas, the horrors of the Fugitive Slave Law, the possibilities for antislavery politics associated with the rise of the Republican party, and John Brown's blow for freedom, there was plenty of temptation to go around for everyone. By and large the nonresistants stuck to their principles. They refused to vote or to participate in acts of violence. But some of the faithful did slip, and certainly everyone considered doing so. All the nonresistants desperately wanted to abolish slavery, and even those who refused to participate in violence could hardly help wishing success for those antislavery workers who did use violence. It was easy to make exceptions to the gospel of love, to assume that "resistant" antislavery laborers were governed by an ethic of coercion that entitled them to use violence on behalf of justice. In the struggle to free the slaves, it had become increasingly difficult to remain dutifully peaceful without regard for the consequences.

The 1850s was a decade replete with events that provoked despair. The new Fugitive Slave Law of 1850 seemed horrifying by itself, but it was made worse by President Franklin Pierce's determination to see the law enforced vigorously. Next came the Kansas-Nebraska Act of 1854. By applying popular sovereignty to territory designated as free by the Missouri Compromise of 1820, the Kansas-Nebraska Act nullifed long-established limits on slavery expansion. The nonresistants despaired that the arrogance and ambition of the "slave power" knew no bounds. In May of 1856 Representative Preston Brooks of South Carolina caned Senator Charles Sumner of Massachusetts into insensibility on the floor of the Senate in answer to insults to Brooks's uncle, South Carolina Senator Andrew Butler, that Sumner had earlier made in his "Crime against Kansas" speech. Again, to the nonresistants there seemed no escaping the wanton cruelty of the slaveholder—the nation was in its grip. Finally, after the election of 1856, the Dred Scott decision opened up all territories, and potentially the Northern free states as well, to slavery, and the slaveocracy indeed appeared on the verge of triumph.[43]

Many Northerners regarded the "slave conspiracy" with fury. Garrison expressed his rage on July 4, 1854 at an outdoor celebration in Framingham, Massachusetts, by leading a religious ceremony marking the end of the Union. After reading from the Scriptures, he set fire to a copy of the Fugitive Slave Law, intoning, "Let all the people say, Amen." They did, and he then set fire to the court decisions that had recently sent Anthony Burns, an escaped slave, back into bondage. Finally, he set fire to the Constitution, saying, "So perish all compromises with tyranny! And let the people say, Amen!" A shout went to the heavens, and he stood before them, his arms outstretched, a priest of freedom and disunionism.[44] Other abolitionists would feed their passion for justice by sending rifles to Kansas or giving money to John Brown. The Garrisonians could not join those activities, but the fury that engulfed them as they faced the Southern "slave power" was all encompassing. At times, it was more than some could bear.

Stearns's defection was the most spectacular, but a few others were equally notable. Stephen S. Foster, the fiery Garrisonian, announced at the New England Non-Resistance Convention of 1855 that he was a nonresistant on the grounds of expediency, not principle. At times, he argued, it might be necessary to fight. He pointed to the pericope where Jesus rebuked the Pharisees with whom he was eating and contended that Jesus had manifested more greatness and heroism on that occasion than at his suffering death. In reply Henry Clarke Wright protested that violence was never justifiable since the inviolability of life was a law of human nature. Unless that law were observed, he said, individuals could experience no true happiness. Foster answered that, in the disordered state of the world, it was necessary to violate some of the laws of our being. The right to liberty, however, was the most sacred of all rights, and thus it should be abolished last.[45]

Foster was arguing that, if forced to choose between liberty and peace—both of which were essential laws of nature—he would choose liberty. As awful as violence was, it was still preferable to slavery. As long as nonviolent methods were the most effective in abolishing slavery, he was a nonresistant. But if the time for violence should arise, he would be ready. Angelina Grimke had also come to that conclusion. Though her Quaker background had made her detest violence in the past, the Fugitive Slave Law had pushed her over the edge. The prospect of escaped slaves being captured in the North and returned to Southern bondage was more than she could bear. As she wrote Garrison,

Although the shedding of human blood is utterly abhorrent to my mind . . . yet the tame surrender of a helpless victim up to the fate of the slave is far more abhorrent. . . . In this case, it seems as though we are compelled to choose between two evils, and all that we can do is take the *least*, and baptize liberty in blood, if it must be so. . . . I now entirely despair of the triumph of Justice and Humanity without the shedding of blood. A temporary war is an incomparably less evil than permanent slavery.

It was clear, she concluded, that the time had come to choose between violence and slavery, and Angelina Grimke had decided that it was immoral to allow another black person to be returned to bondage.[46]

Garrison was sympathetic but unconvinced. The principles of peace, he told her, were eternal. "The spirit of Christ," he added, "infinitely transcends the spirit of Washington, the patriot." Do not yield to temptation, Garrison begged Grimke; continue to follow the way of Christ.[47] Adin Ballou had difficulty even being sympathetic. He was unimpressed with the new generation of abolitionists, who were quick to resort to violence, and he feared that the old guard faithful to the principles of peace was slipping away. "Alas," he said,

> the changes of time have left them few and far between. Their names can be found in connection with certain Declarations, Constitutions, Catalogues and Records grown dusty in neglected archives. But where are *they?* A few (how few!) remain faithful. The rest have re-embraced the War Principle, or have become dumb on the subject, or while professing to be Non-Resistants, themselves, spend their main strength in exhorting fighting people to be sure to fight on the right side. . . .
>
> It is a reasonable fact, that just in proportion as the old dormant pro-slavery multitude are getting roused up and enlisted on the Anti-Slavery side, our Peace Abolitionists are getting out of patience with their moral weapons (which have done the cause so much good service,) and now think they must resort to the *sword*.[48]

Ballou could not believe that those who had "progressed around the moral zodiac into the constellation of INJURIOUS FORCE FOR RIGHTEOUSNESS' SAKE" had found a more excellent way.[49]

For the most part, the other nonresistants agreed with him. Foster did not carry the group at its 1855 meeting, where the participants passed a resolution condemning injurious resistance to evil and a resolution that warned Christian nonresistants that it was wrong to encourage others to use violence, no matter how righteous the cause.[50] Still, Angelina Grimke's remarks had been telling. The Fugitive Slave Law of 1850 had been particularly hard on the nonresistants. For the first time they were put in a position in which they could not say—as they always had in the past—that nonresistants should disobey unjust laws nonviolently and then passively accept the punishment that their actions provoked. In the past it had been the nonresistants themselves who had broken the law and accepted the consequences. They were still prepared to do so. Under the Fugitive Slave Law, however, escaped slaves who followed that strategy would allow themselves to be returned to the South. And that was one scenario that the nonresistants could not stomach.

Henry Clarke Wright revealed the nonresistants' inability to incorporate the Fugitive Slave Law into their usual mode of action in 1852. In November of 1851 Edward Search had written the *Liberator*, asking Wright how he could reconcile the new law with his prior advice to nonresistants to disobey unjust laws passively.[51] Wright did not reply. In July of 1852 Micajah T. Johnson of Ohio wrote to Wright asking whether he would advise an escaped slave voluntarily to surrender to the authorities. If Wright would not offer such advice, Johnson argued, then his case was gone; nonresistants did not respect the authorities that God had ordained, and they were not prepared, as Christ had been, to suffer crucifixion at the hands of those who were evil.[52] Once again, Wright was silent. It was one thing to urge free whites to be willing to suffer on behalf of the slaves, but another to counsel the slaves to accept the consequences of disobedience to the law when those consequences meant meekly returning to bondage.

Besides, there was always the hope that the Fugitive Slave Law could be defied with a minimum of violence. In late 1851 the gentle Samuel J. May, a longtime peace advocate and abolitionist, helped plan a rescue of "Jerry," an escaped slave who had been recaptured in Syracuse, New York. An antislavery mob managed to invade the building where the authorities were holding Jerry, overcome his captors, and whisk him away to Canada. The only injury was a broken arm suffered by a law enforcement official. The Jerry escape became a day of annual celebration for the abolitionists, who were delighted to see the Fugitive Slave Law—which they believed violated the will of God—thwarted. Yet for the nonresistants, defying the law had come at a high price. Opposition to the Fugitive Slave Law could easily lead to violence, and that was a scenario they could never accept with equanimity. May himself was ambivalent about the implications of his role in the Jerry affair. After the rescue attempt he admitted to Garrison, "I could not preach non-resistance very effectively."[53]

The difficulties inherent in forcibly freeing captured slaves became apparent in the Anthony Burns rescue of 1854. An escaped slave who was arrested at the annual New England Anti-Slavery Convention in Boston, Burns was to be sent back to the South. To avoid a repetition of the Jerry affair, the authorities posted a strong guard around him—two artillery companies and two Marine units. To rescue Anthony Burns without violence was impossible. Nevertheless, May told the convention that Burns must be rescued. According to the *Liberator's* report, May "said he was known to be a lover of peace; but his spirit was stirred by such scenes . . . and while he counseled a violent rescue, rather than submission to kidnapping, yet he would have men act not in the spirit of *fighters*, but of *martyrs*."[54] The rescue failed; equally horrible, for the nonresistants, lives were lost. And while no one who saw it could ever forget Bronson Alcott—New England sage and occasional participant at nonresistant gatherings—bravely walking at the head of the crowd into the muzzles of the armed guards, still the spirit of the rescue was problematic for the nonresistants.[55] On an abstract level it was easy to condemn violence, but when the government "kidnapped" escaped slaves and returned them to the hell of bondage, it was hard not to fight back. When fighting back meant using violence, however, nonresistants could never rest easy.

It is not difficult to see why Foster and Grimke concluded that they simply had to choose the lesser of two evils in this situation. Since no option available to them was a happy one, they decided that the least objectionable thing was to do what was necessary to free the slaves, even if that meant that for a time—or at least on occasion—nonresistance had to be abandoned. Yet even in the face of this dilemma, most of the nonresistants held firm. Obedience to the gospel ethic of love remained the central virtue of the movement. By and large, as the 1855 nonresistant society convention revealed, they rejected the path that Grimke and Foster had chosen.

It was particularly easy to reject Foster, since the temptation to use violence to help slaves escape to freedom was greater than the temptation to engage in antislavery political activities. There seemed something so wrenching about the prospect of an escaped slave being returned to the South that even those committed to nonviolence felt called to act. Political antislavery, on the other hand, lacked the possibility of immediate success associated with defiance of the Fugitive Slave Law. When Foster left the 1855 convention he was determined to start a political antislavery party,[56] but few other nonresistants were tempted to get involved in the political process. Charles Stearns may have been foolish enough to think that by working with the antislavery faction in Kansas he was striking a blow for freedom, but the other nonresistants knew better. As Ballou noted, the Free State advocates in Kansas were willing to allow slavery to continue throughout the South; they merely wished to keep it out of Kansas. In addition, they had banished free black immigrants from the territory. Thus Ballou concluded that the struggle in Kansas was not a struggle for true freedom and equality. Therefore it was not a cause worthy of nonresistant involvement. "We trust," he said, "that even the defence of *Freedom in Kansas* with Sharpe's rifles, etc., etc., in spite of all its patriotic and chivalrous glitter, is too low a price for some of us to accept."[57]

Occasionally even those who denounced the use of violence in Kansas fell prey to the temptations of antislavery politics. Samuel J. May had argued against the violence he saw in Kansas,[58] but he could not resist the opportunity to vote for John C. Fremont, the Republican presidential candidate in 1856. Arguing that "a vote is no more nor less than a printed wish" and that the oath of office did not bind political figures to enforce those sections of the Constitution that the abolitionists considered immoral, May decided that he was under no ethical obligation to secede from government. "It seems to me," he said, "to be much rather our duty to meet these oppressors, these tyrants, wherever we may, in Congress and out of Congress; in the churches and out of the churches, and everywhere withstand their unrighteousness. We may be in contact with them daily, without being in union with them a moment." The nonresistants, he noted, were willing to pay taxes to support a proslavery, proviolence government when they could have chosen instead to avoid corruption by living on a Pacific island. Since they were set on living in society, he saw no reason not to participate in it fully. "I really am unable to see," he asserted, "why the same reasons that are urged for our not *voting* under the Constitution, do not prove that we ought not to *live* under the Constitution; but abandon the country, as well as the government, to the inhuman and godless."[59]

Most nonresistants disagreed with May. When Fremont lost, Henry Wright informed May that slavery had triumphed with his consent. Since government was a voluntary association, which May had chosen to join, Wright argued, now he must "quietly consent that Slavery may rule, and receive the behests of the Slave Oligarchy as law, and help execute them."[60] Garrison agreed with Wright's assessment. It was cheering, he said, to see the Republican party give the proslavery Democrats trouble, but to "endorse a party which declares itself ready to carry out all the proslavery compromises of the Constitution, and wholly indisposed to meddle with the institution of slavery in the Southern States" was not worth it. "We shall do our best for Kansas, best for the South, best for the Republic," Garrison concluded, "by a stern adherence to our principles, and refusing to compromise with sin."[61]

Though most resistants remained faithful on most issues, there was no ignoring the mood of violence that had swept the country. The turbulence in Kansas, the attempted rescues of fugitive slaves, the caning of Sumner on the floor of the Senate—all of these events were outward expressions of an inner fury that repeatedly burst forth. In January 1857 a Massachusetts Disunion Convention composed of abolitionists and a few Republicans served notice that the abolitionists' patience was wearing thin. "The sooner the separation takes place," the Convention resolved, "the more peaceful it will be; but . . . peace or war is a *secondary consideration* in view of our present perils. Slavery must be conquered, 'peacefully if we can, forcibly if we must.' "[62]

In the midst of this atmosphere, where violence lurked uneasily below the surface, always threatening to erupt, men and women learned to tolerate brute force. Even the most committed nonresistants were tempted to give their blessings to those who were willing to fight for freedom. Though they disapproved of the methods their colleagues might use, still they fervently supported their goals. The mere thought of slaves asserting their rights in opposition to their masters was enough to send Henry Wright into raptures of ecstasy:

> Oh! I *do* rejoice—I can't help it—God only knows how my very soul exults when I see the slave practically assuming the same rights the masters and their allies claim for themselves; and when I see them standing up in defence of those *rights*, even if they use the murderous means their masters use, I do rejoice. My sympathies are with the slave—I cannot help it—in his object, *not* in his means.[63]

At least as far back as the Mexican War, the nonresistants had chosen sides in violent struggles. Even though they were unwilling to use violence themselves when other people used it, it was hard not to cheer—if only inwardly—for those who fought on the side of righteousness.

Another way in which the nonresistants tolerated violence was by distinguishing between the ethic of love appropriate to nonresistants and the ethic of coercion appropriate to the unregenerate. Henry Wright, for example, believed that slaves had a moral obligation to resist their masters. Ideally, that resistance would be nonviolent. According to Wright, if every slave said, " 'I will be a slave no longer, nor will I resort to violence and blood to resist you' . . . Slavery would instantly cease, without much bloodshed." To those who believed that freedom was a sacred right worth fighting for, however, Wright contended that it was their duty to urge the slaves to resort to armed resistance. Those willing to use arms to protect their own freedom, he said, were obliged to teach that same ethic to the slaves.[64]

The nonresistants had been using that kind of reasoning for years. They had, for example, argued all along that those who believed in the truths of the Declaration of Independence should be willing to apply them to blacks and women as well as to white males. All persons had an equal claim to life, liberty, and the pursuit of happiness, as well as to the right to resist tyranny. But in the fifties, when tempers were on edge, this traditional style of argumentation had a violent ring to it. As Parker Pillsbury explained at the annual meeting of the Massachusetts Anti-Slavery Association in 1857, he had never entirely sympathized with nonresistance. "But now that Non-Resistance people have begun to teach that resistance to tyrants is obedience to God," he said, "perhaps I am a *Non-Resistant*, for I certainly believe that."[65] As they urged the unredeemed to fight injustice according to the best lights they knew, the nonresistants were increasingly inclined to allow them to use violence to achieve just ends.

Garrison recognized that the abolitionists traditionally committed to peaceful means were sounding less and less peaceful. At the New England Anti-Slavery Convention of 1858 he warned, "We are growing more and more warlike, more and more disposed to repudiate the principles of peace, more and more disposed to talk about 'finding a joint in the neck of the tyrant', and breaking his neck." Such an attitude distressed Garrison, for he believed that as the spirit of peace waned, so did the moral power depart from the abolitionist movement. He explained:

> In proportion as we allow the spirit of violence or retaliation to take possession of our minds, and make ourselves familiar with the idea of killing slaveholders and tyrants, I apprehend the Divine Spirit will go out of us, and we shall not have that power over men's minds that we should have, if animated by a different spirit.

Garrison pleaded with the abolitionists to remember that all human beings were sacred before God, even Southern slaveholders. He asked them to temper their passions and to resist the urge to return evil for evil. "Perhaps blood will flow," he concluded, "but it shall not flow through any counsel of mine. Much as I detest the oppression exercised by the Southern slave holder, he is a man sacred before me. He is a man, not to be harmed by my hand, nor with my consent."[66]

In October of 1859, however, John Brown took the lives of slaveholders and Garrison was thrilled. It was the rare nonresistant who failed to be excited by Brown's daring mission on behalf of freedom. Though the nonresistants of course disapproved of his methods, they could not help but praise his goals. As Maria Child wrote to Brown, "Believing in peace principles, I cannot sympathize with the method you chose to advance the cause of freedom. But I honor your gracious intentions, I admire your courage, moral and physical, I reverence you for the humanity which tempered your zeal, I sympathize with your cruel bereavements, your sufferings, and your wrongs. In short, I love you and bless you."[67] For some time, the nonresistants had permitted themselves to approve of goals even when they disapproved of the means employed to reach those goals. They could not condemn slaves who revolted or whites who helped slaves escape—even when violence erupted. Certainly they were not about to condemn John Brown for the task he had undertaken, even if he had used reprehensible means.

The nonresistants had fallen into the habit of applying different ethics to different persons. Rather than demanding that all people obey the gospel of nonresistant love, they had come to recognize that those who were not nonresistants lived by a different code and could be judged according to that code. Here again, it was easy to vindicate John Brown. When Brown was captured and asked upon what principle he had based his actions, he answered, "Upon the golden rule; I pity the poor in bondage that have none to help them; that is why I am here, not to gratify any personal animosity, revenge or vindictive spirit. It is my sympathy with the oppressed and wronged, that are as good as you and as precious in the sight of God."[68] In the eyes of Charles K. Whipple that meant that John Brown had done even better than the Good Samaritan. Like Jesus, Whipple said, Brown had gone out to seek those who were lost that he might save them.[69] An editorial in the *Liberator* agreed with Whipple, calling Brown a "martyr to his sympathy for a suffering race." By the logic of Lexington, Concord, Bunker Hill, and the Declaration of Independence, the *Liberator* claimed, Brown was a hero.[70]

The nonresistants were also attracted to Brown because, after his capture, he faced his execution bravely and without complaint. As Maria Child wrote to Brown, "How I rejoice in you, because you remain so calm and steadfast in the midst of your tribulations! A moral influence goes forth from this, better than anything the world calls success."[71] In fact, except for the violent means Brown had used to defend himself, in every other way he was a model nonresistant—he was an activist who willingly suffered martyrdom in the cause of freedom. If the nonresistants could just overlook the violent means that had put Brown in prison in the first place, they could find much to admire in Brown's example. "Whatever may have been his errors of judgment or calculation," Garrison noted, "his bearing since his capture and during his trial has truly been sublime, and challenges for him all of human sympathy and respect."[72]

The nonresistants shared vicariously in the dramatic actions of John Brown. Though they dared not use the means he had adopted, the prospect of doing something so dramatic on behalf of the slaves thrilled them. For years they had been unwilling to strike out physically in their own cause, and many a Garrisonian lecturer had passed through an angry mob in the care of "a lifeguard of elderly ladies, and protected by a rampart of whale-bones and cotton padding."[73] Agitators by temperament, nonresistance had at times made them feel passive. Brown, on the other hand, had been decisive and daring. As Stephen Foster proclaimed, "I think John Brown has shown himself a *man*, in comparison with the Non-Resistants!"[74] Though the nonresistants were pledged to the ethic of love, still they recognized that no one had ever used the ethic of coercion to seek justice more bravely than John Brown. They envied his extremism. As Maria Child remarked, "Instead of blaming him for carrying out his own convictions by means we cannot sanction, it would be more profitable for us to inquire of ourselves whether we, who believe in 'a more excellent way', have carried our convictions into practice as faithfully as he did his."[75]

The nonresistants yearned to act decisively. The institution of slavery plagued them with an abiding guilt, while their theology told them that they were personally responsible for the betterment of society. They ached to do something that would make a difference. And beneath their passion for justice and their detailed descriptions of the torments of slavery, undoubtedly lay repressed desires for violence and vengeance. As Ronald Walters has noted,

> It is possible that abolitionist pacifism was a mechanism for denying, on the conscious level, subconscious fantasies of violence. Certainly it took lurid imaginations to create the more gruesome antislavery descriptions of insurrections and of Southern brutality. Whatever its psychological components, nonviolence did have an ambivalence that was easily brought to the surface by events, by frustration, and by taunts of anti-abolitionists.[76]

For decades the nonresistants had immersed themselves in the evils of slavery. Its coercion and brutality were daily part of their consciousness. They wanted to destroy slavery, and they wanted to destroy it immediately. After a lifetime of enduring ridicule and ostracism, it would have been strange indeed if John Brown's raid had not appealed to that side of the nonresistant that longed to throw the self into the fray, without care for the consequences. What other course was left when the nation refused to listen to the voices of virtue?

Willing as they were to suffer for the slaves, however, the nonresistants could not bear the thought of the slaves themselves bearing the cross of bondage any longer. As Garrison said on the eve of Brown's execution,

> Whenever there is a contest between the oppressed and the oppressor,— the weapons being equal between the parties,—God knows that my heart must be with the oppressed, and always against the oppressor. Therefore, whenever commenced, I cannot but wish success to all slave insurrections. I thank God when men who believe in the right and duty of wielding carnal weapons are so far advanced that they will take those weapons out of the scale of despotism, and throw them into the scale of freedom. It is an indication of progress, and a positive moral growth; it is one way to get up

to the sublime platform of non-resistance; and it is God's method of dealing retribution upon the head of the tyrant. Rather than see men wearing their chains in a cowardly and servile spirit, I would, as an advocate of peace, much rather see them breaking the head of the tyrant with their chains."[77]

Garrison still was unswayed by the lure of antislavery politics, and he still thought that Charles Stearns had been wrong to take up violence on behalf of the free state party in Kansas, but there was something so compelling about individuals rebelling against the cruel system of slavery that he could not find it in his heart to condemn John Brown as he had once condemned Elijah Lovejoy. For Garrison, Brown was a martyr to be honored.

There was, however, one nonresistant who was not applauding John Brown's raid any more than he had approved Charles Stearns's defection. Even before the eruption at Harper's Ferry, Adin Ballou had objected to the new spirit of violence that pervaded Garrisonian antislavery efforts. He had chosen to ally himself with the Garrisonians, he said, because their tactics seemed most compatible with his own nonresistant, nonpolitical brand of Christianity. But now, he thought, the war spirit was becoming too pronounced in the Garrisonian camp. He could not agree with those who applauded at the Massachusetts Disunion Convention's dictum that slavery must be abolished "peaceably if we can, forcibly if we must." Neither was he pleased with the new hermeneutical assumptions that depicted abolitionism as though it included the main substance of Christianity, or as though it were a natural religion purer than Christianity. Finally he objected to the egotistical, antagonistic, and self-important attitudes increasingly present in abolitionist circles. Political abolitionists, Ballou concluded, could probably not help feeling contempt for the nonresistants' "softness." And nonresistants could not help but be tempted to petition the government to enact laws repealing the Fugitive Slave Law—even though they knew it was wrong to be involved in the work of a government that depended upon the war principle to enforce its laws. For the time being, Ballou suggested, it might be best for nonresistants to retire from the forefront of political controversy and do what good they could as practitioners of simple Christianity.[78]

Nothing that happened at Harper's Ferry made Ballou any happier with his colleagues. J. Miller McKim wrote to Ballou in the *Liberator* asking him to stay in the movement. "I don't think we are nearly as warlike and venomous as you make us out to be," McKim said, "but still we are bad enough to need the antidote of your gentle spirit and peace-breathing doctrines. Don't desert us."[79] Ballou, however, was not convinced that abolitionists were prepared to listen to his message. "Even professed peace men, *ultra* peace men, so called, in many instances go, like hand in glove, with pro-war governments, pro-war politics, pro-war legal coercion, and pro-war *revolutions*," he replied. Moreover, he asserted, some nonresistants held nonresistance to be secondary to antislavery, and that was a conviction to which he could never assent.[80]

Ballou was particularly puzzled that the nonresistants could have been so taken with John Brown's raid. He conceded that Brown might have been sincere and self-sacrificing, but, since his methods were not Christian, Ballou did not see how anyone could conclude that Brown's mission was Christian either. Ballou especially felt betrayed by Garrison. "This man," he said, "became more than an apologist, he became a eulogist of the blood-shedding hero of the Harper's Ferry tragedy."[81] No matter what anybody else thought, Ballou was unwilling to subordinate the gospel of peace to any other goal. Neither was he willing to pretend that Brown—or any unregenerate person—should be praised for being faithful to an ethic that fell below the purity of the gospel. The other nonresistants could accommodate coercion all that they wanted, but Ballou intended to stick to the ethic of love that had always been at the heart of his theology. As he wrote in 1854, "Right duty must be held supreme. Whatever love, or will, or interest, or convenience comes in competition with [it], these must be promptly and unreservedly sacrificed. There must be no compromise of absolute divine principle. This is the indispensable condition of human salvation and progress."[82]

For his part Garrison did not have much sympathy with Ballou's criticisms. In condemning John Brown, Garrison argued, Ballou was only siding with the oppressor against the oppressed. As an ultra peace man, he added, he was always prepared to wish success to every slave revolt once it had commenced. If Ballou could not say the same, Garrison suggested, it was because he lacked a "philosophical view of events." Rather than leading away from nonresistance, John Brown with his righteous violence was a step on the road toward nonresistance. Was there no such thing, Garrison asked, as progress toward the highest Christian position?[83]

Ballou did believe in progress, but he saw no future for the nonresistants' current mode of behavior. "Had Jesus Christ and His apostles undertaken to abolish slavery and other evils in the Roman empire by similar means," he asserted, "we should probably [have] never heard of their doctrine of universal love and good will, nor of them either."[84] And so as the nonresistants headed into the Civil War years—years that would challenge their devotion to the gospel of peace as never before—

they went without Adin Ballou. Ballou was convinced that his friends had deserted the cause, and he believed that the events of the war years proved his case. "What became of the bellicose John Brown Non-resistants?" he asked after the war. "They gradually declined in numbers from that time on and in a few years essentially disappeared. There was no further use for their kind of peace doctrine and they did nothing to propagate or preserve it."[85]

Though Ballou believed that his friends had ceased to be true Christian nonresistants, he did not think that they had given up the cause of peace altogether. It was not the case that they went from radical pacifists to warmongers, but rather that they were, by 1860, different kind of peace reformers than they had been in the beginning. Originally nonresistance was a scripturally based doctrine that applied an ethic of love to all persons. By 1860 the Biblical foundations of nonresistance were no longer essential to many of its adherents. In addition, a few nonresistants—such as Foster and Stearns—had decided that nonresistance was only a strategy of reform to be used when it could successfully be applied, not a way of life to be pursued regardless of the costs.

Though most nonresistants did not follow Stearns and Foster in that conclusion, they did depart from devotion to the ethic of love in another way. Rather than applying the standard of the gospel to all persons, they began to accept the fact that most people lived according to an ethic of coercion. Instead of demanding that those people obey the gospel, the nonresistants chose to judge them by the standards of the world. In that way the nonresistants were able to argue that those who lived according to the violent ethic of the world were morally obliged to do all within their power to fight the evil of slavery. Thus the gospel of love, which demanded that the nonresistants refuse to return evil for evil, had a coercive counterpart that commanded "resistants" to do what was necessary to ensure that all persons enjoyed the blessings of liberty. Whereas self-sacrificial love was the highest value of the gospel ethic, individual freedom was the supreme value of this violent ethic.

It was not unpredictable that the nonresistants should have modified their ethics in such a way. Nonresistance had been plagued by a number of ambiguities from the start. In the first place, though its practitioners had always insisted that the gospel commanded Christians to be nonresistants regardless of the consequences, the nonresistants had simultaneously argued that nonresistance was an efficacious strategy to employ. At the same time that they modeled themselves after Jesus, the martyr, the nonresistants had assumed that obeying the gospel was the best method to ensure the success of their endeavors. It could have taken no one unaware, then, when Stearns and Foster decided that they would practice nonresistance only when it was expedient to do so. Certainly that was not the conclusion Garrison had preached throughout the years, but the message he had spouted was confused enough that it is easy to see why Stearns and Foster reached the conclusion that they did. If nonresistance was a way of life to be practiced even though it had brought Jesus to the cross, then it had been misleading to argue, as the nonresistants had for several decades, that nonresistance was the most efficacious social strategy known to humanity.

In addition, the nonresistants' attitude toward violence had always been ambiguous. Though they had uniformly condemned participation in a government supported by the war principle, few nonresistants had had qualms about telling the people who did run the government how they ought to do their jobs. Nonresistants would not serve in the legislature, but—except for Ballou—they were happy to petition the government to enact laws that they favored. Neither would nonresistants vote, but they were eager to give advice to people who did. In the Mexican War, nonresistants would not fight, but they did not mind rooting for the "righteous" Mexicans to defeat the invading American armies. In reality, they had been telling people how to do their dirty work for a lifetime. What was striking about the 1850s, however, was that it became increasingly clear that the freedom the nonresistants so desperately craved for the slaves could be attained only—or at least most quickly—through violent means. The nonresistants could choose either to give a backhanded approval to those means or to withdraw from the arena altogether and practice nonresistance without regard for the political situation.

Ballou wanted to choose the latter option, but he was virtually alone. In conflict here were two different images of what it meant to be a nonresistant. On the one hand, there was always the image of Jesus, the obedient servant who had quietly done God's will without considering the consequences. On the other hand, there was the image of the nonresistant as agitator, the Garrisonian radical who deliberately stirred people out of their complacency. Garrison had told William Ladd in 1838 that "the more peaceable a man becomes, after the pattern of Christ, the more he is inclined to make a disturbance, to be aggressive, to 'turn the world upside down'. For the sake of quietude, he will make a noise."[86] Though the nonresistants appealed to the image of Jesus the martyr, the predominant model that shaped them was that of the reformer as agitator. They were not satisfied with obeying God and accepting the consequences. Instead, they wanted to shape the results of their activity, and they were willing to use conflict to stir people into action.

There was something problematic about claiming to act in love at the same time that they deliberately sought to create conflict. Focusing on antislavery activities only exacerbated the tendentious quality of their efforts. As Ballou noted, it was difficult to be peaceful and loving at the same time one was fighting the abuses of slavery.

> It is generally easier to be an anti-slavery man on the fighting principle, than on the Peace principle; because anti-slavery is an indignation theme, and whether a man talks or acts, he must deal somewhat largely in indignation. . . . And, generally, we may expect a spice of war about the abolitionist before he gets through; prospective and contingent war, if nothing more. Now when our Peace abolitionists get into a pro-war government, it seldom takes them long, I observe, to dilute their new wine, so that they can put it into old bottles with safety.[87]

The nonresistants were natural activists in any case; they were zealous laborers who expected to change the world. It was unlikely, no matter how often they referred to the crucified Jesus, that they would have been satisfied with so passive a model of reform. Moreover, while they were willing to suffer for their beliefs, it was extremely difficult for them to stand by while the slaves endured bondage year after weary year. The more desperate the political situation became, the more inclined they were to seek immediate ways to end a situation that had become intolerable.

In turning to an ethic of coercion to allow them to encourage resistant antislavery workers, the nonresistants limited the sphere to which they applied the ethic of the gospel. While they continued to believe that the gospel was the only rule of life ordained by God, by 1860 they no longer sought to apply that rule to the unregenerate in society. For that class an ethic of coercion was appropriate. In any number of ways—by petitioning the government, by telling people how to vote, and by rooting for the Mexicans in the Mexican War—the nonresistants had, in the past, also recognized the legitimacy of that other ethic. From the beginning they had, through those activities, tacitly accepted violence. Thus it is incorrect to say that, in the 1850s, the nonresistants suddenly turned away from their peace principles and embraced violence. They did not reject the gospel of peace, but they did embrace, much more openly than ever before, those gray areas of their theology that had implicitly accepted violence. In the hour of the slaves' greatest need, the nonresistants would not abandon them; instead, they would emphasize more than ever before those elements in their theology that allowed them to approve of the "righteous" violence practiced by others.[88]

What had happened in the 1850s to both the nonresistants and the American Peace Society was that both groups felt obliged to circumscribe the realm in which it was appropriate to demand that the gospel of love be obeyed. Both groups tempered the ethic of love with an ethic of coercion. For the American Peace Society, that meant giving the state the broadest powers to carry out its police function. For the nonresistants, it meant recognizing that, while the unregenerate could not be expected to obey the gospel of love, they could be held accountable for acting according to the highest lights available to them. The millennium that had once seemed so imminent to each group now receded into the background as each of them concentrated on removing immediate social ills that precluded the coming of God's reign. While neither group abandoned their commitment to the New Testament ethic of love, each espoused a far more limited type of pacifism than formerly. Both groups believed, however, that God could work to achieve the divine will in history even through a coercive ethic that fell short of the gospel's perfection. That belief—and the conceptual adequacy of their revised, circumscribed pacifism—would be put to the test in the civil war that lay ahead.

THE

CIVIL

WAR

Joshua P. Blanchard was not a happy man in 1861. He had been in-volved in the peace movement most of his life, dating all the way back to his days as a conscientious objector in the War of 1812.[1] A member of the reform party, he had remained active in the American Peace Society, even though his views would never predominate. By 1861 and the beginning of armed conflict between the North and the South, however, he had just about had all he could take of the American Peace Society. Contrary to common sense, not to mention the express command of the gospel—at least in Blanchard's opinion—the society had decided that the war between the states was not a war at all, but a criminal uprising in the South. As the nation's guardian of law and order, the government was obliged, the society argued, to suppress the revolt and punish those who had sparked it.

Blanchard was distraught. It was at the May 1861 annual meeting that the peace society chose to define the war as a criminal rebellion and throw its support behind the Union. "A stranger, unapprised of the purpose of the meeting," Blanchard complained, "would have supposed it for the vindication of war, rather than peace."[2] His old friend Elihu Burritt agreed with Blanchard's assessment. Beckwith, Burritt asserted,

> has assumed from the beginning that this terrible conflict, in which each party is arraying 500000 armed men against the other, is not *war*, but quelling a mob on the part of the Federal Government, that the Northern army of half a million is only a sherifs [sic] *posse* called out to put down an organisation of riotous individuals. I feel that this sophistry and position have shorn the locks of the Society of all strength of principle; and I have been saddened to silence.[3]

Upset as he was over the actions of the American Peace Society, Burritt at least found consolation in Blanchard's firmness. "I have gone as far as I could, without exposing myself to arrest in opposing the war; but I feel powerless and alone," he said. "Dear old Father *Blanchard* of Boston, stands strong as a mountain of iron, and I hope there are a few scattered through the country who hold steadfastly to our principles."[4]

Burritt would eventually move to England rather than endure wartime life in America, leaving Blanchard to uphold the faith. Convinced that the peace society would not recognize a war if it saw one and could not be trusted to condemn a war even if it recognized one, Blanchard turned elsewhere for allies. He was mystified, however, by the stance the nonresistants were taking toward the war. As he pointed out to Garrison in December of 1862, the war was not officially a war to free the slaves; it was a war to save the Union. Yet Garrison was urging an energetic prosecution of the war, even though for years he had been preaching disunionism. Why, Blanchard asked, did Garrison not approve of secession? If the South were given its independence, the free states would be exempted of their constitutional duty to support slavery. Deprived of Northern support, slavery would inevitably die out in the South. So why, Blanchard asked, was Garrison not rejoicing over secession instead of insisting that the Union pursue the war with vigor?[5]

Garrison's answer was simple. We do not sanction evil that good may come of it, he explained. Though secession might eventually have led to abolition, still it would have been wrong to achieve liberation for the slaves at the price of sanctioning a bloody revolt that sought to extend slavery. In Garrison's eyes, the government had been right to oppose the South. "We are with the government in the rectitude of its proceedings on its own plane of action for the suppression of the rebellion," he asserted, "and all the more so as we believe and maintain that it has now the constitutional right, and that it is its highest duty, to decree the emancipation of every slave in the land, and thus terminate the war in the speediest and most effectual way."[6]

Garrison's friend Samuel J. May attempted to make sense out of the nonresistant position by blaming the war on the Colonization Society. Thirty years earlier, he argued, there had been enough moral and religious power to abolish slavery by political means. But those who held the power had used it improperly—they had endeavored to transport the slaves to Africa instead of removing slavery from America, or they had wasted their energies trying to prove that the Bible sanctioned slavery. Because they had misused the power once in their hands, May concluded, now the only thing left to do was support this horrible war until slavery was abolished. The South must be punished till it repented its cruel prejudice against blacks. "It is a miserable way to do it," May conceded, "but it is the way we have chosen, and we must travel it to the end. We have lost our hold upon the slaveholders as fellow-Christians, or fellow-citizens, even; and now we must put them down, utterly down, as wicked rebels against God, and against the best form of civil government God has ever helped men to devise and establish on earth."[7]

Blanchard found none of that convincing. The war was not a war to end slavery, it was a war to save the Union, no matter what Garrison and his friends thought. The only reasonable plan ever offered to end slavery was Garrison's idea of separation—a plan that Garrison now refuted. If anybody thought, Blanchard asserted, that Southern allegiance to the ideals of liberty and equality could be won by coercing the South into a political settlement its people despised, they were badly mistaken. Moreover, Blanchard said, even ignoring

> the fallacious assumptions of our statesmen, that this secession is a rebellion, that ours is the best form of civil government, that God has helped us establish it, etc, I would ask if he has anywhere authorized us to put down those whom we judge to be rebels against him; especially by the criminal murders of war, so abhorrent to his character, and so forbidden in his gospel? I am amazed that an amiable Christian brother should describe such a course of action to the adored God of love. I cannot.[8]

The only answer, Blanchard insisted, was to let the South go—let the Southerners have their independence, and then wait for slavery to collapse under its own weight. For even a complete military conquest of the South would inspire only hatred, not peace, in Southern hearts. And the enormous military force that would be needed to maintain the union of coercion "would only change chattel bondage, in a part of the nation, to a more unrighteous military despotism all over the States."[9]

Though a few others agreed with him, for the most part Blanchard was a voice crying in the wilderness. Disgusted with the American Peace Society, he would join other dissatisfied pacifists in 1866 to form yet another peace organization. Led by Alfred H. Love of Philadelphia, the Universal Peace Union would work for disarmament and uphold the inviolability of human life through the turn of the century.[10] By 1876, however, the society had already said farewell to Joshua P. Blanchard. A child of the eighteenth century, he would not live to celebrate the tenth anniversary of the Universal Peace Union. The work of peace was passing to a new generation.[11]

Blanchard's experience was typical of those peace advocates who were unable to give their blessings to the war. He could not help but feel that the peace society was guilty of the worst kind of mental gymnastics in its determination to deny that the Civil War was actually a war. And the nonresistants' apparent abandonment of their policy of disunionism—not to mention their incessant cheering for the Union war effort—baffled him as well. What had happened to the advocates of peace? Why had they betrayed the cause?

In their own minds, neither the American Peace Society nor the nonresistants had relinquished their peace activism. The ways in which, by 1860, they had come to redefine the sphere to which that activism applied made their response to the Civil War entirely predictable. Beginning with Beckwith's rise to power and supported by the American Peace Society's reactions to the civil disturbances in India and in the United States in the 1850s, the society had come to regard the maintenance of social order as the supreme task of government. No value, not even obedience to the Sermon on the Mount, took precedence over the state's obligation to enforce the law and establish domestic order. By 1860 the society had insisted that war consisted *only* of conflicts between nations. No civil disturbance, however massive, could ever qualify as a war. In defining civil war out of existence and in asserting that the state was obliged at all costs to establish domestic order, the American Peace Society had set the stage for the position it would take in the Civil War. At the same time that the society remained fervently opposed to international warfare, it continued to insist that the state was obliged, according to the mandates of Scripture, to subdue and punish the Southern rebels who had shattered the domestic tranquility.

Similarly, the nonresistants' reaction to the war was, by 1860, a foregone conclusion. The Garrisonian abolitionists had become so accustomed to distinguishing between the ethic of love appropriate to the redeemed and the ethic of coercion pertinent for the unregenerate that they had granted autonomy to the violent moral sphere of the unregenerate. While they remained above the fray themselves, the nonresistants did not hesitate to urge those amenable to violence to use whatever means were necessary to achieve the highest ideals available to them. This "philosophic nonresistance" split in two the ethic of love that had traditionally been the cornerstone of nonresistant thinking. Hints of that split, of course, had long been visible. The nonresistants had been telling people how to vote for years, even though they thought voting was sinful, and they had not been shy about rooting for the Mexicans in 1846, even though they thought all war was wrong. By 1860, however, the nonresistants were desperate to free the slaves. It horrified them that the slaves might suffer additional time in bondage. If the citizens of the North, therefore, were ready to pay the ultimate price to save the Union and free the slaves, the nonresistants were not about to dissuade them.

Moreover, for both the American Peace Society and the nonresistants, there was a feeling that somehow God was behind this great struggle, working out the divine purposes. Convinced that the Union fought—even if unwittingly—for God, the advocates of peace threw themselves behind the Northern war effort. In siding with the North, the peace workers lost the sense of distance that might have allowed them to judge the Union's conduct of the war by the same standard that they applied to the South's. It became all too easy to overlook or condone Union acts of war at the same time that they damned Southerners as unrepentant savages.

In ignoring the Union's acts and concentrating solely upon the errors of the South, the advocates of peace revealed one of the conceptual weaknesses of their pacifism. Applying different moral standards to the two armies was a direct consequence of tempering the ethic of love with an ethic of coercion. The ethic of love had allowed the advocates of peace to maintain a distance between themselves and their culture so that they were free to evaluate it by the light of the gospel they believed. Even the American Peace Society, an apologist for Christian civilization, had had enough independence from its culture to condemn its government's war effort in 1846. But the ethic of love had never allowed either the peace society or the nonresistants to support violent efforts—even those fostered by the state—to free the slaves or to maintain civil order. It was only when they recognized coercion as an independent ethic that the advocates of peace could cheer unreservedly as the North put an end to the rebellious Southern slaveocracy. In the 1860s, moderating the ethic of love for such an end seemed to be a reasonable tradeoff. Loving one's enemies without regard for the consequences was still a virtue, but it was increasingly a luxury appropriate for few.

The American Peace Society: The Fight for Orderly Government

When the American Peace Society first pondered the prospect of secession, it was hopeful about the chances for a peaceful settlement. Predictably, it insisted that the government was obliged to enforce the law against rebels, but prior to the outbreak of hostilities at Sumter the society was willing to entertain the possibility of a nonviolent separation between North and South. Once the South fired on Fort Sumter, however, the society's tolerance disappeared. The society spent the war years demanding that the state revenge itself upon the Southern criminals. Denying that the cause of peace had anything to do with the "police action" being conducted on battlefields across the nation, the peace society concentrated on the need to educate persons to resist the war spirit in the future. Under the guise of law and order, however, the society itself indulged in the war spirit. Though occasional voices of moderation arose, for the most part the society regarded Southerners as subhuman brutes, while it described Northerners and their war efforts in glowing terms. At no time did the society consider applying the "resist not evil" ethic of the Sermon on the Mount to the political situation of the day.

From the 1830s on, it had been George Beckwith's goal to link the cause of peace with the maintenance of orderly government. From the first emergence of nonresistance, with its anarchic tendencies, Beckwith had sought to prove that peace and government went hand in hand. The developments of the 1850s, in which the peace society had argued that war was wrong because it operated outside the rule of law, only enforced that effort. It was not surprising then that the society's initial response to secession should have been to emphasize yet again that the advocates of peace supported the government as it worked to maintain law and order.

An article entitled "The Enforcement of Law a Peace Measure," which appeared in the January–February edition of the 1861 *Advocate*, stated the case clearly. In the first place, it argued, the secession crisis was not an issue of war and peace. Nor, the article continued, was peace a cure-all for every disorder of society. Instead, "for the cure or control of evils like these, we must look, not to Peace, but to Government. . . . It comes not within the province of Peace to prevent or punish crime in general." Having identified secession as crime, the article explained that those committed to peace would naturally give their support to the just application of law. The issue at stake in the present crisis, the article asserted, "is, in its origin and its essential character, a question of obedience to government; and a judicious, yet energetic, unflinching enforcement of its laws would have been precisely the measure of peace needed at the right time to meet the case." Though peace was not directly related to the question, the article did concede that the general influence of peace could have prevented the secession crisis from ever arising. A people committed to peace, it concluded, could never be rebellious: "No people, educated in such views as our cause inculcates, would ever abet or tolerate rebellion or any *violent* resistance to 'the powers that be.' It is the lack of such principles and habits that has occasioned what we now see in the South."[12] In case anyone had missed the point, Beckwith then reprinted his 1839 article on "Peace Compatible with Government" so that everyone could see that it was consistent to oppose war and at the same time believe that government was authorized to punish and coerce its subjects. The Sermon on the Mount did not apply to the state's relationship to its citizens.[13]

Nevertheless, as certain as he was that the present crisis was a law-and-order issue, Beckwith was willing to let the South secede and establish itself as a "Republic of Slaveholders,"[14] if a peaceful settlement could be arranged. Rather than face a war, he said, he was ready to change the Constitution so that the South could secede without violence.[15] The May–June *Advocate* of 1861 was particularly excited about the prospect of a peace congress settling the secession crisis. Why force the South to remain in a political union it despised? the *Advocate* asked. Instead, America could teach the world a great lesson—that war was never necessary. America had already showed the world that a religious people could govern itself; now it was "displaying before the astonished nations another and even sublimer lesson, viz.: that a nation may be dismembered—revolutionized, without the shedding of blood." Such a prospect, the *Advocate* argued, proved something noble about human nature and about the work of the peace society: "How it enobles [sic] our estimate of man to see a great and powerful nation, badgered and robbed by a faction, or fraction of its people, and yet remain calm, conciliatory, kind. . . . Henceforth the 'Peace Society' will no longer be graciously let alone by civil and religious magnates, as a harmless collection of kind-hearted dreamers, but will stand high among the great benevolent institutions which aim to procure the triumph of true religion on earth."[16]

Unfortunately, before the American Peace Society had time to complete the May–June edition of the *Advocate*, the South had fired on Fort Sumter, and Lincoln had issued a call for troops. That was the end of the society's moderation. The first half of that fateful *Advocate* began with a call for peace; the second half closed with a call to arms. The society's position was twofold. In the first place it insisted that the advocates of peace must be loyal to the government. "We trust our friends will, first of all, bear in mind that *Peace is always loyal*," the *Advocate* counseled. "It is not possible for a peace man to be a rebel. We may dislike the government over us, and seek to change it, but never in the way of violent resistance to its authority. We cannot for a moment countenance or tolerate rebellion."[17]

Second, the peace society argued that the battle raging between North and South was not in fact a war, but rather an attempt by the government to suppress a large-scale criminal operation fostered by the South. "It is not strictly war, but a legitimate effort by government for the enforcement of its laws, and the maintenance of its proper and indispensable authority," the *Advocate* explained. "If a million men were mustered to put down by force this climax of all offences, it would still be in form, as it ought ever to be in spirit, only a simple rightful enforcement of the laws—the very laws which the rebels themselves helped to enact— against a combined, wholesale violation of them. It is, or should be, a work of Justice, calm, impartial, awful."[18] As the society had once judged the British attempts to quell the rebellions in India to be a matter of law and order, so now it interpreted the Union's battle with the South in the same manner.[19]

From the annual meeting of 1861 came principles that would guide the society throughout the war. The annual report noted three conclusions to which the society would repeatedly return. The first concerned the magnitude of the Southerners' sin. "We are in the midst," the society asserted, "of a rebellion the most gigantic perhaps that the world ever saw."[20] Convinced, as the previous edition of the *Advocate* had phrased it, that the South was involved in the "gigantic crime of attempting to overthrow the freest and best government on earth,"[21] the society would spend the rest of the war vilifying the South and praising the virtues of the North. It was hard for the advocates of peace to be objective about the Union—much less critical of it—when they were convinced that the North fought on behalf of the Lord. That very attitude, of course, also encouraged them to interpret Southern actions in the worst possible light.

The second argument to emerge from the annual meeting was a familiar one. From every side, members said, people were asking them what the friends of peace should do during this great war. And to everyone who asked, the American Peace Society gave the same answer: "Under our system, such evils could never have occurred; and under no view of the case, is it ours, as a Peace Society, to meet them, and say what ought to be done." The present conflict, the society decreed, had nothing to do with the cause of peace, which endeavored to resolve conflicts between nations, not referee domestic disputes. Since there technically was no war going on in the United States—only a criminal uprising—the principles of peace were not applicable to the present circumstances. The government was merely maintaining law and order, and the advocates of peace, as obedient Christians, ought to obey the government that God had ordained. "It is ours, as loyal citizens," the *Advocate* averred, "to stand firmly by the government, and render such aid as we consistently can in executing its laws, and bringing offenders to condign punishment."[22] Never had the society uttered a firmer endorsement of Romans 13.

Finally, the peace society described the specific sphere in which, as a peace society, it *was* called to act during this hour of trial. Though it did not wish, in the name of Christ, to call for an end to the government's police action against the rebels, nor to advise the government how to conduct that police action, the society did not intend to be passive. Now was the time to renew the work of education to which it had always been dedicated. The society had been convinced since the days of Noah Worcester that war was an evil custom—a bad habit—that otherwise intelligent people resorted to because they had not learned of its futility. Once instructed in the evils of war, the society had asserted, persons would freely choose to reject it. Now the society wished to argue that a proper peace education would also convince people that it was wrong to disobey Paul's injunction in Romans 13 to obey the rulers that God had ordained. "Had the South been trained even to the lowest views of peace, even half as well as New England has been," the society confided, "they would have calmly waited for peaceful, legal means to address their alleged wrongs."[23] In this manner, the society completed the task Beckwith had begun decades ago by making the cause of peace inextricable from support for government. In addition, it reaffirmed a basic theological assumption—namely, that war was the result of uninformed human choices rather than sinful human nature—at the same time that it dedicated itself anew to the task of reeducating humanity so that the present crisis would never be repeated.

The peace society's activities during the rest of the war flowed out of the attitudes toward the Southern rebellion that the society expressed in 1861. The society spent much of its time defending the conclusions of 1861 and cheering the Union on to victory. As a result of the decision to label secession one of the most gigantic crimes in history, the society increasingly regarded Southerners as fanatics untouched by human decency. Gone were the days of the 1850s, when the society had tentatively affirmed that "intelligent, warm-hearted people" could be found even in the South.[24] Unsympathetic with slavery and unfamiliar with Southern customs, the members of the American Peace Society had always been suspicious of Southerners. The society's depictions of the South had inevitably been more like caricatures than descriptions. Now, having branded Southerners as disgraceful criminals and horrified at their treatment of Northern prisoners, the society declared that there was no atrocity that a rebel would not commit.[25] Even Southern women came under fire. "The malice and ferocity of these rebel vixens," one article declared, "often, if not generally, found in the higher circles of Southern society, seem almost incredible."[26]

As merciless aggressors, the Southerners were also, in the opinion of the American Peace Society, entirely to blame for the "evils surrounding the rebellion."[27] The society professed to be grieved by those who claimed that both sides were equally at fault. Such a view, the society answered, ignored the clear fact that rebellion was a crime and that only the South was guilty of it.[28] Particularly offensive were the appeals of the London Peace Society asking the American Peace Society to work to reconcile the North with the South. "Neutrality is plainly impossible," the American Peace Society answered. "We must take sides either with the rebels, or with the government."[29] Similarly, the American Peace Society had no sympathy for the so-called peace party of the Copperhead Democrats. Such a peace party, it claimed, was only a trick of proslavery politicians; true friends of peace did not wish to compromise with the rebels.[30]

As a corollary of blaming the South for all the evils of the war, the society came to glorify the Union's efforts to suppress the rebel criminals. Though the society had to admit that the Union army was not above reproach—in victory, Union troops had a bad habit of "exulting over the rebels"[31]—on the whole the society found much to admire in the Union's police action. Whereas Southerners treated Northern prisoners disgracefully, the North mitigated as many of the evils of war as possible, treating Southern prisoners with respect.[32] Southerners persecuted Quakers who refused to bear arms, but the North treated them leniently.[33] Even when the North turned to conscription to fill up the army, the peace society found much to praise. "If we *must* . . . have the war system in full operation," the society noted, "we see not how our rulers could well have devised a conscription act less liable to objection than the one they have just adopted. . . . The only favor shown is to the poor, the helpless, and suffering."[34]

Absent from the society's characterization of the war was any discussion of Northern atrocities. The society ignored the deplorable state of Union prisoner-of-war camps and spoke not at all of the Union battle tactics that laid to waste the farms of the Shenandoah Valley and made William T. Sherman's name a curse word in Georgia for decades to come. Even though the society chose not to publicize those aspects of the war effort, its members were not unaware of them. As the war dragged on, the society had to steel itself to the suffering and death. It had resolved in 1861 that God willed for the government to maintain law and order, regardless of the cost. In the weary months following that decision, the advocates of peace repeatedly encouraged each other to stand behind their initial resolve. As much as the friends of peace hated to see the corpses pile higher, they had committed themselves to be obedient to God's will.

One of the ways the American Peace Society eased its conscience about the war was by absolving itself of guilt for the deaths the war had caused. Since the rebels were "utterly wrong"[35] in initiating hostilities, there was no use in feeling guilty about the consequences of the rebels' sin. Neither was it the society's job to tell the government how to punish crime. Trying to find a role for the peace society in this crisis was like trying to find a role for the temperance society—neither group, the American Peace Society avowed, had anything to do with the government enforcing laws. The friends of peace could only stand by as the state executed God's will.[36] The suffering and dying would end when the rebels agreed to submit to God's authority, and until that time there was nothing left to do. The killing must go on. "Would you complain of God for executing his laws upon rebels against his throne?" the society asked.[37]

Besides, as the peace society increasingly came to contend, there *was* something vindictive about the work of government, and the friends of peace needed to accept that reality. As Beckwith explained, government's mission was "to restrain and punish wrong-doers by force." The nonresistance of the Sermon on the Mount was an ethic that simply did not apply to the work of the state.[38] The *Advocate of Peace* noted that both the Sermon on the Mount and Romans 13 were part of the gospel,[39] but it was a mistake to confuse one with the other. The Sermon on the

Mount described an ethic for individuals, whereas Romans 13 gave the state authority to chastise transgressors. As an article entitled "The Enforcement of Law Not War" asserted,

> One is a question of personal kindness in social life; the other, of public authority, justice, retribution. As an individual, you ought of course to forgive those who injure you; but as a ruler, you are required, as a Christian duty, to protect society against wrong-doers by bringing them to a suitable punishment. You *must* do so, or you are a ruler only in name. The principles of peace are not applicable to the case. No government, when dealing with incorrigible offenders, ever did or ever can proceed on the principle of turning the other cheek to the smiter, of returning good for evil, and overcoming evil with good. Strict government is the reverse of this.[40]

Members of the American Peace Society opposed to defensive wars could still argue that the government had no right to punish foreign invaders—since it had no jurisdiction to rule over them—at the same time that they insisted that the state was obliged to punish the criminals in its midst.[41] At this point, the idea of applying the ethic of love to individuals and nations alike was obviously dead. Even those who thought the ethic of love was still relevant to defensive wars were unwilling to apply it to the state's internal workings. For better or worse, the society had conceded the existence of an ethic of coercion that was both independent of, and at odds with, the gospel ethic of love.

As they came to accept the reality of that coercive ethic, more and more the friends of peace urged each other not to flinch at its implications. "Numbers can never sanctify crime, nor make its punishment wrong," soothed one *Advocate* article. "If laws were made to be used, and rulers appointed to see them executed, the efforts of our government, however gigantic, to crush our slaveholders' rebellion, are only a legitimate enforcement of law."[42] Another article was even more straightforward. Some people, it noted, felt hesitant about retaliating against the rebels for the barbarities they had perpetrated, but such a reluctance was unfounded. If the government were not serious about retaliation, it would have let the rebels secede. Since the government, however, was determined to punish the Southern criminals, it was ridiculous to be squeamish about it. Indeed, the government was permitted to inflict all the evils necessary to achieve its ends. Thus, the author concluded,

> If an enemy or a rebel does not yield, he must be made to suffer till he will. . . . if [it is] necessary to sacrifice property, comfort, and life itself until the land becomes an Aceldama and a wilderness, it must, on the war principle, be done without hesitation or a twinge. . . . We confess, peace

men as we are, we have often found it very difficult to conceal our lack of respect for the half-war, half-peace way in which our government has treated our rebels. . . . if you will or must have war, better have it throughout in downright earnestness.[43]

By the time Robert E. Lee and Ulysses S. Grant had finally agreed upon peace terms at Appomattox, some members of the peace society had rejected such a vindictive approach to the war. Yet what is surprising is not that some dissented but, rather, that so few chose to do so. At the 1862 annual meeting, Howard Malcom, the society's president, conceded that "the interests of all nations . . . demanded that we should resist the murderous [rebel] assault, even unto death"; yet Malcom followed that remark by asking that peace negotiations begin.[44] For the American Peace Society in 1862 that was an unusual request. In the spring of 1863 an article in the *Advocate* expressed the "tentative thought" that it might be best to let the Southern states go, even if they were engaged in criminal activity.[45] The most conciliatory article of all appeared in the last *Advocate* of 1864. Declaring that the North was partly responsible for the war since it had allowed the slave owners to show disrespect for authority for so many years, an article entitled "How to Close a Civil War" argued that the North should be as lenient toward the South as possible as the war came to an end.[46]

Such voices of moderation, however, were rare. For the most part, the members of the American Peace Society were convinced that the Northern crusaders had a divine mandate to conquer the Southern infidels and rule them with a rod of iron. Even as late as 1866, articles were still appearing in the *Advocate* demanding stern treatment of the erring rebels. Denouncing the "lenity" the government had demonstrated in its handling of the Southern leaders, one article in the March–April edition of 1866 was horrified at the thought that the government might pardon Jefferson Davis. "Pardon Jefferson Davis!" it exclaimed. "On the same principle God ought to have pardoned Satan, and received him back into heaven while reeking with all the guilt of his rebellion still upon him."[47] Whatever else its faults, the peace society did not suffer a crisis of faith during the war. Buoyed by the certainty that the cause of peace was pledged to support law and order, the society may at times have regretted, but never doubted, that God had called it to stand by the state as it executed the awful task of enforcing justice.

Indeed, judging from the annual report the society issued at the end of the war, the American Peace Society remained imperturbably committed to the same doctrines and methods that it had championed before the fighting. Claiming to have "adhered through sunshine and storm to the principles and policy announced by our society from its origin," the society reiterated yet again that "the sole question agitated through all these years of blood has been whether our laws shall be enforced against those who violate them." In looking to the future, the society claimed that its "specific mission" was—as it had ever been—to educate the Christian community to reject the violence of rebellion and war. Without such education, the society argued, more rebellions were in the offing. But if the peace society did its work with vigor, "such an education of our people will be a sure antidote to like evils in the future. . . . God and his gospel, reason, humanity, and the great interests of mankind are all on our side."[48]

Veterans of the fight for peace urged the society to stick to the positions that it had always advocated. Thomas Upham wrote Beckwith, asking the society to return to its old stands. The society should stress once more, Upham argued, that war was evil, that nations were related in Christian fellowship, and that arbitration was a viable alternative to war. Gerrit Smith suggested that it was a good time to petition Congress and the president to establish a Congress of Nations.[49] In short, the American Peace Society seemed determined to proceed as if the Civil War had never happened; the society planned to revive its previous campaigns and seek once again to mold public opinion in favor of peace. The members of the American Peace Society were determined to see the American Civil War only as an unwelcome interruption to their efforts on behalf of peace.

Determined as the peace society was to return to business as usual, however, the fact remained that the society *had* changed in the years between its founding and the signing of peace at Appomattox. By 1865, the society no longer believed that the Sermon on the Mount was an ethic of love that applied to nations and individuals alike, regardless of the consequences. By insisting upon the state's obligation to enforce the law—no matter how drastic the methods necessary—the society had served notice that it regarded law and order as a higher value than the nonresistant love of the Sermon on the Mount. By asserting that war consisted only of international disputes, the society refused to regard civil war as true war. It decreed that all blame lay with those who would resist the government and protested that the state was justified in using any means to restrain and punish those who broke the law. Rather than expecting the state to apply the principles of proportionality or discrimination to its police efforts, the members of the society argued that God had given the government free rein to enforce its will. Thus, though the American Peace Society remained committed to the cause of peace, its interpretation of the state's police function meant that, from 1861 to 1865, the principles of pacifism and holy war were indistinguishable.

The Nonresistants: The Prophets Are Silent in the Land

The Civil War years were a startling time for the nonresistants—startling because, for the first occasion ever, they were not sectarian outsiders out of step with the culture around them. For once the government was acting righteously, and they had no reason to condemn it. For once, their political views coincided with those of most Northerners, and they could unite in a common cause with other citizens. Though the terrible slaughter of the war disturbed the nonresistants, still they felt that God was working through the carnage to create a freer, purer nation. It was not their place, the nonresistants believed, to speak against this providential work, strange and bloody though it was. Rather, it was their calling to be true to the nonresistant gospel of Jesus Christ, while those around them were obedient to the highest moral plane available to them. Nonresistance had not condoned slavery, nor had it initiated hostilities. Neither would it settle the war. Those who had lived by violence and coercion would decide the issue on their own terms. Convinced of the moral superiority of the free North, the nonresistants were content to stand by as Federal soldiers gave their lives for the Union. It was worth granting authority to the ethic of coercion if, as a consequence, the slaves at last gained their freedom.

Garrison endured no turmoil or anxiety about how to regard the war. As long as the Union was proslavery, he explained, he had advocated disunionism. In those days, he had adopted the role of Isaiah and had denounced the Constitution as "a covenant with death, and an agreement with hell." Once the Southern states seceded, however, and forfeited their claim on the proslavery clauses of the Constitution, the North was free to abolish slavery. At that point, Garrison no longer condemned the government with a prophet's rage. "I had no idea," he confessed, "that I would live to see death and hell secede."[50]

Once the Civil War began, Garrison argued, abolitionists had a new role to play. No longer were they agitators, determined to create controversy. Instead, they were observers who were to watch as the events of liberation unfolded. As he wrote in 1861,

> Now that civil war has begun, and a whirlwind of violence and excitement is to sweep through the country, every day increasing intensity until its bloodiest culmination, it is for the abolitionists to "stand still, and see the salvation of God," rather than to attempt to add any thing to the general

commotion. It is not time for minute criticism of Lincoln, Republicanism, or even the other parties, now that they are fusing for a death-grapple with the Southern slave oligarchy; for they are instruments in the hands of God to carry forward and help achieve the great object of emancipation, for which we have so long been striving. The war is fearfully to scourge the nation, but mercy will be mingled with judgment, and grand results are to follow, should no dividing root of bitterness rise up at the North. All our sympathies and wishes must be with the government, as against the Southern desperadoes and buccaneers; yet, of course, without any compromise of principle on our part. We need great circumspection and consummate wisdom in regard to what we say and do, under these unparalleled circumstances. We are rather, for the time being, to note the events transpiring, than seek to control them. There must be no needless turning of popular violence upon ourselves, by any false step of our own.[51]

The nonresistants among the abolitionists, Garrison concluded, could not help but wish success to the cause of freedom; but for the time being their task was simply to watch as the war went on to its consummation. Then it would be time for the nonresistants to speak—and for others to listen—about peace.[52]

In a *Liberator* article aptly entitled "New Occasions Teach Duties," Charles K. Whipple echoed Garrison's sentiments. "It now seems," Whipple remarked, "as if Divine Providence, waiting no longer for the conversion of either South or North, was about to accomplish the deliverance of the slave by the shortest method." The abolitionists, Whipple declared, had three duties before them. First of all, recognizing that the North—though swayed by motives and means other than those of nonresistant abolitionism—now opposed the slave power, the abolitionists ought simply to stand and watch events unfold. Second, they ought to be zealous in their support for the Union, once it was divorced from slavery. Finally, the abolitionists must be on guard against every compromise with slavery; it was their task to see that the Union remained firm in opposing that sinful institution.[53]

If the abolitionists accomplished those three objectives, Whipple was certain that the fight to save the Union would also result in the deliverance of the slaves. Most other nonresistants agreed with him, even though Lincoln had made no such promise at the outset of the war. Garrison believed that the addition of the abolition of slavery as a war aim was inevitable, particularly if the abolitionists did their job of preparing public sentiment to demand emancipation.[54] Just as God had, in the divine providence, brought about this awful war, so, Garrison avowed, God intended to use the war to eradicate slavery. As Garrison explained in May of 1861,

Technically, the war is to restore the old state of things—fugitive slave law, and all; practically, it is a geographical fight between North and South, and between free and slave institutions. Of the great body of soldiers who have enlisted at the North, comparatively few have any intention or wish to break down the slave system; but God, "who is above all, and greater than all," and who

> "—moves in a mysterious way,
> His wonders to perform,"

is making use of them to do a "strange and terrible work," in righteousness. I neither deprecate his justice, nor desire to see peace through compromise. I believe this state of things is hopeful, compared with what it was six months ago.[55]

For the nonresistants, the war was God's judgment on a society that had chosen to live by violence and coercion. They were confident that God would, through the war, eliminate the evil institution of slavery that had for too long been a blot on the nation's character.

Even given that conviction, however, the nonresistants had to do some fancy stepping to support the use of violence as a means of abolishing violence. It was one thing to claim that their peace principles were "as beneficent and glorious as ever,"[56] and another thing to refuse to compromise them. Almost all of the nonresistants followed Garrison and Whipple in supporting the war, but they were able to do so only by conceding that the ethic of coercion was independent of the ethic of love. As nonresistants, they continued to be obedient to the Sermon on the Mount, eschewing consequential reasoning and refusing to return evil for evil. For the vast majority of the Northern population who were not nonresistants, however, they recommended a less exalted course of action. Samuel J. May, for example, noted that he could not "exhort or counsel others to go to war," since he thought war was wrong. Certainly he would not go to war himself. Yet knowing in his heart that slavery was an abomination before God, neither would he seek to prevent those who wished to join the North in its battle against the Southern slaveocracy. "I shall not hinder any, whose sense of duty may impel them thither," he proclaimed.[57]

Garrison had to face such a sense of duty in his own household. One of his sons, William Lloyd, Jr., had decided in 1858 to be a nonresistant. Another son, Frank, was still a child in 1861, and Garrison asked the principal of the Boston Latin School to excuse Frank from the school's military drills. Two other sons, Wendell Phillips and George Thompson, had reached no decision by the time the war started. Each was of draftable age. Eventually Wendell Phillips decided to follow in his father's footsteps, declaring himself to be a nonresistant. He refused on moral grounds to hire a substitute to fight in his place, but he did consent to pay a three hundred dollar fine to avoid military service. Garrison approved of that action and was delighted that Wendell had chosen the path of nonresistance.[58]

George Thompson Garrison, the oldest son, chose in 1863 to enter the army as a second lieutenant in command of a company of black soldiers. In 1862, prior to the Emancipation Proclamation, Garrison had urged George not to enter the army. "If I had no conscientious scruples as a peace advocate against enlisting so long as the government is struggling, avowedly and solely, to maintain 'the Union as it was, and the Constitution as it is,'—the old 'covenant with death and the agreement with hell,' " he explained, "I do not see how I, or any other radical abolitionist, could consistently fight to maintain it."

By 1863 the abolition of slavery had become an official war aim. Garrison deeply regretted that George had not chosen to adopt the principles of peace that he considered sacred, yet he supported George's decision to enlist. Like all other Union soldiers, George ought to do his best to be true to the highest moral principles he was capable of following. "I have nothing but praise to give you," Garrison said, "that you have been faithful to your highest convictions, and, taking your life in your own hands, are willing to lay it down . . . if need be, in the cause of freedom, and for the suppression of slavery and the rebellion. True, I could have wished you could ascend to what I believe a higher plane of moral heroism and a nobler method of self-sacrifice; but as you are true to yourself, I am glad of your fidelity, and proud of your willingness to run any risk in a cause that is undeniably just and good."[59]

Garrison's recognition of the ethic of coercion could hardly have been clearer. Indeed, he had already worked out a theory in which he contended that Northern citizens had a moral obligation to go to war. Arguing that Garrisonian abolitionism in the political realm translated into support for the Declaration of Independence's claim that all human beings were equal and in the religious realm meant adherence to the Golden Rule, Garrison claimed that the war had brought home the meaning of oppression to the North. Previously, he said, Northerners had supported the Declaration of Independence, but had not cared enough to apply its principles to the slaves. Now that Northern property had been stolen and Northern rights trampled, however, people at last understood the oppression that the slaves had so long endured.[60] Garrison believed that anyone who considered voting to be a moral act should also be eligible to be drafted into the army. Only nonresistants, who abstained from governmental involvement, should be exempted.

Otherwise, all men—including "peacemen" who voted—could be called on to support the state with their blood, since their willingness to vote had already revealed their support for a "war-making Constitution."[61]

Presenting the Declaration of Independence as nonresistance in political clothing, however, could be tricky. For one thing, the South was claiming that the right of revolution delineated in the Declaration gave it license to throw off the federal government and start a new nation. Having claimed the Declaration of Independence for himself, Garrison was not about to let the South use it to give secession political legitimacy. As a result, he was forced to argue that secession had nothing to do with either disunionism or with the Declaration of Independence. Disunionism, he asserted, had called upon people, in the name of a "Higher Law," peacefully to repudiate the "covenant with death" that the Constitution had made with slavery. Clearly secession differed from disunionism. And while it was true that the Declaration of Independence had urged resistance to tyrants, this too had nothing to do with secession, since it was the South that for years had played the tyrant over the slaves.[62] Nor did Garrison believe that the South could claim the Declaration's decree that all governments derived their just powers from the consent of the governed as a legitimate way out of its constitutional attachment to the Union. "This is as stupid and monstrous a perversion of the language of the Declaration as is the rendering of Christ's injunction, 'Take, eat—this is my body'—by the Romish Church, so as to prove the doctrine of transubstantiation," he fumed.[63]

Having thus denied that the Southern revolt was a legitimate war for independence—though he did not add, as the American Peace Society did, that it was not a war at all—Garrison chose to depict the struggle as a contest between the lawless and the law-abiding. Under this theory, Lincoln was obliged—whatever his views as a private individual—to enforce the laws and maintain the Constitution. Just as he had no constitutional right, before secession, to abolish slavery, so after secession did he have a constitutional responsibility to preserve the Union.[64] Garrison was convinced that Lincoln, in overseeing the Union war effort, had done nothing more than execute faithfully his oath of office.

Nevertheless, by choosing to characterize the North as law-abiding and the South as lawless, Garrison and his followers signaled their determination to lay all the blame for the war on the South. The Garrisonians had always prided themselves on their objectivity—on their willingness to criticize any institution or person that erred. For over twenty-five years, as an editorial in the *Liberator* noted in 1861, they had refused to participate in government, choosing instead to criticize and condemn all parties and administrations. That impartiality, the article argued, empowered them to pass a fair judgment on the present state of affairs— and that judgment was that "the conduct of the Secessionists combines all conceivable perfidy and crime, and that they are brigands and pirates on a scale unparalleled in the annals of human depravity."[65] As Charles Whipple would later add, one party was wholly in the right, and the other wholly in the wrong—and only the abolition of slavery could put things right.[66]

Other "impartial" nonresistants added their voices. Henry Wright announced that he could not help but rejoice that the present offense against God—that is, the war—had finally come. Lincoln, of course, would later use that same text from Scripture in his second inaugural address, but he assumed that the "offense" was slavery and that both North and South were to blame:

> The Almighty has His own purposes. "Woe unto the world because of offenses. For it must needs be that offenses come; but woe to that man by whom the offense cometh." If we shall suppose that American slavery is one of those offenses which, in the providence of God, must needs come, but which having continued through His appointed time, He now wills to remove, and that He gives to both North and South this terrible war, as the woe due to those by whom the offense came, shall we discern therein any departure from those divine attributes which the believers in a living God always ascribe to Him?[67]

Wright, however, assumed that the offense was the war, which he blamed entirely on the South. He praised the North for answering violence with violence and thereby paving the way for the liberation of the slaves:

> My sense of justice, my sympathy with human suffering, my compassion, my reason, my conscience, my non-resistance, my hatred of war and slavery, my desire for the purity, perfection, and happiness of human nature—all prompt me to say to . . . the North, "I BLESS YOU FOR PREFERRING WAR TO SUCH A PEACE!" Be this your slogan: "DEATH TO SLAVERY! the sum of all villainy, 'the concocted essence of theft, rape, robbery, prostitution, incest, piracy and murder!' "[68]

Though they portrayed themselves as unbiased observers, the non-resistants were blatant partisans. Convinced that the North fought for liberty, they dismissed Southerners as depraved tyrants and accepted whatever means Lincoln had to use to achieve his ends. "In the present war," Wright concluded, "fidelity to freedom is true allegiance to the Government, for the Republic is fighting for liberty. . . . God will bless the object, though, ignobly, bloody means are used to attain it."[69] Given the nonresistants' presumption that the South was wholly to blame for the war and that God blessed the Northern struggle for freedom, it is easy to see why the nonresistants had no sympathy for pacifists who urged them to condemn the violence enveloping the nation. Alfred H. Love, a Quaker from Philadelphia, wrote the *Liberator* repeatedly, urging Garrison to hold to his principles and seek to win others to nonresistance, but Garrison was not impressed.[70] E. H. Heywood was a frequent correspondent, reiterating the refrain that war was wrong—"not an evil merely, but a sin and a crime."[71] H. H. Brigham wrote as well, imploring Garrison to speak out on nonresistance. "It appears to us," Brigham argued, "that the time to rebuke sin . . . and speak against it, is while sin abounds."[72]

To all who asked him to be a prophet of peace, Garrison gave the same answer: "There is a time to be silent as well as to speak. . . . this is not the best period for an abstract ethical discussion of the question of Non-Resistance. Especially do we consider it very unfortunate for any one, claiming to be a Non-Resistant, who so enforces the doctrine as to give 'aid and comfort' to traitors and their copperhead sympathizers at this particular crisis."[73] Though Garrison continued to print articles and speeches by nonresistants opposed to the war, he gave his partners in pacifism little encouragement. "Ardently as my soul yearns for universal peace, and greatly shocking to it as are the horrors of war," he explained, "I deem this a time when the friends of peace will best subserve their holy cause to wait until the whirlwind, the fire and the earthquake are past, and then 'the still small voice' may be understandingly and improvingly heard."[74]

The London Peace Society was particularly disappointed with the nonresistants. We do not believe, the society stated, that the American Civil War is a war of freedom; we believe its object is to conquer the South. And even if it were a war of freedom, we would not support it. How, the London pacifists asked, can you stand quietly by and let brute force decide complex questions of moral right? The only evil you can see, the society complained, is the evil of slavery, but we believe that war is an even worse sin, and we will oppose it in every instance.[75]

Even criticism from respected pacifists, however, was not enough to sway the nonresistants. The London Peace Society, Garrison noted, had accused abolitionists of abandoning peace activism and of urging Americans to butcher one another. Since most abolitionists had never been nonresistants in the first place, Garrison replied, such criticism could hardly hold. And those abolitionists who were nonresistants had refused to go to battle.[76] Charles Whipple agreed, perplexed that the London society seemed determined to side with the Southern slaveocracy in this battle for freedom. "Does Peace seem supremely lovely to you," he asked, "when it comes by the consent of the weaker party to bear gross oppression without resistance? Is Peace the *one* thing needful when it leaves one party established as tyrant and the other as slave?"[77]

Arguing that there "are other principles to be advocated" in the present struggle besides the question of peace, Whipple insisted that agitating for peace would only give aid and comfort to the South:

> The Peace men in this country, always an insignificant minority, and now fewer than ever—rarely making converts in favorable periods, and now making none—see no prospect of success in labors for the cause of peace at present. Moreover, those of them that are Abolitionists see that all and more than all that they can do is needed for the cause of freedom . . . and that, while their labor is successful and mightily effective in that field, every word now uttered in advocacy of peace is prejudicial to liberty, chiming with the party cry now raised by those who wish only the success of the rebels, and have no sympathy with what *we* recognize as "peace principles."[78]

The power of truth and love, Whipple concluded, could accomplish much with the average person or savage, but the Southern slaveholders and the poor whites who supported them were "a class worse than any of these." The most depraved and hardened people on earth, Southerners would perhaps have been persuaded in a thousand years through Northern kindness and forbearance to abolish slavery. Given the present opportunity to abolish slavery through force, Whipple was determined that he and the other nonresistants would not be a stumbling block in the path of freedom.[79]

Predictably the Londoners were not convinced. I know you will deny it, Henry Richard wrote Whipple, but I believe you are in too feverish an atmosphere to listen to sober reason. The government may be conducting the war, but it is the abolitionists who demand that it continue. Why, Richard demanded, had the nonresistants refused to learn from history? Did they not realize that combatants always claimed that their enemies were depraved? How could the nonresistants think that their case was unique or that their Southern compatriots were peculiarly satanic? All that the nonresistants had done, in Richard's view, was to trade what they had learned from the gospel of peace in favor of the standard arguments used to justify war. "In truth my dear Sir," Richard admonished, "if your reasoning be sound, Peace Societies may as well break up at once, and acknowledge that their whole foundation is a rotten one."[80]

Richard's remark about the nonresistants' estimate of Southern depravity was revealing. Like those of the American Peace Society, the nonresistants' discussions of Southerners had always had the quality of caricature, being little more than moral assessments—usually negative— of the Southern character rather than flesh-and-blood descriptions of individuals. Though Garrison had argued in 1858 that he would always regard the Southern slaveholder as a human being, "sacred before me" and "not to be harmed by my hand, nor with my consent,"[81] during the war years the nonresistants routinely spoke of Southerners not as human beings, but as brutes to be broken. Maria Child set the tone when she wrote, in the summer of 1861, that the North was not dealing with "Southern brethren," but with "fierce, malignant, savage enemies . . . rendered utterly barbarous by long practice of a hellish system."[82] Accustomed to thinking of Southerners as coldly cruel oppressors who could torture a slave at the blink of an eye, the nonresistants piled up the epithets. Criminal, depraved, perfidious, savage, tyrannical, rebellious, diseased, even benumbed vipers[83]—no appellation was too degrading to describe a Southerner.

It was impossible for the nonresistants to love and respect people whom they regarded as despicable savages. Garrison tried to temper that language by invoking the Golden Rule. "All we threaten to do," he said, "in the excess of our wrath, as a retaliatory measure, is to abolish their iniquitous and destructive slave system, and thus give them light for darkness, good for evil, heaven for perdition! . . . let us return them good for evil, by seizing this opportunity to deliver them from their deadliest curse—that is Christian."[84] Abolishing slavery, Garrison argued, would establish the South as the garden of God.[85]

Hidden under Garrison's disclaimers, however, beneath the traditional nonresistant phrases of returning good for evil, lay other desires. The nonresistants had awaited the day of emancipation for decades. Now that it was at hand, they wanted to be sure that white Southerners were prepared to welcome blacks as their equals. Fully aware that whites would not voluntarily embrace racial equality, the nonresistants prepared to conquer the South and coerce it into submission. No one called for more stringent measures against the seceded states than did the nonresistants. They quarreled with Lincoln's plans for reconstruction on the grounds that merely granting amnesty to the rebellious states would not make them loyal. Congress must, the Garrisonians insisted, establish military control in the South after the war. Only later—perhaps much later—would it be possible to restore civil government. Until then, as Garrison put it, "the Government is solemnly bound to be omnipresent, omniscient, and omnipotent in every part of the South."[86] Charles Whipple went so far as to argue that military rule should continue in the South until the freed blacks were financially independent and the whites were thoroughly penitent.[87]

Nor were the nonresistants willing, once the war had ended, to forgive and forget the sins they perceived in those who had fought for the South. The Civil War, Maria Child declared, had not been a tournament or a game; it was a "death-grapple" between freedom and despotism. "Those who eulogize the bravery of Lee, and shake hands with Jeff Davis," she insisted, "have no right ever to touch the hands of Grant, Sherman, Sheridan. . . . I never wanted greater severity shown to the South than was necessary to restrain them from further evil. But there is a right and a wrong in this matter, which ought not to be confounded by a desire to exhibit magnanimity."[88] Garrison concurred, asserting that in the South "the powers of hell are still strong and defiant, resolved upon sowing whatever evil is possible, in the spirit of diabolical malignity."[89] In 1866, when asked to sign a petition to release Jefferson Davis from prison, he refused, answering that if "Davis, with his colossal guilt, escaped the gallows, hanging ought certainly to be forever abolished."[90]

Perhaps Garrison and his friends were returning good for evil and love for hate, but if so, both were far removed from the noncoercive ideal they had championed as advocates of the government of God. For the nonresistants the war ended not in peace, but in acrimony. They persisted in demanding, if not punishment, at least unceasing vigilance in the government's treatment of the South. Formerly they had insisted that social change was possible only through individual conversions, not through institutional reforms. Now, in the name of nonresistance and noncoercion, they were calmly entertaining the possibility of holding the South at gunpoint till Southern whites at last agreed to be moral. Joshua Blanchard and E. H. Heywood had each warned that military tyranny would only impel Southern whites to hate blacks and the North more fiercely, but the nonresistants put their faith in the Northern army and in the hope that the next generation of Southerners, educated by wise volunteers from the North, would be a different people.[91] Time would show that hope to be futile.

The nonresistants' determination to depend upon institutional reform in the South was a natural consequence of a prior theological decision. Once they concluded that all persons and groups were not in every instance duty bound to obey the Sermon on the Mount, the nonresistants granted autonomy to the ethic of coercion that the unregenerate practiced. Garrison admitted as much when he argued that nonresistance was, on the personal level, the Golden Rule, and, on the political level, the Declaration of Independence. In the early years of the movement the nonresistants had stressed the distinction between the two, always noting that the Declaration of Independence fell below the perfection of the gospel. By the Civil War, however, they regarded the ideals of the Declaration as the political expression of nonresistance. In the old days nonresistance had no concrete political expression; it was a righteous way of living that went beyond the sinful limitations of the political realm. By the 1860s, however, the nonresistants believed that those who lived in the world ought to defend the highest ideals of their culture. The death grapple between freedom and despotism was no time to introduce abstract questions of peace and war. Though they continued to practice nonresistance themselves, the nonresistants sought no converts during the war. The prophets of peace were silent in the land.

Granting autonomy to the ethic of coercion also entailed engaging in consequential reasoning. The ethic of love had rejected consequential reasoning as unworthy of a savior who had willingly accepted death on the cross rather than disobey God. By allowing for an ethic of coercion, however, the nonresistants could urge those who accepted violence to use it in the cause of liberty. The desire to achieve results—rather than simply practice obedience to the gospel—had admittedly been present in the movement from the beginning. The nonresistants had petitioned the government and advised people how to vote even when they refused to be involved in a government founded upon violence. Yet even then they had never ceased to encourage the unregenerate to abandon the ways of the world and convert to nonresistance. In their desire to end one form of violence, however, the nonresistants were willing to incite others to war. Slavery was an institution so evil—and the slaves themselves had already endured the cross so long—that the nonresistants considered themselves justified in urging others to use violence to abolish violence. It was a small thing to ask unregenerate Northerners to sacrifice their lives to liberate the slaves.

Unfortunately the nonresistants developed no norms to govern the ethic of coercion. While they had a goal—liberty—they set no ethical standards by which to judge the way in which they progressed toward that goal. Like the members of the American Peace Society, the nonresistants refused to discriminate between the justice of the war and the just (or unjust) means used in the war. Having abandoned their role as sectarian outsiders, they had no distance from which to evaluate the government's conduct of the war. The nonresistants wanted to free the slaves, and they wanted the war to continue until abolition was included among the Union war aims. Other than that, they were uninterested in how the war was fought. The *Liberator* raised no complaints against Northern tactics or excesses; it was easy to regard the Northern forces as God's avenging armies and to chalk up the desolation of the South as its just reward for centuries of cruelty to the slaves. In their new role as advocates for the state, rather than agitators against it, the only thing the nonresistants found to complain about was excessive lenience towards the South. For the nonresistants, as for the American Peace Society, the Civil War was a holy war.

It was the identification of God and Union that provided an apocalyptic note to the peace activists' perceptions of the war. They saw a cosmic drama between good and evil being played out before them.[92] That apocalyptic vision revealed, in turn, a great deal about the peace activists' emotional responses to the war. As social psychologist Herbert C. Kelman has observed, it is possible to consent to mass violence only when we cease to regard our victims as fully human. The advocates of peace had always assumed the moral superiority of the North and had yearned for decades to remake the South along Yankee lines. Nevertheless, as long as they regarded Southerners as potential converts, the friends of peace might depict them in stereotypical ways, but they necessarily regarded them as human beings like themselves. When the war came, however, and provided a release from decades of suspicion and repressed hatred, the moral restraints that had previously forbade, or at least controlled, violent urges were weakened. The advocates of peace, identifying themselves entirely with the North, no longer regarded Southerners as members of the human community. That was a significant shift. "To accord a person community," Herbert C. Kelman has asserted, "is to perceive him—along with one's self—as part of an interconnected network of individuals who care for each other, who recognize each other's individuality, and who respect each other's rights."

By appealing to dualistic images—good versus evil, right versus wrong—the advocates of peace objectified and dehumanized their Southern colleagues while claiming divine righteousness for themselves. As Charles Stearns had discovered in Kansas, it was much easier to consent to others' deaths when one no longer regarded one's enemies as human. Kelman has noted the same phenomenon in modern settings. When a person dehumanizes others, Kelman concluded, "he loses his capacity to care for them, to have compassion for them, to treat them as human beings. He develops a state of psychic numbing and a sense of detachment which sharply reduce his capacity to feel."[93] As they looked South and saw nothing but rebel vixens and benumbed vipers, the advocates of peace imagined themselves involved in an apocalyptic battle that at all costs must be won. Love was, for the moment, out of the question. First the rebellion had to be quelled; ultimate evil must taste defeat; then there would be time for kindness, conversion, and the renewing of millennial hopes.

That scenario gave rise to a pervasive sense of destiny and finality. Divine judgment, not love or forbearance, was the only acceptable response to a people whose sin was beyond measure. As early as 1837, Garrison had predicted just such a judgment. Lamenting the stubbornness of the slave states, he admitted that

> I have relinquished the expectation, that they will ever, by mere moral suasion, consent to emancipate their victims. I believe that nothing but the exterminating judgments of heaven can shatter the chain of the slave, and destroy the power of his oppressor. . . . Repentance, if it come at all, will come too late. Our sins have gone up over our heads, and our iniquities unto the clouds, and a just God means to dash us in pieces as a potter's vessel is broken.[94]

By 1861 moral suasion had failed; God had grown weary of sin; and now a time of bitter purification was necessary so that, in the aftermath, believers could once again follow a loving Jesus into a nonviolent kingdom. In the present, however, the Northern armies marched for God. And the Southern forces that met them could be shown no mercy, for they had rejected the voices of God's prophets and had sided with evil. On this the American Peace Society and the nonresistants were in accord. As Charles Sumner, renowned in 1846 for proclaiming that every war was disobedient to God, put it in 1861: "Against this rebellion we wage war. It is our determination, it is our duty to crush it. . . . Only by crushing this rebellion can union and peace be restored."[95]

It was more than a little odd that the crusaders for peace should have ended up as apologists for war. Yet from the earliest days of the movement the peace reformers had struggled to balance means and ends. They had sought to follow Jesus without regard for the consequences at the same time that they had energetically labored to convert the world into the millennial kingdom. That juggling act was never easy, and by the Civil War the advocates of peace no longer had the heart for it. Other values such as law and order and freedom from tyranny had taken precedence over the ethic of love outlined in the Sermon on the Mount.

It was a cruel irony that prompted the American Peace Society and the nonresistants to support war in the name of peace. Though they continued to cherish dutiful obedience to the Prince of Peace, they no longer assumed that political success necessarily gravitated to those who in love refused to return evil for evil. Some situations were so dire and the stakes so high that the millennial kingdom was best served by violence. The God of the New Testament was a God of righteousness as well as love, and on some occasions, people could be so enmeshed in sin that they were blind to both love and justice. When moral suasion failed and the cosmic struggle for good lay in the balance, it was necessary to coerce people into righteousness.

As reformers who every day faced their own inner demons, controlled them, and dedicated themselves anew to selfless service to God, the advocates of peace understood the enormity of that cosmic battle for good. Yet they had won it within themselves in the past and they expected to fight and win it every day that they were on earth. They were also determined to love their neighbors as themselves and to work with them in creating a society worthy of the millennium. Thus, when in 1861 their compatriots to the South fell from the grace of God, the advocates of peace concluded that the best way to love their neighbors was to compel them to return to the gospel. In time, the friends of peace believed, the South would rise again—not to condemn them, but to give thanks that Yankees had had such great love for the nation that they had given their lives for their friends, both black and white, Northern and Southern.

6

CONCLUSION

The advocates of peace were extraordinarily ambitious reformers. Convinced that Christianity was a faith to be enacted in the social sphere and not merely a spiritual experience confined to their private lives, they felt responsible for persuading Americans to live peacefully in love for one another. Lives of love required discipline and self-control, but the friends of peace never doubted the human capacity to be true to the gospel's high calling. God would empower all who, putting selfish concerns aside, devoted themselves in disinterested benevolence to molding the social order to the divine will. The power to obey the Sermon on the Mount, they were convinced, was readily available to those who sought it, and the dawning of the millennium awaited only a determined application of the New Testament ethic of love.

Having set for themselves the task of converting their nation to the love ethic of Jesus, the advocates of peace were nevertheless divided by two markedly different reforming temperaments. The members of the American Peace Society were, by and large, prosperous and even eminent persons whose culture had treated them well. Temperamentally they were at home in that culture, and they assumed that reform meant improving—not rejecting—the godly institutions already at work in American society. The nonresistants, on the other hand, were "come outers" who found American culture more godless than godly. They wanted to overturn it and establish a realm in which regenerated persons would be free of institutional coercion, obeying God not out of fear but out of a spontaneous desire to do so.

Both groups of peace activists were deeply engaged in the benevolent projects of the period. In time antislavery activity came to dominate the reform movements. The members of the American Peace Society had a mixed response to the antislavery campaign. Some were sympathetic to colonization, the most conservative antislavery reform, while others supported the more far-reaching goals of political immediatism. That diversity represented a division that would be the source of continual controversy among the members of the peace society. Conservatives led by George Beckwith desired above all else to preserve the group's public reputation, hoping to concentrate on a narrow institutional reform that would outlaw offensive wars between nations. The moderates, sparked by leaders such as Elihu Burritt, Samuel E. Coues, Amasa Walker, and J. P. Blanchard, wanted to condemn defensive wars as well. They were less concerned with guarding the peace society's reputation than with exhorting it to positions that would generate more sweeping social changes.

Despite those differences, the factions of the American Peace Society were united in their desire to maintain congenial ties with their colleagues in the larger benevolent enterprise. Whether they were more extreme or more conservative than those colleagues, the members of the peace society had a strong need to be in community with other Christians engaged in reform. That need set them apart from the nonresistants, who valued righteousness over community with less zealous reformers. The nonresistants' needs for intimate friendships were no less real than those of the members of the peace society, but the nonresistants were unwilling to soften their radical program of reform. "Compromise" and "gradual" were words that sounded to the nonresistants like "treason" and "blasphemy." They wanted to overturn society, not repair it. To them, both the moderates and the conservatives of the peace society had betrayed God by being too cautious. And though the nonresistants craved affirmation and acceptance, they had to look to their own cohort for those affections. Their insistence on condemning those who were less radical than them isolated the nonresistants from the larger community of reform and from American society in general.

In spite of those temperamental differences, a common ethical assumption guided both the nonresistants and the American Peace Society. They sought, above all else, to follow the New Testament ethic of love without regard for the consequences. Quite simply, they wanted to imitate Jesus. They also assumed, however, that in selflessly obeying the ethic of love they were initiating an efficacious method of social change. Though they applauded Jesus the martyr, they assumed that, in imitating him, their efforts would lead not to the cross, but to success. Thus they failed to appreciate the tensions inherent in their conceptions of peace reform. As they spoke of peace and its benefits, they unconsciously used images that worked at cross purposes with one another. Even in describing themselves, they invoked symbols that clashed. Was the peace reformer a nonresistant martyr or an indefatigable agitator? A prophet without honor or a defender of the status quo? A sheriff who enforced the laws mercilessly or a pilgrim following in Jesus' bleeding steps? A sensible educator or a daring anarchist? A dutiful reformer or an effective strategist?

No one could act consistently with each of those images. As violence erupted over the slavery issue, the advocates of peace increasingly found themselves moderating the ethic of love with consequential reasoning. Achieving results became more important than witnessing faithfully. In the early days of the movement, the peace reformers had assumed that the Sermon on the Mount was directly applicable to the political affairs of nations as well as to the devotional lives of individuals. As the years passed, however, and the advocates of peace made exceptions to the ethic of duty, the Sermon on the Mount came to have less and less relevance for the political realm. An ethic of coercion took its place, at least in certain situations.

During the crisis of the Civil War, the American Peace Society and the nonresistants were convinced that a coercive ethic ought to guide both the federal government and those citizens who had consented to that government by participating in the political process. Always sympathetic to the North, during the war the advocates of peace identified themselves with Northern interests far more completely than before. Previously biased characterizations of the South hardened into apocalyptic descriptions pitting rebel demons against Yankee angels. Frustrated that moral suasion had failed and certain that Southern defeat was a necessary prelude to repentance and reformation, the friends of peace were ready to entertain coercion as a means toward purification.

Emotional factors also came into play. Both the nonresistants and the

American Peace Society had cherished a vision of the entire nation uniting in goodness to welcome the reign of God. Through many arduous years, in the face of numerous setbacks and much public indifference, the peace reformers had labored to make that vision a reality. Secession and slavery, however, rendered the vision unattainable. The war, on the other hand, provided an environment in which the friends of peace could release the frustration and anger that they had been forced to repress for so long. After decades of denying themselves the psychological satisfaction of openly hating their enemies or of wishing them dead, the advocates of peace were at last in a situation where killing Southern slaveholders seemed virtuous. Revenge, covered by the assurance that the killing served God's greater good, undoubtedly seemed sweet.

Finally, the war touched other sensitive points of the reformers' psyches. For the American Peace Society, supremely confident of the redemptive capacities of Christian institutions, Southern secession was rebellion against a government ordained by God. The members of the peace society had always set a tremendous store on law and order; an abiding fear of anarchy and chaos coupled with an enduring respect for authority had marked the society from its beginning. The Civil War threatened the society's deepest sense of rightness and security, and the society's desire to reestablish social order prompted it to deny the Southern army the dignity of combatant status. Eager to restore its culture to its proper order, the peace society was willing to bless any efforts the federal government devised to crush the Confederate uprising.

For the Garrisonians, at last finding themselves attuned to the political climate of the day, the war offered a chance to break out of the ghetto that radical abolitionism had created for them. As Lawrence Friedman has emphasized, immediatist abolitionists were deeply convivial people. In condemning American society as sinful, however, the Garrisonians had marked themselves as separate from it. Yet their yearning for acceptance and friendship—their "insatiable longings for fellowship," as Friedman put it—remained. In identifying their cause with God's and God's cause with the Union, the nonresistants at last found the acceptance and love they had yearned to receive from their culture for over three decades.[1]

Nevertheless, by granting autonomy to the ethic of coercion, during the war the antebellum peace reformers became crusaders uninterested in the gospel of love. Though they remained committed in theory to peace reform, their social analysis in the Civil War offered little to distinguish it from the holy war ethic of the Old Testament. Rather than prophets, the advocates of peace became apologists for their war-torn society. Having decided that the Sermon on the Mount did not directly apply to the political crisis of the day, the crusaders for peace proceeded to banish it from their moral discourse altogether. The only way for Northerners to love their Southern neighbors, it seemed, was to annihilate them.

Such an end was a far cry from the confident proclamations of earlier decades that predicted the imminent arrival of God's kingdom. In their great test, the advocates of peace were unable to suggest ways that their compatriots might seek justice at the same time that they consistently applied the lessons of peace. Indeed, the peace reformers were unable to admit to themselves their own inconsistencies and inadequacies. Stubborn to the end, they persisted in arguing that their wartime ethical analysis was the very model of pacific restraint and forbearance. Few of their contemporaries agreed. For most Americans, Rev. A. H. Quint of Massachusetts had it right when in 1866 he denounced the American Peace Society as a "humbug" and a "living lie."[2] It was easy, too, to see why the London Peace Society in 1861 accused the nonresistants of "hounding on their countrymen to mutual slaughter."[3]

Regardless of whether they succeeded in obeying the ethic of love, however, both the nonresistants and the American Peace Society conscientiously strove to bring peace to a troubled world. Undoubtedly they overestimated the extent to which their theology adequately described or could serve to reshape reality. Often they were blind to the ways that their ideas reflected their own particular interests rather than those of humanity as a whole. Even so, in their theological reflections, as well as in their plans for implementing peace, they pioneered ideologies and strategies that continue to appear in modern discussions about war and peace. In both their errors and their insights, their successes and their failures, they have left to future generations a story that points to the elusiveness of peace and justice. Social harmony and good will are fragile human creations, never more so—sadly enough—than when reformers seek to love their neighbors as themselves.

NOTES

Introduction

1. Quoted in Peter Walker, *Moral Choices: Memory, Desire, and Imagination in Nineteenth-Century American Abolition* (Baton Rouge: Louisiana State University Press), pp. 280–85.

2. Both groups appealed to the pacifism of the early church. In addition, the American Peace Society's analysis of the Christian's relationship to the state had similarities to Thomas Aquinas and John Calvin, who argued that the work of the state was complementary to that of the church. Christians thus did not need to feel ambivalent about involvement in the state, for God had ordained the work of government not in answer to the devastation of the Fall, but as a part of the original plan of creation. (See Thomas Aquinas, *On Kingship*, p. 233; and John Calvin, *Institutes of the Christian Religion*, pp. 321–25; both found in William Ebenstein, ed., *Great Political Thinkers: Plato to the Present* [New York: Holt, Rinehart and Winston, 1969].)

In arguing that God established the state after the Fall to preserve corrupted human life, the nonresistants echoed an argument advanced by sixteenth-century Anabaptist groups like the Swiss Brethren, who insisted that government was meant for the fallen, not for the redeemed. The redeemed would, out of love for the sinful world, give their support to the state, but they would define themselves as a regenerate people called out from the mass of sinners to emulate true obedience to the gospel. (See John Howard Yoder, ed. and trans., *The Schleitheim Confession* [Scottdale, Pa.: Herald Press, 1973], pp. 11–16.)

For a good historical survey of Christian teachings on the state, see Roland H. Bainton, *Christian Attitudes toward War and Peace* (Nashville: Abingdon Press, 1960).

3. In his classic study of religion and reform, Whitney R. Cross discussed ultraism as a religious conversion that prompted individuals to seek perfection in their own lives. Having made that commitment, individuals discovered that the reforms they sought were social in nature and could be achieved only through organized political action. Unfortunately, the powerful individualistic religious experience that prompted the impulse for reform blended poorly with group political activism. Radical reformers always struggled to bridge the gap. Moderates, on the other hand, did not envision the reforms that would lead to the kingdom to be as revolutionary (or "ultra") as the radicals imagined. (*The Burned-Over District* [New York: Harper and Row], pp. 173, 206, 236–38, 276–78.)

4. For an excellent account of immediatism among young abolitionist "missionaries," see Lawrence J. Friedman, *Gregarious Saints: Self and Community in American Abolitionism, 1830–1870* (Cambridge: Cambridge University Press, 1982), pp. 11–40.

5. Bertram Wyatt-Brown, *Yankee Saints and Southern Sinners* (Baton Rouge: Louisiana State University Press, 1985), pp. 44–73.

6. In 1834–35, for example, Garrison was mobbed in Boston and led

through town by a rope around his neck. Mobs in New York City sacked Lewis Tappan's house and destroyed three churches, a school, and twenty homes in the African American community. Amos Dresser, a theological student, was given twenty lashes by a vigilante committee in Nashville for possessing abolitionist literature and then was mobbed by Northern antiabolitionists in Marblehead, Massachusetts, less than a year later. In Cincinnati, proslavery vandals tore apart James G. Birney's printing office (where he produced the antislavery *Philanthropist*) and wrecked his home as well. In Berlin, Ohio, a mob attacked abolitionist Marius Robinson in the middle of the night, stripping, tarring, and feathering him and leaving him in the middle of the woods. (John L. Thomas, *The Liberator: William Lloyd Garrison* [Boston: Little, Brown and Company, 1963], pp. 187–200.)

7. As James Brewer Stewart noted, Southern anger was in part a reaction to the "great postal campaign" launched by the American Anti-Slavery Society in 1835. Hoping to saturate the country with abolitionist literature but aiming in particular at ministers, elected officials, and newspaper editors, the abolitionists' pamphleteering endeavor was unprecedented. They sent over 175,000 items from the New York City post office in July 1835. In response, citizens in Charleston, South Carolina, stole the incoming mail from New York on July 29, 1835. The next evening they hung effigies of Garrison and Arthur Tappan and set them afire with abolitionist newspapers. President Andrew Jackson approved of the Southern response, asking Congress to ban abolitionist literature from the United States mail. (*Holy Warriors: The Abolitionists and American Slavery,* American Century Series [New York: Hill and Wang, 1976], pp. 69–70.)

8. Lewis Tappan, who with his brother Arthur helped create the influential "Tappanite empire" of antislavery reform, joined the Massachusetts Peace Society in 1817. In 1828, he became a member of the first board of directors of the American Peace Society, and he filled various offices in the society for the next twenty-five years. (Stewart, *Holy Warriors,* pp. 15–18.) Gerrit Smith, who gained fame for his work with the Liberty party, gave five hundred dollars to the American Peace Society in 1838 and was a vice-president of the society from 1839 until his death. In 1858 Smith gave an address entitled "Peace Better Than War" at the society's annual meeting. The society distributed thousands of copies to the public. Later turning to violent means, Smith was one of the conspirators who helped fund John Brown's raid. (See Ralph Volney Harlow, *Gerrit Smith: Philanthropist and Reformer* [New York: Russell & Russell, 1972], pp. 108–109, 401; and Gerrit Smith, "Peace Better Than War," *Advocate of Peace* [July and August 1858]: 97ff.) William Jay, son of Justice John Jay, was a New York judge and a Tappanite. A longtime member of the American Peace Society, he published a number of pamphlets for the society, including a review of the causes of the Mexican War, and was serving as the society's president at his death in 1859.

9. Aileen Kraditor, *Means and Ends in Abolitionism* (New York: Pantheon Books, 1969), pp. 8–10, 20–32. Kraditor's book is a superb analysis of radical and moderate reformers in the antislavery movement. For a comparison of the social psychology of immediatist abolitionists and of antislavery gradualists, see Friedman's *Gregarious Saints.* Also informative is Carleton Mabee's, *Black Freedom: The Nonviolent Abolitionists from 1830 through the Civil War* and Ronald G. Walters, *The*

Antislavery Appeal: American Abolitionism after 1830 (Baltimore: The Johns Hopkins University Press, 1976).

10. Kraditor, *Means and Ends*, pp. 44–62.

11. Ibid., p. 72.

12. Abraham Lincoln, "Second Inaugural Address," in Conrad Cherry, ed., *God's New Israel: Religious Interpretations of American Destiny* (Englewood Cliffs, N.J.: Prentice-Hall, 1971), p. 196.

13. See Bodo, *The Protestant Clergy and Public Issues* (Princeton: Princeton University Press, 1954); Cole, *The Social Ideas of the Northern Evangelists* (New York: Columbia University Press, 1954); Donald, "Toward a Reconsideration of the Abolitionists," pp. 19–36, in *Lincoln Reconsidered* (New York: Alfred A. Knopf, 1956); Foster, *An Errand of Mercy: The Evangelical United Front, 1790–1837* (Chapel Hill: University of North Carolina Press, 1960); and Johnson, *A Shopkeeper's Millennium: Society and Revivals in Rochester, New York, 1815–1837*, American Century Series (New York: Hill and Wang, 1978). Critiques include Lois W. Banner, "Religious Benevolence as Social Control: A Critique of an Interpretation," *Journal of American History* 60 (1973): 23–41; and John L. Hammond, *The Politics of Benevolence: Revival Religion and American Voting Behavior* (Norwood, N.J.: Ablex Publishing, 1979).

14. See Hammond, "Revivals, Consensus, and a Political Culture," *Journal of the American Academy of Religion* 46 (September 1978): 293–314, for an explication and critique of the cultural unity theory.

15. See Donald, "Toward a Reconsideration of the Abolitionists"; Elkins, *Slavery: A Problem in American Institutional and Intellectual Life* (Chicago: University of Chicago Press, 1959); Foner, *Free Soil, Free Labor, Free Men: The Ideology of the Republican Party before the Civil War* (New York: Oxford University Press, 1970); Sewell, *Ballots for Freedom: Antislavery Politics in the United States, 1837–1869* (New York: Oxford University Press, 1976); and Trefousse, *Radical Republicans: Lincoln's Vanguard for Racial Justice* (New York: Alfred A. Knopf, 1969). I am much indebted to James Brewer Stewart's delineation of abolitionist historiography. See his "Garrison Again, and Again, and Again, and Again . . ." *Reviews in American History* (December 1976): 539–45.

16. Perry, *Radical Abolitionism: Anarchy and the Government of God in Antislavery Thought* (Ithaca: Cornell University Press, 1973); Kraditor, *Means and Ends;* Walters, *Antislavery Appeal;* and Wyatt-Brown, *Yankee Saints and Southern Sinners.*

17. DeBenedetti, *The Peace Reform in American History* (Bloomington: Indiana University Press, 1980); Demos, "The Antislavery Movement and the Problem of Violent Means," *New England Quarterly* 37 (1964): 501–26; Pease and Pease, "Freedom and Peace: A Nineteenth-Century Dilemma," *Midwest Quarterly* 9 (October 1967): 23–40; Tyler, *Freedom's Ferment: Phases of American Social History from the Colonial Period to the Outbreak of the Civil War* (New York: Harper & Row, 1962). Other works that use a declension theory include Arthur C. F. Beales, *A History of Peace: A Short Account of the Movement for International Peace* (New York: Dial Press, 1931); Amos Arnold Hovey, *A History of the Religious Phase of the American Movement for International Peace to the Year 1814* (Ph.D. dissertation, University of Chicago, 1930); and Donald Dayton and Lucille Dayton, "A Historical Survey of Attitudes toward War and Peace within the American Holiness

Movement" (Paper delivered at the Seminar on Christian Holiness and the Issues of War and Peace, Winona Lake, Indiana, July 7–9, 1973).

18. Curti, *The American Peace Crusade, 1815–1860* (New York: Octagon Books, 1965); and Brock, *Radical Pacifists in Antebellum America* (Princeton: Princeton University Press, 1968). Brock's work on the antebellum period is excerpted from his larger book *Pacifism in the United States from the Colonial Period to the First World War* (Princeton: Princeton University Press, 1968). Other works by Curti include *Peace or War: The American Struggle, 1636–1936* (New York: W. W. Norton, 1936) and "Non-Resistance in New England," *New England Quarterly* 2 (1929); 34–57.

19. Allen, *The Fight for Peace: The Peace Movement in America* (New York: Macmillan, 1930; facsimile reprint, Jerome S. Ozer, 1972), p. vii. David Clifton Lawson, in *Swords into Plowshares, Spears into Pruninghooks; The Intellectual Foundations of the First American Peace Movement, 1815–1865* (Ph.D. dissertation, University of New Mexico, 1975), goes against the scholarly stream by defending the American Peace Society as a responsible organization dedicated to achieving realizable (albeit limited) goals, as opposed to the nonresistants, whom he characterizes as "dilettantes building castles in the sky" (p. 20).

20. In his book *Nevertheless: The Varieties and Shortcomings of Religious Pacifism* (Scottdale, Pa.: Herald Press, 1971), John Howard Yoder develops this point at length.

21. Walters, *Antislavery Appeal*, p. xii.

22. Perry, "Versions of Anarchism in the Antislavery Movement," *American Quarterly* 20 (1968): 770.

23. See Friedman, *Gregarious Saints;* Stewart, "Garrison Again"; Walters, *Means and Ends;* and Wyatt-Brown, *Yankee Saints and Southern Sinners.* Mathews has written a number of valuable works, including "Religion and Slavery: The case of the American South," in Christine Bolt and Seymour Drescher, eds., *Anti-Slavery, Religion, and Reform: Essays in Memory of Roger Anstey* (Kent, England: Wm. Dawson & Sons; Hamden, Conn.: Archon Books, 1980): pp. 207–23. See also his *Slavery and Methodism: A Chapter in American Morality, 1780–1845* (Princeton: Princeton University Press, 1965); and *Religion in the Old South,* Chicago History of America (Chicago: University of Chicago Press, 1977).

No one has written a systematic study of the theology of antebellum peace reform, but two writers have produced excellent studies of the way in which the nonresistants realigned elements of their ideology in the 1850s and 1860s. In *Radical Abolitionism* Lewis Perry argued that, for the nonresistants, "the general goal of ending force became less important than the specific goal of ending one manifestation of force: slavery" (p. 301). In *Gregarious Saints,* Lawrence J. Friedman contended that two elements characterized the nonresistants: conviviality and austere piety. He maintained that the nonresistants accepted violence in the Civil War because it afforded the possibility of immediate success to their antislavery campaign and because it allowed them, for the first time, to form social bonds with a variety of Northerners.

24. James H. Moorhead, "Social Reform and the Divided Conscience of Antebellum Protestantism," *Church History* 48 (1979): 418–19.

25. Jonathan Edwards, *The Nature of True Virtue,* in *Works of Jonathan Edwards,* Vol. 8: *Ethical Writings,* ed. by Paul Ramsey (New Haven: Yale University Press, 1989), pp. 540, 547–60; "Personal Narrative," pp. 57–72 and "A Divine and

Supernatural Light," pp. 102–111 in Clarence H. Faust and Thomas H. Johnson, editors, *Jonathan Edwards: Selections,* American Century Series, rev. ed. (New York: Hill and Wang, 1962).

26. Jonathan Edwards, *A History of the Work of Redemption,* in *Works of Jonathan Edwards,* Vol. 9, transcribed and ed. by John F. Wilson (New Haven: Yale University Press, 1989), p. 459.

27. Jonathan Edwards, *An Humble Attempt to Promote Explicit Agreement and Visible Union of God's People in Extraordinary Prayer* in *Works of Jonathan Edwards,* Vol. 5: *Apocalyptic Writings,* ed. by Stephen J. Stein (New Haven: Yale University Press, 1972), p. 360. Edwards was convinced not only that the millennium would first dawn in America but also that New England was "the most likely of all American colonies, to be the place whence this work shall principally take its rise." (Edwards, *Some Thoughts concerning the Present Revival of Religion in New England,* in *Works of Jonathan Edwards,* Vol. 4: *The Great Awakening,* ed. by C. C. Goen [New Haven: Yale University Press, 1972], pp. 353, 358.)

28. James F. Maclear, "The Republic and the Millennium," in Mulder and Wilson, eds., *Religion in American History: Interpretive Essays* (Englewood Cliffs, N.J.: Prentice-Hall, 1978), p. 184.

29. Francis Wayland, "Encouragements to Religious Efforts," in *American National Preacher* 5, no. 3 (1830): 39–46, quoted in Maclear, "Republic and the Millennium," pp. 188–89.

30. Nancy Hardesty, *Women Called to Witness* (Nashville: Abingdon Press, 1984), pp. 50–51, 60–69.

31. Moorhead, "Social Reform and the Divided Conscience," p. 420.

32. William Ladd, in John Hemmenway, ed., *The Apostle of Peace: Memoir of William Ladd,* Peace Movement in America (Boston, 1872; facsimile reprint, Jerome Ozer, 1972), p. 268. Lydia Maria Child, a nonresistant, expressed the idea this way: "Now my own opinion is that the perfection of the *individual* is the sure way to regenerate the mass. . . . 'If *I* am lifted up, I will draw *all* men unto me.' " (*Lydia Maria Child, Selected Letters, 1817–1880,* ed. Milton Meltzer and Patricia G. Holland [Amherst: University of Massachusetts Press, 1982], p. 161.)

33. Robert H. Abzug, *Passionate Liberator: Theodore Dwight Weld and the Dilemma of Reform* (New York: Oxford University Press, 1980), pp. 59–74. For another account see James W. Fraser, *Pedagogue for God's Kingdom: Lyman Beecher and the Second Great Awakening* (Lanham, Md.: University Press of America, 1985), pp. 103–15.

34. Peter Gardella, *Innocent Ecstasy: How Christianity Gave America an Ethic of Sexual Pleasure* (New York: Oxford University Press, 1985), pp. 46–47.

35. Quoted in Gardella, *Innocent Ecstasy,* p. 53.

36. Stewart, *Holy Warriors,* p. 39.

37. Quoted in Walters, *Antislavery Appeal,* p. 82.

38. Ibid., pp. 79–80.

39. Walker, *Moral Choices,* pp. 284–85, 292.

40. William Lloyd Garrison, in Walter M. Merrill and Louis Ruchames, eds., *The Letters of William Lloyd Garrison* (Cambridge: Belknap Press of Harvard University Press, 1971), vol. 3, p. 269.

41. Hammond, *Politics of Benevolence,* pp. x, 3–4, 53.

42. D. H. Meyer, *The Instructed Conscience* (Philadelphia: University of Penn-

sylvania Press, 1972), p. 116. See Moorhead's discussion of Meyer's point in "Social Reform and the Divided Conscience," pp. 421–22.

43. Richard T. Hughes and C. Leonard Allen, *Illusions of Innocence: Protestant Primitivism in America, 1630–1875*, foreword by Robert Bellah (Chicago: University of Chicago Press, 1988), pp. xiii–xiv, 13–14.

44. See Hughes and Allen for an excellent discussion of Southern primitivism and slavery in *Illusions of Innocence*, pp. 188–203.

1. Early Advocates of Peace

1. David Low Dodge, *Memorial of Mr. David Low Dodge, Consisting of an Autobiography. Prepared at the Request of his Children: with a Few Selections from His Writings* (Boston: S. K. Whipple & Co., 1854), pp. 62, 78–81. For selections from Dodge's *Memorial of Mr. David Low Dodge*, see pp. 104–13 of Peter Mayer, ed., *The Pacifist Conscience* (New York: Holt, Rinehart and Wilson, 1966).

2. Dodge, *Memorial of Mr. David Low Dodge*, pp. 20–26; Mayer, *Pacifist Conscience*, pp. 104–6.

3. Dodge, *Memorial of Mr. David Low Dodge*, p. 62; Mayer, *Pacifist Conscience*, pp. 109–10; Peter Brock, *Radical Pacifists in Antebellum America* (Princeton: Princeton University Press, 1968), pp. 15–16; Allen Johnson and Dumas Malone, eds., *The Dictionary of American Biography*, vol. 5 (New York: Charles Scribners' Sons, 1930), p. 345.

4. *Dictionary of American Biography*, 5:345; William E. Dodge, *Memorials of William E. Dodge*, comp. and ed. D. Stuart Dodge (New York: Anson D. F. Randolph and Company, 1887), p. 5. The Higginsons were cousins of Dodge's wife, Sarah. In 1811 their Boston firm went bankrupt when the embargo placed on shipping (because of the Napoleonic wars) ruined their shipping interests. Dodge's New York branch survived, but the Dodge–Higginson partnership had to be dissolved.

5. Dodge, *Memorial of William E. Dodge*, p. 6.

6. Dodge, *Memorial of Mr. David Low Dodge*, p. 89.

7. Devere Allen, *The Fight for Peace*, The Peace Movement in America (New York: Macmillan, 1930; facsimile reprint, Jerome S. Ozer, 1972), p. 7.

8. W. Freeman Galpin, *Pioneering for Peace: A Study of American Peace Efforts to 1846* (Syracuse: Bardeen Press, 1933), pp. 13–14; *Dictionary of American Biography*, 5:345.

9. Dodge, *Memorial of Mr. David Low Dodge*, p. 95. See also Curti, *American Peace Crusade, 1815–60*, p. 8; David Low Dodge, "Letter," *Advocate of Peace* 2, no. 4 (September 1983): 92–94. Galpin, in *Pioneering for Peace*, is the only commentator to argue that Dodge was not a complete nonresistant. According to Galpin, Dodge "never seems to have become a pure non-resister. He admits that personal self-defense was a right not condemned by God," though Dodge designated it as "presumptuous." (p. 14) Though Galpin is normally a reliable guide, I disagree with his interpretation here, as my own analysis will indicate.

10. Henry Ware, *Memoirs of the Rev. Noah Worcester, D.D.*, The Peace Movement in America (Boston: James Munroe and Company, 1844; facsimile reprint, Jerome Ozer, 1972), pp. 5–7. See also *Dictionary of American Biography*, 20:528–29.

11. Ware, *Memoirs of the Rev. Noah Worcester*, pp. 6–20, 18–57, 61–63.

12. Ibid., pp. 64–66.

13. Curti, *American Peace Crusade*, p. 11; Galpin, *Pioneering for Peace*, p. 23.

14. Galpin, *Pioneering for Peace*, pp. 25–26.

15. Noah Worcester, *A Circular Letter from the Massachusetts Peace Society, Respectfully Addressed to the Various Associations, Presbyteries, Assemblies and Meetings of the Ministers of Religion in the United States* (Cambridge, Mass.: Hilliard and Metcalf, 1816), pp. 4, 14.

16. Carleton Mabee, *Black Freedom: The Nonviolent Abolitionists from 1830 through the Civil War* (London: Macmillan, 1970), p. 9; Brock, *Radical Pacifists in Antebellum America*, pp. 268–79.

17. Thomas Dawes, *Address to the Massachusetts Peace Society, at Their Second Anniversary, Dec. 25, 1817* (Boston: Massachusetts Peace Society, 1818), p. 2.

18. "Second Annual Report," printed with Dawes' *Address to the Massachusetts Peace Society*, p. 16. For more discussion of the Ohio societies, see Galpin, *Pioneering for Peace*, pp. 64–65.

19. Clyde Winfield McDonald, Jr., *The Massachusetts Peace Society, 1815–1828: A Study in Evangelical Reform* (Ph.d. Dissertation, University of Maine, 1973), pp. 223, 237–38.

20. McDonald, *Massachusetts Peace Society*, pp. 124, 151–59, 237–38.

21. Frederick West Holland, "The History of the Peace-Cause," Boston Public Library Archives, p. 12.

22. Curti, *American Peace Crusade*, p. 23; Dodge, *Memorial of Mr. David Low Dodge*, p. 101.

23. Minutes of the New York Peace Society, Library of Congress Archives, Washington, D.C. The December 30, 1826 minutes reported that the society received twenty-eight dollars from some of the Friends—an event, the minutes concluded, "which was cheering." Many authors have wondered why Dodge was not more financially generous to the society, particularly in light of his claim that from 1809 to 1815 he spent much of his "time, strength, and money" in the cause of peace (Dodge, "Letter," *Advocate of Peace* 2, no. 4 (September 1838): 93. No one has offered a definitive answer.

24. Holland, "History of the Peace-Cause," p. 13; *Memoir of Samuel Joseph May*, ed. Thomas J. Mumford (Boston: Roberts Brothers, 1873), p. 48.

25. No author, "Memoirs of Worcester," *Christian Examiner and Religious Miscellany* 37 (November 1844): 378.

26. Holland, "History of the Peace-Cause," p. 15.

27. Dodge, *Memorial of Mr. David Low Dodge*, pp. 89, 101.

28. David Low Dodge, *The Mediator's Kingdom Not of This World: But Spiritual*, Peace Movement in America (Boston: Ginn & Company, 1905; facsimile reprint, Jerome S. Ozer, 1972), pp. 155–56, 158.

29. David Low Dodge, *War Inconsistent with the Religion of Jesus Christ*, Peace Movement in America (Boston: Ginn & Company, 1905; facsimile reprint, Jerome S. Ozer, 1972), p. 111. Twentieth-century discussions of the Christian's relationship to the state have made much of this distinction. In 1932 Reinhold Niebuhr published *Moral Man and Immoral Society* (New York: Charles Scribner's Sons, 1960), a book that became a classic in theological circles and a handbook among the "Christian realists" of the period. In this and in a later work *An Interpretation of Christian Ethics* (New York: Seabury Press, 1979), Niebuhr argued that groups were invariably more selfish and less capable of altruism than were individuals. The New Testament, in articulating an ethic of vicarious self-sacri-

fice and nonresistant love, was therefore not directly applicable to the political realm. Only individuals, as they became converted to the gospel of love, could hope to attain the purity of the New Testament ethic. Institutions were impervious to conversion; they always remained mired in sin and selfishness. Yet Niebuhr did not conclude that the New Testament was irrelevant to politics. Although the Sermon on the Mount could not be directly transformed into a realistic social ethic, it could provide an impetus for groups to seek justice. Even though groups could not escape sin and selfishness completely, they could learn judiciously to balance power with power so as to make social justice (if not self-sacrificing love) a relevant corporate ethic.

In the last thirty years, a Mennonite writer named John Howard Yoder has attacked Niebuhr's conclusions. As he explained in *The Politics of Jesus* (Grand Rapids, Mich.: William B. Eerdmans, 1972), Yoder believed that Niebuhr was wrong to conclude that Jesus set forth an ethic that applied only to individuals. Instead, Yoder insisted, Jesus' ethic was political as well as individual. It was an ethic of the kingdom, relevant even to institutions insofar as those institutions consisted of persons who had experienced regeneration. For Yoder, groups as well as individuals were obliged dutifully to obey Jesus' ethic of love.

30. See Charles Chatfield, "The Bible and American Peace Movements," in Ernest R. Sandeen, ed. *The Bible and Social Reform* (Philadelphia: Fortress Press; Chico, Calif.: Scholars Press, 1982), pp. 107–11.

31. Alexander McLeod, *A Scriptural View of the Character, Causes, and Ends of the Present War* (New York: n.p., 1815), p. 121. For pictures of McLeod and Dodge, as well as a brief summary of their positions, see *American Presbyterians: Journal of Presbyterian History,* 63, nos. 1 and 2 (1985): 60–61.

32. McLeod, *Scriptural View of the Character, Causes, and Ends of the Present War,* p. 109.

33. Nathan O. Hatch, "Sola Scriptura and Novus Ordo Seclorum," in Nathan O. Hatch and Mark A. Noll, eds., *The Bible in America: Essays in Cultural History* (New York: Oxford University Press, 1982), pp. 62–64. The quotation from Worcester is from his *Bible News of the Father, Son, and Holy Spirit* (Concord, N.H.: 1810).

34. Noah Worcester, "Review of Some Passages in Dr. McLeods's 'Five Discourses' on the Late War," *Friend of Peace* 5 (ca. 1816): 18; and "Review of Dr. M'Leod's Argument from the New Testament," *Friend of Peace* 6 (ca. 1816): 8–16.

35. Hatch, "Sola Scriptura," pp. 74–75. The quotation from Finney is from his *Memoirs* (New York: 1876), pp. 42–46.

36. David Low Dodge, *Remarks upon an Anonymous Letter, Styled, "The Duty of a Christian in a Trying Situation." Addressed to the Author of a Pamphlet. Entitled, "The Mediator's Kingdom Not of This World," Etc.* (New York: Williams & Whiting, 1810), pp. 22, 24.

37. For an example of this view, see McLeod's *Scriptural View of the Character, Causes, and Ends of the Present War,* pp. 110–12.

38. Dodge, *War Inconsistent with the Religion of Jesus Christ,* pp. 83–93, 61, 56–58.

39. William Ellery Channing, "First Discourse on War," in *Discourses on War* (Boston: Ginn & Company, 1903), p. 33.

40. Dodge, *War Inconsistent with the Religion of Jesus Christ,* pp. 101–10, 47, 52; *Mediator's Kingdom,* p. 149.

41. Dodge, *War Inconsistent with the Religion of Jesus Christ*, pp. 6, 8, 16, 18, 28, 30, 44, 52–56.

42. Ibid., pp. 78–82.

43. Ibid., pp. 77–78, 82. Dodge also argued that, before the Fall, animals were docile and harmless, free from violent urges.

44. Dodge, *Mediator's Kingdom*, pp. 161–64.

45. Ibid., pp. 125, 127, 148; *War Inconsistent with the Religion of Jesus Christ*, p. 6.

46. Dodge, *Mediator's Kingdom*, pp. 132–37, 160.

47. Ibid., pp, 161–65.

48. Noah Worcester, *Solemn Review of the Custom of War*, The Peace Movement in America (Boston: S. G. Simpkins, 1933; facsimile reprint, Jerome S. Ozer, 1972), pp. 10–16; [Philo Pacificus], "Six Letters From Omar to the President," *Friend of Peace* 1 (n.d.): 21.

49. Worcester, *Solemn Review of War*, pp. 5–6; Worcester, "Review of Some Passages in Dr. M'Leod's 'Five Discourses' on the Late War," *Friend of Peace* 5 (ca. 1816): 22–27.

50. Worcester, "Review of Dr. M'Leod's Argument from the New Testament," pp. 10–16.

51. Dodge, *War Inconsistent with the Religion of Jesus Christ*, pp. 95–97.

52. Dodge, *Remarks upon an Anonymous Letter*, p. 40.

53. Noah Worcester [Philo Pacificus], "On Estimating the Characters of Men Who Have Been Concerned in Sanguinary Customs," *Friend of Peace* 3 (1815): 29.

54. Worcester [Philo Pacificus], "On Estimating the Characters of Men," p. 29.

55. Worcester, *Solemn Review*, p. 22; [Philo Pacificus], "Review of the Arguments of Lord Kames in Favor of War," *Friend of Peace* 2 (1815): 34.

56. Worcester, *A Circular Letter from the Massachusetts Peace Society*, pp. 4, 14.

57. Worcester, *Solemn Review*, pp. 23–24, 4–7.

58. William Ladd, *The Essays of Philanthropos on Peace and War*, Garland Library of Peace (New York: Garland Publishing, 1971), p. 7. See also Holland, "The History of the Peace-Cause," p. 27; and John Hemmenway, *The Apostle of Peace: Memoir of William Ladd*, Peace Movement in America (Boston: 1872; facsimile reprint, Jerome S. Ozer, 1972), p. 38.

59. Hemmenway, *Apostle of Peace*, pp. 38–46.

60. Ladd, *Essays of Philanthropos*, p. 168.

61. Independent of American developments, pacifists in England and France also formed peace societies after the Napoleonic wars. The London Peace Society was the most prominent of these groups. American peace societies and the London pacifists maintained contact throughout the antebellum period, and in the 1840s a number of international peace conferences were held in Europe. Elihu Burritt was the American most involved in the international peace movement. For a good account of the international peace congresses, see Curti, *American Peace Crusade*, pp. 166–88.

62. William Ladd Letter File, Library of Congress Archives, Washington, D.C.; reprinted in Hemmenway, *Apostle of Peace*, pp. 229–31.

63. Holland, "History of the Peace-Cause," pp. 27–28; Hemmenway, *Apostle of Peace*, p. 59, 95–101.

64. William Ladd Letter File, Library of Congress Archives, Washington,

D.C. See also William Ladd, *On the Duty of Females to Promote the Cause of Peace*, Garland Library of War and Peace (New York: Garland Publishing, 1971). Welcoming women as coworkers, however, did not mean that Ladd thought that women should venture beyond their proper "sphere." Like many other peace reformers, Ladd was uneasy at having women join the American Peace Society, though he was glad for them to start women's auxiliaries. But even more radical reformers who welcomed women as full members of peace societies emphasized the special role that women in their roles as nurturers of the new generation could play in raising peace-loving children. Thus, in her essays in the *Advocate Of Peace*, the society's journal, Garrisonian abolitionist and nonresistant sympathizer Lydia Maria Child emphasized woman's special role as nurturer of peace. An example of Lydia Maria Child's writing is available in her "Christmas Thoughts on Peace" in the March 1844 edition of *Advocate of Peace*. For a discussion of the potentially radicalizing effects of the "woman's sphere" argument, see Nancy Hardesty, *Women Called to Witness* (Nashville: Abingdon Press, 1984).

65. Lawrence J. Friedman, *Gregarious Saints*, p. 18.

66. James Brewer Stewart, *Holy Warriors*, pp. 40, 46.

67. William Ladd Letter Collection, Library of Congress Archives, Washington, D.C.

68. The one pacifist with the common touch was Elihu Burritt, whose League of Universal Peace and Brotherhood won thousands of adherents in the 1840s. Most of Burritt's converts, however, were in England.

69. William Ladd, *Essays of Philanthropos*, pp. 10; 83; *Address Delivered at the Tenth Anniversary of the Massachusetts Peace Society, December 25, 1825* (Boston, 1826), pp. 3, 16–17.

70. Edwin L. Whitney, *The American Peace Society: A Centennial History* (Washington, D.C.: American Peace Society, 1928), p. 20.

71. American Peace Society, "Circular Letter of the American Peace Society," *Harbinger of Peace* 1, no. 1 (May 1828): 6–9; Worcester, "Friendly Remarks on the Letter from Mr. Jay," *Friend of Peace* 11 (ca. 1817): 32.

72. Ladd, "Prospectus," *Harbinger of Peace* 1, no. 1 (May 1828): 21. Whitney reports that Ladd printed 1,500 copies of each month's edition of the journal. Each *Harbinger* was twenty-four pages long. The journal ran from May 1828 to April 1831; about 50,000 copies in all were printed (Whitney, *American Peace Society*, p. 28).

73. "First Annual Meeting of the American Peace Society," *Harbinger of Peace* 2, no. 1 (May 1829): 4; Galpin, *Pioneering for Peace*, p. 215.

74. Whitney, *American Peace Society*, p. 29. At this point, the society switched from a monthly to a bimonthly format. To make the journal look more respectable, the society changed it from a twenty-four page, duodecimo-sized production to a thirty-two page octavo-sized one.

75. "Fourth Report of the American Peace Society," *Calumet* 1, no. 7 (May–June 1832): 211–12.

76. "The Sixth Annual Report of the Windham County Peace Society," *Calumet* 1, no. 9 (September–October 1832): 258–59.

77. The first annual meeting of the American Peace Society lists him among the board of directors. See "First Annual Meeting of the American Peace Society," *Harbinger of Peace* 2, no. 1 (May 1829): 4; and Curti, *American Peace Crusade*, p. 69.

78. Brock, *Radical Pacifists in Antebellum America,* p. 47; Barnes, *Antislavery Impulse,* p. 153.

79. He would return to this theme in his "Extract from an Address on the Power and Valu [sic] of the Sunday-school System, March, 1834," printed on pages 295–300 in Jonathan Dymond, *An Inquiry into the Accordancy of War with the Principles of Christianity,* with notes by Thomas Smith Grimke (Philadelphia: I. Asmead and Company, 1834). Ladd and others made it a standard argument.

80. Thomas Grimke, *Address on the Truth, Dignity, Power, and Beauty of the Principles of Peace, and on the Unchristian Character and Influence of War and the Warrior* (Hartford, Conn.: George F. Olmstead, 1832), pp. 4–11, 29; Brock, *Radical Pacifists in Antebellum America,* p. 48.

81. Grimke, *Address on the Truth, Dignity, Power,* p. 29; quoted in Galpin, *Pioneering for Peace,* p. 102.

82. Grimke, *Address on the Truth, Dignity, Power,* pp. 42–8. David Low Dodge himself noted that the common sentiment regarding the Revolutionary War as a sacred event in American history was the biggest obstacle for the cause of peace to overcome (*Memorial of Mr. David Low Dodge,* p. 101).

83. Brock, *Radical Pacifists in Antebellum America,* p. 49; Allen, *Fight for Peace,* pp. 376–77.

84. Grimke, *To the People of the State of South-Carolina* (n.p.: n.d.), p. 15.

85. Brock, *Radical Pacifists in Antebellum America,* p. 51.

86. Charles DeBenedetti, *The Peace Reform in American History* (Bloomington: Indiana University Press, 1980), p. 40.

87. William Allen, "Defensive War Vindicated, II," *Calumet* 2, no. 1 (May–June 1834): 13–18; and "Defensive War Vindicated," *Calumet* 1, no. 17 (January–February 1834): 529–30, 525.

88. Thomas Grimke, "Defensive War," *Calumet* 2, no. 5 (January–February 1835): 142–50; "Defensive War, II," *Calumet* 2, no. 6 (March–April 1835): 166–67, 177.

2. Schism

1. Hemmenway, *Apostle of Peace,* pp. 268, 275.

2. The second edition of the *Liberator* (January 8, 1831) included an editorial criticizing David Walker's *Appeal* to the Southern slaves to be prepared to fight for their freedom. "Believing as we do," Garrison wrote, "that men should never to evil that good may come of it; and that we ought to suffer, as did our Lord and his apostles, unresistingly . . . believing all this, and that the Almighty will deliver the oppressed in a way which we know not, we deprecate the spirit and tendency of this appeal. Nevertheless, it is not for the American people, as a nation, to denounce it as bloody and monstrous. Mr. Walker but pays them in their own coin, but follows their own creed, but adopts their own language" (p. 6).

It was typical of Garrison to add the final rejoinder. He never let Americans forget that they had won their political independence by violence, and he never ceased to insist that it was inconsistent for a people who celebrated the bloody War of Independence to contend that blacks had no right to resort to violence to achieve freedom. Garrison denounced the use of violence in both cases, but as long as most people continued to applaud the Revolution, he wanted them to know that they were being hypocritical if they did not also welcome black violence on behalf of liberation.

Though the American Peace Society tried to avoid the incendiary comparison of slave rebellions with the Revolution, Noah Worcester had noted the parallel in 1816. In answer to Alexander McLeod's defense of the War of 1812 as a just war, Worcester pointed out that, should they choose to revolt, slaves could claim a "violation of right" and a "rational prospect of success." If the principles of war were to be cultivated, he asked, "what better can we reasonably expect, than that the blacks who are held in slavery among a free people, will be formed into a terrifick army by the permission and providence of the 'God, to whom vengeance belongeth', and be suffered to distress and destroy their oppressors?" (*Friend of Peace* 5 [1816]: 28.)

3. Garrison, *Letters*, 2: 278–79.

4. Hemmenway, *Apostle of Peace*, pp. 73–74.

5. Garrison, *Letters*, 2: 391.

6. Hemmenway, *Apostle of Peace*, p. 77.

7. Edwin L. Whitney, *The American Peace Society: A Centennial History*, pp. 31–32; "Literary Notices," *Advocate of Peace* 2, no. 3 (August 1838): 68.

8. "Resolves in Favor of Peace," *Calumet* 2, no. 13 (May–June 1833): 413; "Resolutions Regarding the Cause of Peace," *Calumet* 1, no. 15 (September–October 1833): 471, 473.

9. George C. Beckwith, "Report of the Rev. George C. Beckwith's Agency on Behalf of the American Peace Society," *Advocate of Peace* 1 (June 1837): 31–32.

10. Allen, *Fight for Peace*, pp. 97–98. The American Peace Society continued for the next thirteen years to petition Congress to pass a resolution on stipulated arbitration and a Congress of Nations. At times the *Advocate of Peace* even published sample petitions for readers to copy and send to congressional representatives under their own names. (See the back cover of the November 1838 edition for an example.) Congress finally reported on these petitions in 1850, though it took no action on them. A. C. F. Beales, a modern British historian of the peace movement, considered the Massachusetts resolution and the congressional report to be "prodigious" achievements for the society. See his *History of Peace: A Short Account of the Organized Movement for International Peace* (New York: Dial Press, 1931), p. 86.

11. The Connecticut Peace Society lasted until 1837. An unusually active society, it had proposed to the American Peace Society in 1832 that its journal be expanded and that a vice-president in charge of developing statewide societies be appointed in every state of the Union. When the American Peace Society failed to act on that plan, the Connecticut society forged ahead with its own journal. (Galpin, *Pioneering for Peace*, pp. 89, 91–92.)

12. "Address to the Friends of Peace," *Advocate of Peace* 1 (June 1837): 2.

13. "Second Volume," *Advocate of Peace* 2 (June 1838): 1.

14. "Address to the Friends of Peace," *Advocate of Peace* 1 (June 1837): 8.

15. Thomas, *Liberator*, pp. 50–51.

16. Garrison, *Letters*, 2: 93, 97; Hemmenway, *Apostle of Peace*, p. 161.

17. Holland, "The History of the Peace-Cause," pp. 7, 30.

18. Hemmenway, *Apostle of Peace*, pp. 112, 116–18.

19. William Ladd, *An Essay on a Congress of Nations*, with an introduction by James Brown Scott (New York: Oxford University Press, 1916; reprint of 1840

edition). See Curti's summary of Ladd's argument in *American Peace Crusade, 1815–1860*, pp. 58–59.

20. "Mr. Ladd's Tour," *Advocate of Peace* 2 (April 1839): 264.

21. William Ladd, "Mr. Ladd's Address at the Anniversary," *Advocate of Peace* 3 (August 1840): 181.

22. William Ladd, "Letter from William Ladd," *Liberator*, November 23, 1838, p. 188; "Prospectus of the *Liberator*," Jan. 5, 1838, p. 4.

23. William Ladd, "Ladd's Letter," *Advocate of Peace* 1 (December 1837): 131.

24. William Allen, "Dr. Allen's Letter to Mr. Ladd," *Advocate of Peace* 3 (December 1837): 112–17.

25. William Ladd, "Mr. Ladd's Answer to Dr. Allen's Letter," *Advocate of Peace* 3 (December 1837): 123.

26. Quoted in Galpin, *Pioneering for Peace*, pp. 107–8.

27. Grimke, "Notes to Jonathan Dymond on War," in Dymond's *Inquiry into the Accordancy of War* (Philadelphia: I. Asmead and Company, 1834), p. 159.

28. "Cooperation among the Friends of Peace," *Advocate of Peace* 3 (December 1837): 108.

29. John Demos, "The Antislavery Movement and the Problem of Violent 'Means,' " *New England Quarterly* 37, no. 4 (December 1964): 515.

30. David Low Dodge, "Letter," *Liberator*, December 21, 1838, p. 204.

31. William Lloyd Garrison, "Remarks from Mr. Ladd's Letter," *Liberator*, November 23, 1838, p. 188.

32. Garrison, *Letters*, 3: 456.

33. "Withdrawal from the Non-Resistant Society" and "To Correspondents," *Non-Resistant*, August 12, 1840, n.p. The constitution claimed that nonresistants belonged to a kingdom not of this world, a kingdom without sexual inequalities or geographical and national boundaries. "Constitution of the New-England Non-Resistant Society," *Non-Resistant*, January 1839, p. 1.

34. Friedman, *Gregarious Saints*, pp. 11–28, 43–57; Stewart, "Garrison Again, and Again, and Again, and Again . . .," pp. 542–45.

35. Friedman, *Gregarious Saints*, pp. 48–55; Jane H. Pease and William H. Pease, *Bound with Them in Chains: A Biographical History of the Antislavery Movement*, Contributions in American History, number 18 (Westport, Conn.: Greenwood Press, 1972), pp. 28–59; Walters, *Antislavery Appeal*, pp. 16–17.

36. Kirk Jeffrey, "Marriage, Career, and Feminine Ideology in Nineteenth-Century America: Reconstructing the Marital Experience of Lydia Maria Child, 1828–1874," *Feminist Studies* 2 (1975): 115–25; Margaret R. McGavran, "The Role of Domesticity Transcended," in Howard R. Quint and Milton Cantor, eds., *Men, Women, and Issues in American History* (Homewood, Ill.: Dorsey Press, 1975), 2: 181–84.

37. Pease and Pease, *Bound with Them in Chains*, pp. 194–95; Johnson and Malone, *Dictionary of American Biography*, 6: 558.

38. Johnson and Malone, *Dictionary of American Biography* 6: 542–43; Wendell Phillips Garrison and Francis Jackson Garrison, *William Lloyd Garrison, 1805–1879; The Story of His Life, Told by his Children* (New York: Century Company, 1885; reprint ed., New York: Negro Universities Press, 1969), 2: 366–81; Pease and Pease, *Bound with Them in Chains*, p. 26; Friedman, *Gregarious Saints*, pp. 144, 149–51.

39. Perry, *Childhood, Marriage, Reform: Henry Clarke Wright* (Chicago: Univer-

sity of Chicago Press, 1980), p. 51; Adin Ballou, *Autobiography of Adin Ballou*, completed and edited by his son-in-law, William S. Heywood, The American Utopian Adventure, series 2 (Lowell, Mass.: Vox Populi Press, Thompson and Hill, 1896), pp. 277–78. The *Non-Resistant* was never a wild success. By 1840 it had only 1,000 subscribers, and its editors were tiring of their work (Brock, *Radical Pacifists in Antebellum America*, p. 117). The paper folded in 1842. Ballou was elected president of the society in 1843. He revived the paper in 1845, issuing it from Hopedale for three months, from January 1 to March 29. At that point the journal had only 280 subscribers, and Ballou gave up, sending the faithful 280 his *Practical Christian* instead ("Suspended," *Nonresistant*, new series, March 29, 1845, p. 118). In January of 1848, Ballou combined the two to form the *Non-Resistant and Practical Christian*, dedicated to "absolute truth, essential righteousness, individual responsibility, social reform, human progress," and "ultimate perfection." (See the masthead, January 22, 1838.) Again, his attempt to issue the *Non-Resistant* was shortlived.

40. Friedman, *Gregarious Saints*, p. 35.

41. Stewart, *Holy Warriors*, pp. 89–90.

42. Mabee, *Black Freedom*, pp. 20–26; "Declaration of Sentiments," in William H. Pease and Jane H. Pease, eds., *The Antislavery Argument* (Indianapolis: Bobbs-Merrill, 1965), p. 60.

43. Mabee, *Black Freedom*, pp. 38–40.

44. Merton L. Dillon, *Elijah P. Lovejoy, Abolitionist Editor* (Urbana: University of Illinois, 1961), pp. 1–59; citation from the St. Louis *Observer*, January 9, 1834 (quoted by Dillon on page 32).

45. Dillon, *Elijah P. Lovejoy*, pp. 156, 160–70; Mabee, *Black Freedom*, pp. 40–41.

46. Mabee, *Black Freedom*, pp. 46–47.

47. *Liberator*, January 5, 1838, p. 2; Henry Clarke Wright, "Recompense To No Man Evil for Evil," December 1, 1837, p. 194.

48. Stephen B. Oates, *To Purge This Land with Blood: A Biography of John Brown* (New York: Harper & Row, 1970), pp. 41–42.

49. Mabee, *Black Freedom*, pp. 46–48; Walters, *Antislavery Appeal*, pp. 10–13.

50. Thomas, *The Liberator*, pp. 220–21.

51. Walters, *Antislavery Appeal*, pp. 10–13; Stewart, *Holy Warriors*, pp. 76–83, 90–94.

52. Since government came from God, Garrison had to admit that it was good, but because government was God's concession to the Fall, he did not think it was good for much. Human governments, he said, "are the result of human disobedience to the requirements of heaven; and they are better than anarchy just as a hail-storm is preferable to an earthquake, or the small-pox to the Asiatic cholera." Quoted in Wendell Phillips Garrison and Francis Jackson Garrison, *William Lloyd Garrison: The Story of his Life*, 2: 150–51.

53. All of this did not mean that Garrison would not compromise when he worked with less radical reformers. He realized that his goals would not materialize overnight, but by insisting upon ultimate ends, as Aileen Kraditor has noted, his own intransigence made compromises favorable to his position possible. (*Means and Ends in Abolitionism*, p. 28)

54. Ballou, "Reply to Henry Grew," *Non-Resistant*, February 12, 1840, n.p.; also printed in the *Liberator*, February 7, 1840, p. 24.

55. Both Ballou and Whipple thought that it was at times permissible physically to restrain evildoers. Ballou argued that nonresistance did not imply passivity, though it would not answer injury with injury, it nevertheless was bound to offer "the utmost moral resistance" to evil. In the case of "maniacs," the insane, the "delerious sick," "ill natured children," the intoxicated, and the "violently passionate," the nonresistant could apply "uninjurious, benevolent physical force" to restrain them. While such force could not "kill, maim or otherwise absolutely injure any human being," it could justifiably be used to "promote the safety, welfare, the holiness and happiness of all human beings." (Ballou, *Christian Non-Resistance in All Its Important Bearings,* with an appendix by William S. Heywood (Philadelphia: Universal Peace Union, 1910; reprint edition, New York: Da Capo Press, 1970), pp. 3, 15–19.

In his work entitled *Non-Resistance Applied to the Internal Defence of a Community* (Boston: R. F. Wallcut, 1860), Charles K. Whipple contended that nonresistants could operate successfully as a police force. Echoing Ballou, he asserted that "Non-Resistance objects, not to government, but to an anti-Christian mode of governing; not to physical force, but to injurious force; not to the restraint of malefactors, but to a system which contents itself with punishing, without attempting, or wishing, to reform them. It objects, in short, only to violations of the Golden Rule" (p. 4).

Whipple suggested that, providing the will of God—rather than the desires of the majority—could be made the law of the land, nonresistants would serve as police officers. These officers would confront criminals with righteousness and love. If law-breakers resisted that love and killed an officer, then two more would come to the scene. The community, in addition, would help the officers apply noninjurious force in apprehending criminals. Once arrested, the criminals would go to a "House of Reformation," and the community would make certain that the offender's family was not in want. In the House of Reformation, criminals would be instructed by those who understood them—by persons who were morally superior yet kind to them. In the end, Whipple was convinced, most criminals would reform themselves; and even if the system did not have a 100 percent cure rate, Whipple was convinced that it would reform far more people than the prisons of his day did (pp. 15–29).

56. Garrison, "Remarks," *Liberator,* December 7, 1838, p. 196.

57. Samuel J. May, "Non-Resistance," *Liberator,* December 20, 1839, p. 204.

58. Garrison, *Letters,* 2: 328.

59. "Constitution of the New-England Non-Resistant Society," *Non-Resistant,* January 1839, p. 1.

60. Adin Ballou, *Primitive Christianity and Its Corruptions,* edited by William S. Heywood (Lowell, Mass.: Vox Populi Press, Thompson and Hill, 1899), 2: 91–92. The constitution of the New England Non-Resistant Society made the same point, arguing that Jesus had abrogated the penal code of the Old Testament. ("Constitution," *Non-Resistant,* January 1839, p. 1).

61. Ballou, *Christian Non-Resistance,* p. 88; *History of the Hopedale Community,* ed. William S. Heywood (Lowell, Mass.: Vox Populi Press, Thompson and Hill, 1897), p. 1.

62. Henry Clarke Wright, *Man-Killing, by Individuals and Nations, Wrong— Dangerous in all Cases* (Boston: 1841), p. 16.

63. Garrison, "Remarks," *Liberator*, December 7, 1838, p. 196; Ballou, *Autobiography*, p. 340.

64. Wendell Phillip Garrison and Francis Jackson Garrison, *William Lloyd Garrison: The Story of His Life*, 2: 18.

65. Garrison, *Letters*, 2: 67.

66. "The Non-Resistant," *Non-Resistant*, January 1839, n.p.; Henry Clarke Wright, "To Die Is Gain," *Non-Resistant*, March 2, 1839, n.p.

67. Lewis Perry has also noted this ambivalence. See his *Radical Abolitionism*, pp. 75–76.

68. Adin Ballou, *Practical Christian Socialism: A Conversational Exposition of the True System of Human Society* (Hopedale, Mass.: Adin Ballou; New York: Fowlers and Wells, 1854), p. 155; *Christian Non-Resistance*, pp. 23–25. Note also this statement in the New England Non-Resistance Society's Declaration of Sentiments: "we cordially adopt the non-resistant principle; being confident that it provides for all possible consequences, will ensure all things needful to us, is armed with omnipotent power, and must ultimately triumph over every assailing force." ("Declaration of Sentiments," *Non-Resistant*, January 1839, p. 1.)

69. Garrison, "Remarks from Mr. Ladd's Letter," *Liberator*, November 23, 1838, p. 188.

70. "Safety of the Non-Resistant Pledge"; "Correspondence"; Henry Clarke Wright, "Clerical Opposition," *Non-Resistant*, March 2, 1839, n.p.

71. Lydia Maria Child, *Lydia Maria Child: Selected Letters, 1817–1880*, ed. Milton Meltzer and Patricia Holland (Amherst: University of Massachusetts Press, 1982).

72. Adin Ballou, "Letter from Adin Ballou," *Liberator*, August 2, 1839, p. 124; "Petitioning," *Non-Resistant*, June 15, 1839, n.p.

73. Thomas, *Liberator*, p. 190; Stewart, *Holy Warriors*, pp. 76–89.

74. Ballou, *Primitive Christianity*, 2: 74, 179; John Humphrey Noyes, *The Berean: A Manual for the Help of Those Who Seek the Faith of the Primitive Church* [Putney, Vt.: Office of the Spiritual Magazine, 1847], pp. 276–77. Noyes visited Garrison in the spring of 1837 and impressed him so favorably with his come-outer view of government that Garrison's biographer John L. Thomas has argued that Noyes converted Garrison to perfectionism. (*The Liberator*, pp. 227–32) After their meeting, Noyes wrote Garrison a letter stating that the millennial age would begin when the federal government was overthrown. Garrison ran Noyes's letter in the October 5, 1837, edition of the *Liberator*. For an insightful analysis of the significance of Noyes's eschatological theories for the development of nonresistant thought, see Perry's *Radical Abolitionism*, pp. 65–72, 153–57, 298–301.

75. Adin Ballou, *The Scriptural Doctrine of the Second Advent: An Effectual Antidote to Millerism, and All Other Kindred Errors* (Milford, Mass.: Community Press [Hopedale], 1843), pp. 3, 12, 21–25.

76. Noyes, *Berean*, pp. 276–98, 378–80, 382–85.

77. John Humphrey Noyes, "Declaration of Sentiments," *Liberator*, October 5, 1837, p. 166; *Berean*, pp. 338, 450.

78. Henry Clarke Wright, "Letter From Henry C. Wright," *Liberator*, April 2, 1841, p. 56.

79. Ballou, "Communities," *Practical Christian,* September 15, 1840, quoted in *History of the Hopedale Community,* p. 17.

80. Lydia Maria Child, *Selected Letters,* p. 90.

81. Garrison, *Letters,* 3: 17, 24.

82. Ballou, *Primitive Christianity,* 2: 182.

83. Adin Ballou, *Non-Resistance in Relation to Human Governments* (Boston: Non-Resistance Society, 1839), p. 4.

84. Executive Committee of the New England Non-Resistance Society, "National Organizations," *Liberator,* January 4, 1839, p. 4. Ballou made the same point in his speech on nonresistance at the society's first anniversary meeting. See pages 4–11 of his *Non-Resistance in Relation to Human Governments.*

85. Garrison, *Letters,* 2: 408.

86. "Constitution of the New-England Non-Resistance Society," *Non-Resistant,* January 1839, p. 1.

87. "First Annual Meeting of the New-England Non-Resistant Society," *Non-Resistant,* December 7, 1839, n.p.

88. Walters, *Antislavery Appeal,* pp. 70–71; Perry, *Radical Abolitionism,* p. 48.

89. Walters, *Antislavery Appeal,* pp. 72, 78, 80–83.

90. James A. Thome, "James A. Thome Condemns Licentiousness," in Pease and Pease, *The Antislavery Argument,* p. 93.

91. Theodore Dwight Weld, "Theodore Dwight Weld Shows Slavery as It Is," Ibid., p. 96.

92. Lydia Maria Child, "Lydia Maria Child Plays Up the Atrocity Theme," in Pease and Pease, *Antislavery Appeal,* pp. 87–88.

93. William Lloyd Garrison, "Strident Denunciation," in Richard W. Leopold, Arthur S. Link, and Stanley Coben, eds., *Problems in American History,* vol. 1, 3rd ed. (Englewood Cliffs, N.J.: Prentice-Hall, 1966), p. 307.

94. Perry, *Radical Abolitionism,* pp. 23–31.

95. James Henley Thornwell, "The Rights and Duties of Masters," in Robert L. Ferm, ed., *Issues in American Protestantism: A Documentary History from the Puritans to the Present* (Gloucester, Mass.: Peter Smith, 1983), p. 189.

96. Donald Mathews, "Religion and Slavery: The Case of the American South," pp. 217–18. See also Wyatt-Brown, *Yankee Saints and Southern Sinners,* pp. 156–69.

97. Hughes and Allen, *Illusions of Innocence,* pp. 189–99; quotation from page 192.

98. Garrison, *Letters,* 2: 705.

99. "Peace Convention," *Liberator,* October 19, 1838, p. 168; Garrison, *Letters* 2: 465.

100. Lewis Perry, *Childhood, Marriage and Reform: Henry Clarke Wright,* p. 29; Oliver A. Taylor, "Sketches, Statistics, Etc., of the Theological Seminary at Andover," *American Quarterly Register* 11 (1839): 69.

101. Garrison and Garrison, *The Life of William Lloyd Garrison,* 2: 226–28.

102. George C. Beckwith, "Address to the Friends of Peace," *Advocate of Peace* 1 (June 1837): 8, 11; "Address to Pastors and Churches," *Advocate of Peace* 1 (December 1837): 99. See also the "Tenth Annual Report of the American Peace Society," *Advocate of Peace* 2 (June 1838), for a description of peace advocacy as a

"conservative reform" that worked "with, not against, the agents of Christianity." (p. 9) The "Disclaimer of the American Peace Society," *Advocate of Peace* 2 (November 1838) also noted that the society sought only to regulate intercourse between nations, not to remove government from the earth or to abolish self-defense (p. 143).

103. Beckwith wanted to replace the 1837 amendment with the following sentence: "The object of this society shall be to illustrate the inconsistency of war with Christianity, to show its baneful influence on all the great interests of man and to devise means for insuring universal and permanent peace." Quoted in Galpin, *Pioneering for Peace*, p. 121. It is interesting to note that Beckwith claimed personally to agree with the 1837 constitution. As a matter of policy, however, he thought it best to keep the society's platform as broad as possible.

104. Peter Brock, *Radical Pacifists*, pp. 60–61; Allen and Malone, *Dictionary of American Biography*, 19: 123–24; Thomas C. Upham, *The Manual of Peace*, Peace Movement in America (New York: Leavitt, Lord & Co., 1836; facsimile reprint by Jerome S. Ozer, 1972), pp. 161–71, 394–403; Hardesty, *Women Called to Witness*, pp. 54–55. Upham first attended the Tuesday Night Meeting in December 1839, four years after the Palmer sisters started the group.

105. William Paley, *The Principles of Moral and Political Philosophy*, British Philosophers and Theologians of the Seventeenth and Eighteenth Centuries, Rene Wellek, ed. (New York: Garland Publishing, 1978), pp. 61, 313, 637–44.

106. Wilson Smith, *Professors and Public Ethics: Studies of Northern Moral Philosophers before the Civil War* (Ithaca, N.Y.: Cornell University Press, 1956), pp. 30–36, 45–65, 188–93; E. Brooks Holifield, *The Gentlemen Theologians: American Theology in Southern Culture, 1795–1860* (Durham, N.C.: Duke University Press, 1978), pp. 134–35.

107. See, for example, the excerpt from Jonathan Dymond in "The Rights of Self-Defence," *Advocate of Peace* 2 (August 1838): 49–55; "The Sixth Annual Report of the Windham County Peace Society," *Calumet* 1, no. 9 (September–October 1832): 258–59.

108. William Allen, "Dr. Allen's Letter to Mr. Ladd," *Advocate of Peace* 2 (August 1838): 49–55; William Ladd, "Mr. Ladd's Answer to Dr. Allen's Letter," Ibid., pp. 120–23.

109. Francis Wayland, *The Elements of Moral Science*, 3rd ed. (Boston: Gould, Kendall and Lincoln, 1836), p. 396. In his preface to the first edition of the *Elements*, Wayland explained that it was using Paley's moral philosophy text in his classes at Brown that prompted him to write a book in order to refute Paley. (Francis Wayland and H. L. Wayland, *A Memoir of the Life and Labors of Francis Wayland, DD. LL.D.* [New York: Sheldon and Company, 1867; reprinted by Arno Press, 1972], 1: 381.)

110. Wayland, *Elements of Moral Science*, 3rd ed., pp. 393–96.

111. In his article entitled "Wayland's Moral Philosophy," Charles K. Whipple pointed out that Wayland had violated the Sermon on the Mount in order to protect the police function of the state. "Dr. Wayland," he said, "here turns his back upon the Gospel. He cannot find, in the instruction of our Savior and the apostles, any thing in the slightest degree, resembling the spirit of his assertion—'It is necessary that the depradations of individuals upon society should

be prevented.' This is not a Christian principle!" (*Non-Resistant*, July 20, 1839, n.p.)

112. William Ellery Channing, "Second Discourse On War," in *Discourses on War*, p. 67.

113. Beckwith's first discussion of this topic was in the 1839 article discussed in the text. Later he repeated his points in his 1842 introduction to Upham's *Manual of Peace* (Boston: American Peace Society) and in the preface to his own *Peace Manual* (Boston: American Peace Society, 1847).

114. George Beckwith, "Peace and Government: Or, the Strictest Principles of Peace Not Incompatible with the Legitimate Powers of Government," reprinted in *Non-Resistant*, March 16, 1839, and April 6, 1839, n.p.

115. See, for example, the "Address to Pastors and Churches," *Advocate of Peace* 1 (December 1837): 104; and "The Duty of Ministers with Respect to the Cause of Peace," *Advocate of Peace* 2 (December 1838): 156.

116. See "Exposition of the American Peace Society," *Advocate of Peace* 2 (February 1839): 201.

117. See "Documents on a Congress of Nations," *Advocate of Peace* 2 (November 1838): 140; Thomas Upham, "Circumstances Favorable to an International Congress," *Advocate of Peace* 2 (January 1839): 175–76. In the next decade, Elihu Burritt would make free trade—and its presumed tendency to promote pacifism—a part of the peace movement's creed. The London Peace Society would also stress the ameliorating effects of free trade.

118. William Ladd, "Letter from William Ladd," *Liberator*, November 23, 1838, p. 188. The society's emphasis on the practicality of its reforms was so pronounced that Amasa Walker's address to the annual meeting in 1841 was even entitled "The Cause of Peace Practicable." *Advocate of Peace* 4 (August 1841): 32–38.

119. "Address to the Friends of Peace," *Advocate of Peace* 1 (June 1837): 7; "Prejudices in Favor of War," *Advocate of Peace* 1 (March 1838): 157; Thomas Upham, "Safety of Pacific Principles," *Advocate of Peace* 2 (March 1839); 217–22, and 2 (May 1839): 265–70.

120. Francis Wayland did no better in explicating an ethic of duty than the American Peace Society did. Wayland rejected Paley's claim that personal happiness was the chief aim of virtue. Yet as Edward Madden has indicated in his *Civil Disobedience and Moral Law in Nineteenth-Century American Philosophy* (Seattle: University of Washington Press, 1968), Wayland managed to sneak utilitarianism in through the back door. Wayland argued in the *Elements* that human beings should obey God's will without regard for the consequences, but then he added that God willed those things that worked for humanity's happiness (pp. 20–21). Thus, Wayland jettisoned utilitarianism as a basis for human action but then reincorporated it by ascribing a utilitarian ethic to God.

3. The Gap Widens

1. Merle Curti, ed., *The Learned Blacksmith*, Garland Library of War and Peace (New York: Garland Publishing, 1971), pp. 1–4.

2. Curti, *Learned Blacksmith*, p. 10.

3. Elihu Burritt, *Ten-Minute Talks on All Sorts of Topics,* with an autobiography by the author (Boston: Lee and Shepard, 1874), pp. 17–18.

4. Merle Curti, *The American Peace Crusade, 1815–1860* (New York: Octagon Books, 1965), pp. 89–90; Peter Tolis, *Elihu Burritt: Crusader for Brotherhood* (Hamden, Conn.: Archon Books, 1968), pp. 12–22; Burritt, *Ten-Minute Talks,* pp. 18–19; Elihu Burritt, "Home Operations," *Advocate of Peace and Universal Brotherhood* 1 (April 1846): 104. Burritt was fond of putting leaflets on trains, under the theory that people would read anything there, even tracts that they would not read if they were home.

5. Curti, *American Peace Crusade,* pp. 143–65; Elihu Burritt, *The Works of Elihu Burritt* (London: Charles Gilpin, 1848), pp. 143–44.

6. International peace conferences began in London in the summer of 1843. There had been exchanges of visitors and literature between the American and British movements for some time, and by 1843 a weekly French peace newspaper had been established. Beckwith, Amasa Walker, the Tappan brothers, and fourteen other American delegates attended the first conference, where the principle that "war is inconsistent with the spirit of Christianity and the true interests of mankind" was first articulated. From 1848 to 1851, at the urging of Elihu Burritt, four additional international congresses took place. The highlight was the 1849 Paris conference, where Victor Hugo gave a stirring address on a Congress of Nations. (Curti, *American Peace Crusade,* pp. 133–43, 167–80; "The First General Peace Conference," *Advocate of Peace* 5 [October–November 1843]: 109–14; 118, 125–26.)

7. Nathaniel P. Rogers, "Moral Suasion and the Ballot-Box," *Liberator,* June 28, 1844; "Marvelous Inconsistency," *Liberator,* November 22, 1844, p. 188; Edmund Quincy, "Mr. Burritt and the Vice-Presidency," *Liberator,* August 20, 1847, p. 134.

8. George Beckwith, "Specifics for Peace," *Advocate of Peace* 7 (May–June, 1847): 52–53.

9. Burritt, *Learned Blacksmith,* pp. 136–37.

10. Meetings of the society would continue sporadically through the 1850s.

11. A whimsical example was reported in an article in the January 15, 1841 edition of the *Herald of Freedom.* When challenged by a citizen who wanted to test his devotion to nonresistance, Stephen Foster freely gave away his coat in accordance with Matthew 5:40 ("if any one would sue you and take your coat, let him have your cloak as well"). (p. 186)

12. On June 7, 1844, the society's records reported a debt of $3,636.35. (Library of Congress, Manuscript Collections, Records of the American Peace Society, Vol. 1.)

13. Henry Clarke Wright, "Letter from the General Agent," *Non-Resistant,* November 2, 1839, n.p.

14. Johnson and Malone, *Dictionary of American Biography,* 19: 338–39. Oberlin was the hot spot in the West for peace activities. Two societies operated there during the 1840s—a nonresistant one and a more moderate group. Because of his close friendship with Amasa Walker, Burritt was a welcome visitor to the campus. Others on the faculty were also active in peace work. One professor—Hamilton Hill—as well as Asa Mahan, the college president, attended the 1849 Paris international peace convention. Most of those involved were moderate

peace reformers like Burritt. (See Barbara Zikmund, *Asa Mahan and Oberlin Perfectionism* [Ph.D. dissertation, Duke University, 1969] for an account of reform activities at Oberlin.) The most famous of the radicals was Amos Dresser, a "Lane rebel" who transferred to Oberlin. Well known in abolitionist circles for having suffered a public beating in Nashville, Tennessee, when he dared to travel south with abolitionist literature in his suitcase, Dresser wrote an antiwar book entitled *The Bible against War* in 1849.

15. One of Ladd's fondest dreams was to win the West for peace. It was during his long awaited journey to western New York state that he was struck down with the illness that soon ended his life.

16. The August 1842 and the September 1842 editions of the *Advocate of Peace* ran selections from Judd's sermon. Judd was a member of the reform group. He based his assessment of the Revolution on his conviction that all war was immoral. Despite the outrage that greeted his sermon, Judd's description of the Revolution was not entirely unsympathetic. As he explained, in the sermon "he confesses that [the Revolutionary War] to have been the holiest war on record; but he would dispel the illusion of war, by entering its most sacred retreats, and showing that an essential evil cleaves to the system, and that immoralities are inborn in its purest sources." (Sylvester Judd, *A Moral Review of the Revolutionary War, or Some of the Evils of That Event Considered*, Peace Movement in America [Hallowell, Maine: 1842; facsimile reprint, Jerome S. Ozer, 1972], p. 3.)

17. "Testimonies from the Right Source," *Advocate of Peace* 5 (September 1844): 248–49.

18. Records of the American Peace Society, 1, December 19, 1844.

19. "Action of Methodist Conferences on Peace," *Advocate of Peace* 6 (June–July 1845): 70–71; "Correspondence," *Advocate of Peace* 6 (September–October 1845): 117.

20. "Notices and Receipts," *Advocate of Peace* 7 (September–October 1847): 119.

21. "Miscellaneous," *Advocate of Peace* 7 (January–February 1848): 190–91; "Receipts," *Advocate of Peace* 7 (July–August 1848): 240; "Resolutions on Peace," *Advocate of Peace* 7 (October–November 1848): 274–76.

22. Hemmenway, *Apostle of Peace*, p. 268.

23. Holland, "History of the Peace-Cause," p. 9.

24. In 1834 the Massachusetts Peace Society had refused to condemn defensive wars. (Curti, *American Peace Crusade*, p. 72)

25. "First Annual Meeting of the New-England Non-Resistant Society," *Non-Resistant*, November 2, 1839, n.p.

26. George C. Beckwith, "Course of the Society," *Advocate of Peace* (January–February 1847): 3; Beckwith, "Introduction," to Thomas C. Upham, *The Manual of Peace: Exhibiting the Evils of War and Remedies of War* (Boston: American Peace Society, 1842), pp. 7–8.

27. George C. Beckwith, *The Peace Manual: or, War and its Remedies* (Boston: American Peace Society, 1847), p. 7.

28. Holland, "History of the Peace-Cause," p. 51.

29. Curti, *American Peace Crusade, 1815–1860*, pp. 89–90; Tolis, *Elihu Burritt: Crusader for Brotherhood*, p. 121.

30. Holland, "History of the Peace-Cause," p. 85.

31. Records of the American Peace Society, 1, October 20, 1841, May 27, 1845, and May 28, 1845.

32. Records of the American Peace Society, 1, June 23, 1845 and November 3, 1845; Burritt quoted in Galpin, *Pioneering for Peace,* p. 164.

33. Holland, "History of the Peace-Cause," p. 85.

34. Curti, *American Peace Crusade,* p. 92. Curti claims that Rev. A. Foster joined with Garrison, but I believe that he meant Stephen S. Foster. Aaron Foster had been an occasional agent of the American Peace Society for several years. Burritt's account of the anniversary meeting indicated that Stephen S. Foster participated in the discussions—an event highly unlikely for an avowed non-resistant like Foster, unless he had accompanied Garrison to the meeting for strategic purposes. ("Eighteenth Anniversary," *Advocate of Peace and Universal Brotherhood* 1 (June 1846): 135.

35. Curti, *American Peace Crusade, 1815–1860,* pp. 92–93; Walker quoted in Allen, *Fight for Peace,* p. 413.

36. Burritt quoted in Allen, *Fight for Peace,* pp. 414–15.

37. Curti, *American Peace Crusade,* pp. 93–94; Records of the American Peace Society, 1, May 26, 1846, and June 10, 1846.

38. Records of the American Peace Society, 1, June 5, 1846, and June 10, 1846.

39. Elihu Burritt, "To the Readers of the Advocate of Peace," and "To the Members of the American Peace Society," *Advocate of Peace and Universal Brotherhood,* 1 (December 1846): 275–78.

40. Holland, "History of the Peace-Cause," p. 87.

41. "Course of the Society," *Advocate of Peace* 7 (January–February 1847): 2–3; "Misconceptions Concerning the Society," *Advocate of Peace* 7 (March–April, 1847): 31–34.

42. George C. Beckwith, "Note," *Advocate of Peace* 7 (July–August 1848): 233.

43. George C. Beckwith, *The Peace Manual: or, War and its Remedies* (Boston: American Peace Society, 1847), 11.

44. Garrison, *Letters,* 3: 264.

45. As we have seen, this did not mean that they did not want to have political influence. The Garrisonians were happy to petition the state for legislation that they favored, and they openly supported some political candidates over others. They hoped for the best from politics and the people who participated in government, but they refused to become personally involved. Since the government of the United States depended on violence and sanctioned slavery, no true Christian could be a part of it.

46. Quoted in Kraditor, *Means and Ends in American Abolitionism,* p. 200. The slogan was a citation from Isaiah 28:18: "your covenant with death will be annulled, and your agreement with Sheol will not stand; when the overwhelming scourge passes through you will be beaten down by it." (RSV)

47. Garrison, "The Annual Meeting at New-York," *Liberator,* April 22, 1842, quoted in Kraditor, *Means and Ends in American Abolitionism,* p. 198.

48. The resolution declared that "secession from the present United States government is the duty of every abolitionist; since no one can take office, or throw a vote for another to hold office, under the United States Constitution, without violating his anti-slavery principles, and rendering himself an abettor of the slaveholder in sin." Quoted in Perry, *Radical Abolitionism and the Politics of Anarchy,* p. 161.

49. Kraditor, *Means and Ends in American Abolitionism*, pp. 198, 206–7.

50. "Second Annual Meeting of the New England Non-Resistance Society," *Liberator*, September 18, 1840, p. 159.

51. Garrison and Garrison, *William Lloyd Garrison: The Story of His Life, Told by His Children*, 3: 80.

52. In this analysis of disunionism, I have particularly depended upon Kraditor and Perry. Kraditor explained disunionism as a moral imperative similar to immediate emancipation and individual perfectionism. She considered it a natural development from the original nonresistant position. Kraditor also argued that the Garrisonians developed disunionism later than nonresistance because only later was the view of the Constitution as an antislavery document fully articulated. For Kraditor, disunionism was not a sectional issue, since it accused both North and South of complicity in the sin of slavery and encouraged all people, regardless of where they lived, both to accept responsibility for participating in a sinful political system and to renounce that system. (pp. 197–215) Perry, on the other hand, asserted that disunionism replaced nonresistance as the antigovernment movement of Garrisonianism. Though an effective substitute for nonresistance, disunionism was not, in Perry's opinion, a "happy application of nonresistance principles, for instead of viewing slavery as but one horrible instance of the ubiquitous sinful habit of governing and coercing, it made slavery a sectional issue and identified Northern governments with liberty." For Perry, Garrison's insistence that the Non-Resistance Society use the motto "No union with warriors or war-makers" as a parallel to the abolitionist "No union with slave-holders" slogan was at best an awkward way to resolve the tensions between disunionism and nonresistance. (*Radical Abolitionism and the Politics of Anarchy*, p. 161) In my analysis, I have used Perry's idea of disunionism as an antigovernment alternative to nonresistance but I have agreed with Kraditor that disunionism was neither incompatible with nonresistance nor a sectional issue. What is new in my discussion is the suggestion that disunionism not only resolved the nonresistants' dilemma of having reached an organizational dead end, but also served as a radicalizing principle.

53. Quoted in Garrison, *Letters*, 3: 298.

54. Garrison, *Letters*, 3: 299, 301.

55. Garrison, *Letters*, 3: 17.

56. Thomas, *The Liberator*, pp. 351–53.

57. Henry Steele Commager, *Theodore Parker* (Boston: Beacon Press, 1947), pp. 74–101; Robert C. Albrecht, *Theodore Parker*, Sylvia E. Bowman, ed., Twayne's United States Authors (New York: Twayne Publishers, 1971), pp. 69–71; Theodore Parker, "The Transient and the Permanent," in H. Shelton Smith, Robert T. Handy, Lefferts A. Loetscher, *American Christianity: An Historical Interpretation with Representative Documents* (New York: Charles Scribner's Sons, 1963), 2: 141–47.

58. Garrison and Garrison, *The Life of William Lloyd Garrison*, 3: 145–47; Kraditor, *Means and Ends in American Abolitionism*, p. 92; Wayland, *Elements*, 3rd ed., p. 398; Moorhead, "Social Reform and the Divided Conscience of Antebellum Protestantism," 421–22.

59. Quoted in Garrison and Garrison, *Life of William Lloyd Garrison*, 3: 145–46.

60. Henry Clarke Wright, "Letter from the General Agent," *Non-Resistant*,

September 7, 1839, n.p.; *Liberator,* December 25, 1846, p. 150, quoted in John Demos, "The Antislavery Movement and the Problem of Violent 'Means,' " 517.

61. Hughes and Allen, *Illusions of Innocence,* pp. 14–16, 188–98.

62. "The Non-Resistants," *Liberator,* October 1, 1840, p. 158.

63. Garrison, *Letters,* 3: 632.

64. Charles Stearns, "The Character of God—Sacredness of Life," *Liberator,* March 27, 1846, p. 52.

65. *Liberator,* September 29, 1847 and November 10, 1848.

66. Henry C. Wright, *Anthropology: Or, The Science of Man: In Its Bearing on War and Slavery* (Cincinnati: E. Shephard, 1850), pp. 5–25, 46, 52, 57.

67. Adin Ballou, *Christian Non-Resistance,* pp. 1–2, 59; *Primitive Christianity and Its Corruptions,* 2: 169.

68. Ballou, *Autobiography,* pp. 438–39, 446–48.

69. Henry Clarke Wright, "The Bible Question," *Liberator,* April 1, 1853, p. 52.

70. "War for Slavery," *Liberator,* June 5, 1846. Garrison wrote to Charles Whipple in 1846: "No matter what may be the success of American arms, it cannot alter the criminality of the war. The more success, the more crime, and the more guilt. The more Mexicans slain, the more murders committed. It is a distinct, all-crushing pro-slavery movement." (*Letters,* 3: 353.)

71. See Friedman's *Gregarious Saints,* pp. 202–95, for a discussion of the ways in which the nonresistants unashamedly rooted for the Mexicans. Friedman argues that such an attitude was an abandonment of the nonresistant ethic, which should have deplored the violence, not picked sides.

72. "Channing's Duty of the Free States," *Southern Quarterly Review,* 2–3 (1842): 175.

73. Mabee, *Black Freedom,* pp. 250–51; Stewart, *Holy Warriors,* pp. 108–11.

74. Stewart, *Holy Warriors,* pp. 109–18.

75. Wyatt-Brown, *Yankee Saints and Southern Sinners,* pp. 188–99.

76. Stewart, *Holy Warriors,* pp. 115–25. A number of excellent discussions of abolitionist racial prejudices are available. See, for example, Jane H. Pease and William H. Pease, "Ends, Means, and Attitudes: Black-White Conflict in the Antislavery Movement," *Civil War History* 17 (1972): 117–28; Friedman, *Gregarious Saints,* pp. 160–95; Mabee, *Black Freedom,* pp. 61–66; and Ronald T. Takaki, *Iron Cages: Race and Culture in Nineteenth-Century America* (New York: Alfred A. Knopf, 1979).

77. Charles Sumner, *The True Grandeur of Nations* (Boston: William D. Ticknor and Company, 1845), p. 4.

78. David Donald, *Charles Sumner and the Coming of the Civil War* (New York: Alfred A. Knopf, 1960), p. 114.

79. Theodore Parker, *Speeches, Addresses, and Occasional Sermons,* 3 vols. (Boston: Horace B. Fuller, 1871), 1: 114, 117–18.

80. Francis Wayland, *Sermons Delivered in the Chapel of Brown University* (Boston: Gould, Kendall, and Lincoln, 1849), pp. 272–74, 269–70.

81. Garrison, *Letters,* 3: 339.

82. Records of the American Peace Society, 1, June 5, 1846 and June 10, 1846.

83. "Eighteenth Annual Report," *Advocate of Peace and Universal Brotherhood* 1 (June 1846): 139.

84. Joshua P. Blanchard, "Mexican War," *Advocate of Peace and Universal Brotherhood* 1 (July 1846): 168.

85. "More Vengeance," *Advocate of Peace* 7 (May–June, 1847): 68–70.

86. "Petitions Respecting the Mexican War" and "The Mexican War: What Shall Be Done to Hasten Its Termination?" *Advocate of Peace* 7 (January–February 1847): 16–21.

87. William Jay, *A Review of the Causes and Consequences of the Mexican War*, 2nd ed., The Anti-Slavery Crusade in America (Boston: 1849; reprinted by Arno Press, 1969), pp. 31–32, 66–74, 100, 130, 173. The Tappanite American and Foreign Antislavery Society helped circulate Jay's book as well (Mabee, *Black Freedom*, p. 253). Francis Wayland was one of the judges for the Society's essay contest. "Home Operations," *Advocate of Peace* 7 (May–June 1847): 71.

88. "Annual Report," *Advocate of Peace* 7 (July–August 1847): 85.

89. "Resolutions on Peace," *Advocate of Peace* 7 (November–December 1847): 134–37; "Miscellaneous," *Advocate of Peace* 7 (January–February 1848): 166–67.

90. DeBenedetti, *The Peace Reform in American History*, pp. 50–52.

91. "Twentieth Anniversary of the American Peace Society," *Advocate of Peace* 7 (July–August 1848): 216.

92. "Mr. Walker's Remarks," *Advocate of Peace* 3 (June 1840): 164; "Annual Report," *Advocate of Peace* 5 (June–July 1844): 216; "Miscellaneous," *Advocate of Peace* 7 (March–April 1848): 189. The most blatant article contrasting the elevated Christian sentiments of New England with the depravity of the South and West was a postwar essay by Rev. Aaron Foster entitled "The American Church on the Subject of War." Foster concluded that those states with the most Christian ministers and laypeople had opposed the war, whereas those with the fewest supported it. He credited the free states that were "older and more thoroughly Puritan in character" and the slave states such as Georgia, Kentucky, and North Carolina, which had strong Methodist, Baptist, and Presbyterian influences, for opposing the war. There were two "old free states" that favored the war— Pennsylvania and Virginia—but Foster explained that religion had never been prominent in either of them. The "new" states that favored the war—such as Maine, Michigan, Illinois, Missouri, Arkansas, Texas, Mississippi, and Alabama—he said, were simply states "whose people have been very much restricted in their religious and educational advantages." *Advocate of Peace* 7 (October–November 1848): 269–72. The American Peace Society in general claimed that the war could have been prevented if only the cause of peace had been active long enough in the West to enlighten its inhabitants. Efforts to send peace materials to the West continued throughout the war. (See "Publications for Ministers at the West," *Advocate of Peace* 7 (January–February 1847): 21; "Notices and Receipts," *Advocate of Peace* 7 (September–October 1847): 119; "Special Efforts for Funds," *Advocate of Peace* 7 (November–December 1847): 142–43.

93. Garrison, *Letters*, 1: 34.

94. Walters, *Antislavery Appeal*, pp. 129–38; Garrison, *Letters*, 1: 249–50.

95. Wyatt-Brown, *Yankee Saints and Southern Sinners*, p. 43.

96. "Letters from Henry C. Wright," *Liberator*, (July 28, 1843), p. 120; Elihu Burritt, "Universal Brotherhood. Great Social Movement," *Advocate of Peace and Universal Brotherhood*, 1, no. 3 (March 1846): 79.

4. The Trauma of the 1850s

1. Charles Stearns, "Physical Restraint," *Liberator*, October 31, 1845, p. 176;

"Non-Resistance," *Liberator,* October 12, 1845, p. 164; "The Character of God—Sacredness of Life," *Liberator,* March 27, 1846, p. 52.

2. Charles Stearns, "Letter from Kansas," *Liberator,* March 16, 1855, p. 43; "State of Affairs in Kansas," *Liberator,* July 27, 1855, p. 120.

3. Charles Stearns, "Letter from Kansas," *Liberator,* September 14, 1855, p. 145; "Letter from Kansas," *Liberator,* December 21, 1855, p. 207; "The Civil War in Kansas," *Liberator,* January 4, 1856, p. 2.

4. Charles Stearns, "The Civil War in Kansas," *Liberator,* January 4, 1856, p. 2.

5. Charles Stearns, "Letter From Charles Stearns," *Liberator,* February 15, 1856, p. 27.

6. "Annual Meeting" *Advocate of Peace* 9 (July–August 1851): 36–37. For a complete account of the internal machinations in the American Peace Society from 1846 to 1851, see Curti, *American Peace Crusade,* pp. 87–102.

7. "Peace Petitions to the President," *Advocate of Peace* (November 1843): 370.

8. "A Word to Good Men on Peace," *Advocate of Peace* (August 1852): 129.

9. "Home Affairs," *Advocate of Peace* 10 (March 1852): 48.

10. One figure who drew much attention was the Hungarian patriot Louis Kossuth, who toured the United States in the early 1850s to try to arouse popular sympathy for the Hungarians, who were rebelling against Austria, and to persuade the U.S. to intervene in the eventuality that Russia went to the aid of Austria. The American Peace Society condemned Kossuth for tempting the friends of peace into compromising the peace principles of peace for the sake of liberty (see William Jay, *The Kossuth Excitement: A Letter from the Hon. William Jay, President of the APS* (Boston: American Peace Society, 1852); and "Kossuth and the Peace Society," *Advocate of Peace* 10 [January 1852]: 9). Predictably, Garrison criticized Kossuth not simply for inciting Americans to violence, but for ignoring the plight of the slaves when he sought aid for the oppressed. (Garrison, *Letters,* 4: 102.)

11. "Home Items," *Advocate of Peace* (October 1853): 366–67; "Addresses," *Advocate of Peace* (June 1853): 310.

12. William Jay, "Annual Address: The Eastern War an Argument for the Cause of Peace," *Advocate of Peace* (June 1855): 274.

13. George C. Beckwith, "Introduction," to Thomas C. Upham, *Manual of Peace,* p. 12.

14. William Ladd, "Mr. Ladd's Address at the Anniversary," *Advocate of Peace* 3 (August 1840): 44. "Philanthropist," the author of an article entitled "A Common Mistake," made the same argument in *Harbinger of Peace* in 1830. See p. 215 of the January 1830 edition.

15. William Jay, "Annual Address," *Advocate of Peace* (June 1855): 274.

16. "Report," *Advocate of Peace* (June 1855): 289–90.

17. "Demoralization Inseparable from War," *Advocate of Peace* (August–September, 1855): 321–322.

18. *Advocate of Peace* (December 1855): 384; Records of the American Peace Society, vol. 2, December 5, 1855.

19. "The True Remedy," *Advocate of Peace* (December 1855): 369–70.

20. "B," "International War," *Advocate of Peace* (February 1856): 20–22; "How Shall an End Be Put to the Practice of International War?" *Advocate of Peace* (March 1856): 35–39.

21. "Military Disobedience," *Advocate of Peace* (March 1856): 38–39; "European Peace," *Advocate of Peace* (May 1856): 66–67.

22. "The True Course of Peace," *Advocate of Peace* (February 1856): 17–18.

23. "The Safe Defence" *Advocate of Peace* (February 1856): 26.

24. In 1858, for example, the American Peace Society published Amasa Walker's *Le Monde: or, In Time of Peace Prepare for War.* Walker's work argued that the only way to avoid war was to abandon preparations for it. Beckwith printed a favorable account of the book in the *Advocate* in that same year. ("Folly of Preparations for War," *Advocate of Peace* (November–December 1858): 182–85. Favorable articles on disarmament also appeared in the *Advocate* in 1859. ("Resolves on Disarmament," *Advocate of Peace* [July–August 1859]: 308–9; and Amasa Walker, "Letter from Hon. Amasa Walker," *Advocate of Peace* [September–October 1859]: 336–38). In addition, "B" of Castleton, Vermont, continued to contribute articles to the *Advocate* after Beckwith returned to edit it.

25. "Report," *Advocate of Peace* (June–July 1856): 83.

26. Curti, *American Peace Crusade,* pp. 212–13.

27. "Report," *Advocate of Peace* (June–July 1856): 83–86. It was a common strategy to prove that the peace society's efforts were successful by comparing the current situation to what it would have been without the labors of the society. It was an article of faith for the group to claim success for their efforts, no matter how little concrete evidence was available. Even when the society's representatives were discouraged in the 1850s—when they freely admitted that the people to whom they spoke were often more interested in the slavery question than in peace—they managed to conclude that it was only the tireless efforts of the American Peace Society that prevented greater disasters from occurring (see "Some Extracts From Reports of Agents," *Advocate of Peace* [June–July 1856]: 99; and "Report," *Advocate of Peace* [July–August 1858]: 119–20). One writer reached the most nebulous conclusion possible in 1859, when he noted that there was no doubt that progress had been made, but precisely how much, it was impossible to say with entire confidence. ("Progress Already Made in the Cause of Peace," *Advocate of Peace* [July–August 1859]: 303.)

28. "The Late French Revolution: Its Probable Bearings on the Peace of Europe and the World," *Advocate of Peace* (May–June 1848): 193–95. The article went on to assert that the American Peace Society had never approved of the mob rule that followed the French Revolution but noted that this time the mob was under control and the provisional government showed promise. By implication the author was not about to quarrel with the questionable means that had attained this desirable result.

29. "A Word to Peace Men Just Now: Their Duty in the Present Crisis of Our Country," *Advocate of Peace* (October–November 1856): 147–50. Amasa Walker made a similar argument in his May address at the American Peace Society's annual meeting. See "The Duty of Peace Men in Regard to Kansas," *Advocate of Peace* (August–September 1856): 116–17.

30. "Divine Retribution," *Advocate of Peace* (March–April 1858): 37.

31. "Practical Questions on Peace," *Advocate of Peace* (May–June 1858): 69–71.

32. "Mutiny or Rebellion?" *Herald of Peace,* London (February 1, 1858): 13, "Our Future in India," Ibid., 20–23.

33. "Annual Meeting of the Peace Society," *Herald of Peace* (June 1858): 68; "Thanksgiving for Victories in India," *Herald of Peace* (May 1859): 199–200.

34. "Discrimination Necessary in Peace: Enforcement of Law against Criminals Not the Same as War," *Advocate of Peace* (May–June 1859): 266.

35. Rev. Frederick D. Huntingdon, "Christ the Pacificator," *Advocate of Peace* (June–July 1852): 88–104; Allen and Malone, *Dictionary of American Biography*, 9: 413.

36. "B," "Peace Principles," *Advocate of Peace* (March–April 1857): 234.

37. "Misconceptions on Peace," *Advocate of Peace* (March–April 1858): 35–36.

38. "How to Do away with War," *Advocate of Peace* (September–October 1859): 321.

39. Oates, *To Purge This Land with Blood*, pp. 22–24, 130–37, 168–71.

40. Garrison and Garrison, *William Lloyd Garrison: The Story of his Life, as Told by His Children*, 3: 487–88; Oates, *To Purge This Land with Blood*, pp. 114–15, 181–86.

41. Oates, *To Purge This Land with Blood*, pp. 284–302, 312–15.

42. "The Harper's Ferry Affair," *Advocate of Peace* (March–April 1860): 64.

43. Stewart, *Holy Warriors*, pp. 164–68.

44. Garrison and Garrison, *The Life of William Lloyd Garrison as Told by His Children*, 3: 412–13; Thomas, *Liberator*, p. 387.

45. "Meeting of the New-England Non-Resistance Society," *Liberator*, March 30, 1855, p. 50; "New England Non-Resistant Convention," *Liberator*, April 13, 1855, p. 60.

46. Angelina Grimke, "Feelings of a Woman," *Liberator*, July 7, 1854, p. 106.

47. "Peace Forever, War Never," *Liberator*, July 28, 1854, p. 117.

48. Ibid.

49. Adin Ballou, "Meeting of the N.E. Non-Resistant Society," *Liberator*, March 16, 1855, p. 43.

50. "Meeting of the New England Non-Resistant Society," *Liberator*, March 30, 1855, p. 50.

51. Edward Search, in *Liberator*, November 14, 1851, p. 107.

52. Micajah T. Johnson, "Non-Resistance," *Liberator*, July 23, 1852. In a book published in 1863, Wright would speak to the issue clearly. Arguing that self-abnegation was the "most sacred and ennobling demand of Human Nature" and that self-preservation at the expense of others was a denial of the noblest elements of human nature, Wright nevertheless admitted that self-abnegation in favor of slavery was "mean" and "cowardly." Since slavery was the sum of all villainy, refusing to combat it meant giving life to the most godless institution on earth. That was one bit of sacrifice that Wright was unable to advise. "The one great lesson of the hour," he asserted, "is, SELF-ABNEGATION FOR FREEDOM, SELF-PRESERVATION AGAINST SLAVERY!" Wright did not, however, go on to conclude that freedom could best be preserved by killing slaveholders. Instead, he continued to insist that the battle for liberty was a war to be conducted in the realm of ideas. Nonresistants, he said, must convert the slaveholders through their ideas, not through weapons of death. They must be ready to die, but not kill, for freedom. (*The Self-Abnegationist, or the True King and Queen* [Boston: Bella Marsh, 1863], pp. 10–13, 122, 131–32.)

53. William J. Pease and Jane H. Pease, "Freedom and Peace: A Nineteenth-Century Dilemma," *Midwest Quarterly* 9, no. 1 (1967–68): 34–36.

54. Pease and Pease, "Freedom and Peace: A Nineteenth-Century Dilemma," p. 36.

55. Madelon Gedell, *The Alcotts: Biography of a Family* (New York: Clarkson N. Potter, 1980), pp. 329–32.

56. "Mr. Foster's Views," *Liberator*, February 19, 1858, p. 31; "Political Anti-Slavery Convention," *Liberator*, June 15, 1860, p. 93.

57. Adin Ballou, "Freedom in Kansas vs. Christian Non-Resistance," *Liberator*, May 2, 1856, p. 69; see also "Peace and War," *Liberator*, April 4, 1856.

58. "Letter from Samuel J. May," *Liberator*, September 12, 1856, p. 152.

59. Samuel J. May, "The Impact of a Vote," *Liberator*, October 24, 1856, p. 171; and "The Old War Better Than the New," *Liberator*, October 31, 1856, p. 174. May had once been as consistent as anyone in opposing political participation. In 1845, in opposition to the antislavery Liberty party, he wrote that freedom would come only through moral means, not through political partisan instruments. It did no good, he argued, to pass a law if public sentiment was unready to obey it. Of those abolitionists who had flocked to the Liberty party, May commented that he deplored their loss of confidence in the sufficiency of truth. ("The Liberty Bell Is Not of the Liberty Party," *Liberty Bell* [1845]: 159–61.)

60. Henry Clarke Wright, "An 'Infernal Covenant'—The Parties to It—Slavery Triumphant—Duty of the North," *Liberator*, December 5, 1856, p. 195.

61. Garrison, *Letters*, 4: 408–9.

62. Garrison, *Letters*, 4: 419.

63. Henry Clarke Wright, "Slave-Hunting in Cincinnati—The Fugitive and Geo. Washington," *Liberator*, July 3, 1857, p. 108.

64. Henry Clarke Wright, "Resistance to Tyrants Obedience to God," *Liberator*, January 23, 1857, p. 16.

65. "Annual Meeting of the Massachusetts Anti-Slavery Society," *Liberator*, February 13, 1857, p. 27. The New England Anti-Slavery Convention, led by the nonresistant Edmund Quincy, had much earlier issued a pamphlet entitled the *Address of the New England Anti-Slavery Convention to the Slaves of the United States with an Address to President Tyler, Faneuil Hall, May 31, 1843.* The pamphlet argued that the self-evident truths of the Declaration of Independence gave to the slaves a right and a duty to throw off the government that oppressed them. Every slave, the pamphlet insisted, was obliged, whenever it was possible, peaceably to escape to the North. (Pease and Pease, *Antislavery Argument*, pp. 212–23.) In the late 1850s, Wright increasingly stressed the slaves' duty to resist their masters. He became less diligent, however, in asserting that that resistance should be peaceful. In response to his urging, in 1859 the citizens of Natick, Massachusetts, passed a resolution that "it is the right and duty of the slaves to resist their masters, and it is the right and duty of the people of the North to incite them to resistance, and to aid them in it." Coming soon after John Brown's raid on Harper's Ferry, such a resolution could hardly have sounded pacific in nature. Wright claimed that, since the resolution did not specify the means of resistance to be used, no one could complain that he was inciting the slaves to violence. Though he opposed John Brown's means, he said, he did support his goals. Henry Wilson wrote a letter of complaint to Wright, arguing that though his resolution may have meant nothing more than a general, or even peaceful opposition to slavery, still the language of the resolution made it sound as if Wright were suggesting violent resistance. Such indiscriminate language, Wilson noted, could only increase alarm in the South. (Henry Clarke Wright, "Great Meeting in Natick," *Liberator* December 9, 1859, p. 196; Henry Wilson, "Letter

from Hon. Henry Wilson to Henry C. Wright," *Liberator,* January 13, 1860, p. 7.)

66. "The New England Anti-Slavery Convention," *Liberator,* June 4, 1858, p. 90.

67. Meltzer and Holland, *Lydia Maria Child, Selected Letters, 1817–1880,* p. 324. John Brown had decided not to use violence except to defend himself. Lewis Perry has argued that Garrison managed to turn that resolution into a virtue, since, in this reading of the events, Brown's greatest sin was advocating self-defense. (*Radical Abolitionism,* p. 259.)

68. Meltzer and Holland, *Lydia Maria Child, Selected Letters,* p. 323.

69. Charles K. Whipple, "John Brown, and his Movement," *Liberator* October 28, 1859, p. 170. Whipple also thought that Brown's actions were not nearly so reprehensible as the actions of those who captured Brown. "To gain one's freedom by killing the kidnapper is to do evil that good may come of it," he admitted. "But if Brown is not to be praised for fighting, even for liberty, what is to be said of [Governor] Wise, and the military ruffians of the Slave Power, who shed blood in defence of slavery?"

70. "The Tragedy at Harper's Ferry," *Liberator,* October 28, 1859, p. 170.

71. Meltzer and Holland, *Lydia Maria Child, Selected Letters,* p. 328.

72. Garrison, *Letters,* 4: 661.

73. Baltimore *Patriot,* quoted in *Liberator,* June 2, 1854; cited in Wyatt-Brown, *Yankee Saints and Southern Sinners,* p. 124.

74. *Practical Christian,* November 26, 1859, p. 3; quoted in Perry, *Radical Abolitionism,* p. 259.

75. Meltzer and Holland, *Lydia Maria Child, Selected Letters,* p. 336.

76. Walters, *Antislavery Appeal,* p. 28.

77. Garrison, *Letters,* 4: 604; Brock, *Radical Pacifists in Antebellum America,* p. 237.

78. "Practical Christian Anti-Slavery," *Liberator,* September 16, 1859, p. 145.

79. J. Miller McKim, "Practical Christian Anti-Slavery," *Liberator,* September 30, 1859, p. 154.

80. Adin Ballou, "Adin Ballou in Reply to J. Miller McKim," *Liberator,* November 4, 1859, p. 176.

81. Adin Ballou, *Autobiography,* pp. 416–19.

82. Adin Ballou, *Practical Christian Socialism: A Conversational Exposition of the True System of Human Society* (Hopedale, Mass.: published by the author; New York: Fowlers and Wells, 1854; New York: AMS Press Reprint Series, Communal Societies in America, n.d.), p. 116.

83. "The Practical Christian," *Liberator,* January 13, 1860, p. 7.

84. Ballou, *Autobiography,* p. 422.

85. Ballou, *Autobiography,* p. 421.

86. "Remarks From Mr. Ladd's Letter," *Liberator,* November 23, 1838, p. 188.

87. Adin Ballou, "Gerrit Smith's 'Armed Police,' " *Liberator,* February 10, 1854, p. 21.

88. Both Lewis Perry, in his *Radical Abolitionism* (pp. 232–68, 301) and Friedman, in *Gregarious Saints* (pp. 198–221) have made this same point. It is a significant argument because it counters the standard historical explanations, which assume that the nonresistants began by unambiguously rejecting violence and then later unreservedly embraced it. In rejecting that interpretation, Perry

stated that "we should not assume that abolitionists were abruptly dissuaded from cherished convictions by some clamorous event, nor that they finally found nonresistance inadequate. Instead, they found their doctrine ambiguous enough to condone and even demand violence—usually by men other than themselves. This process was almost from the start of nonresistance" (pp. 232–33).

Friedman contended that in the Garrisonians "a dual commitment to moral suasion and violent means was evident from the start. . . . Whereas violence became more attractive as time passed, most immediatists never relinquished their peace principles. Therefore, we are seeking explanation for a transformation not from pacifism to advocacy of force but from a rough equilibrium between moral suasion and violent means to a situation where commitment to violence gained general but never total hegemony" (pp. 196–97).

5. The Civil War

1. Brock, *Radical Pacifists in Antebellum America*, pp. 3, 27.

2. J. P. B., "American Peace Society," *Liberator*, September 27, 1861, p. 156.

3. Curti, *Learned Blacksmith*, p. 139.

4. Ibid., p. 140.

5. Joshua P. Blanchard, "No Union with Slaveholders," *Liberator*, December 5, 1862, p. 195.

6. Ibid.

7. "Letter from Samuel J. May," *Liberator*, May 29, 1863, p. 85.

8. J. P. Blanchard, "Letter to Rev. Samuel J. May," *Liberator*, July 10, 1863, p. 112.

9. Joshua P. Blanchard, "Separation," *Liberator*, February 24, 1865, p. 32.

10. *A Brief Synopsis of Work Proposed, Aided and Accomplished by the Universal Peace Union during the Last 31 Years, (From 1866 to 1897) under the Direction of Its President, Alfred H. Love, of Philadelphia* (n.p., n.d.), pp. 2–3.

11. Alfred H. Love, "Our First Decade Meeting," *Voice of Peace* 3, (October 1876): 105.

12. "The Enforcement of Law a Peace Measure," *Advocate of Peace* (January–February 1861): 165–67.

13. "Peace Compatible with Government," *Advocate of Peace* (January–February 1861): 170. The society also invoked the support of William Ladd, arguing that he had said nothing in his 1837 debate with William Allen to make anyone suppose that the peace society had ever objected "to the use of the sword of the magistrate in punishing crimes." See "William Ladd on the Government Question," *Advocate of Peace* (March–April 1862): 37–38.

14. "Peace at Home," *Advocate of Peace* (March–April 1861): 199.

15. J. A. Copp, J. W. Parker, George Beckwith, "The Present Crisis in Our Country: Plea for Its Peaceful Solution in any Event," *Advocate of Peace* (March–April 1861): 200–1.

16. "Proofs of Peace in Progress," *Advocate of Peace* (May–June 1861): 229–31.

17. "Rebellion Actually Begun," *Advocate of Peace* (May–June 1861): 258.

18. Ibid., p. 259.

19. Francis Wayland was one member of the American Peace Society who did not go along with the society's insistence that a civil war was by definition not a

war. Wayland had become president of the society in February of 1859, after the death of William Jay, but by January of 1861 he was determined to resign. Beckwith visited him at his home in Rhode Island to attempt to persuade him to stay on but met with no luck. (Records of the American Peace Society, vol. 2, February 1, 1859 and January 21, 1861.)

In his 1865 edition of *The Elements of Moral Science*, Wayland revised his section on warfare. Rather than condemning all wars as contrary to the revealed will of God—as he had in the past—he now made an exception to that rule. With the example of the Southern revolt obviously in his mind, he explained that, in cases where a nation sought to overthrow a just government and replace it with one of brute force, then "force must be repelled by force." In this, he added, "the whole people may unite, and strive to the utmost to transmit to their children the legacy of liberty which they have received from their fathers." Nevertheless, Wayland concluded, the just war to protect a righteous government ought never to become a crusade; rather, it should employ only so much violence as was necessary to repulse the enemy. "Their object," he stipulated, "is simply to repel injury; and when this is accomplished, the sword should be returned to its scabbard, and the offending nation be treated as brethren as soon as they have by their conduct shown themselves worthy of this relation." (*The Elements of Moral Science*, revised and improved edition (Boston: Gould and Lincoln, 1865), pp. 392, 394.)

20. "Annual Report," *Advocate of Peace* (July–August 1861): 268.

21. "Rebellion Actually Begun," *Advocate of Peace* (May–June 1861): 259.

22. "Annual Report," *Advocate of Peace* (July–August 1861): 268–69; "Resolutions," Ibid., p. 270.

23. "Annual Report," *Advocate of Peace* (July–August 1861): 269.

24. "Home Items," *Advocate of Peace* (October 1853): 366.

25. "Barbarities of Rebellion," *Advocate of Peace* (November–December 1863): 372.

26. "Rebel Women," *Advocate of Peace* (July–August 1862): 116.

27. "Report," *Advocate of Peace* (May–June 1862): 83.

28. "Lack of Discrimination on Peace," *Advocate of Peace* (September–October 1863): 330.

29. "English Views of Our Present Duty," *Advocate of Peace* (November–December 1862): 172. The American Peace Society deplored everything about the British reaction to the war. Having given support to the British suppression of the revolts in India, the society felt betrayed when the English government granted belligerency status to the South. To be consistent, the society complained, the British should regard the Southern rebels just as the American Peace Society had regarded the Indian ones—as criminals in need of punishment. ("Our Complaints against England," *Advocate of Peace* (January–February 1863): 197–98.)

30. "Foreign Misconceptions of Our Affairs," *Advocate of Peace* (July–August 1863): 300.

31. "Exultation over Rebels," *Advocate of Peace* (November–December 1862): 164.

32. "Meliorations of War," *Advocate of Peace* (January–February 1863): 209.

33. "Fidelity of Quakers to Their Principles," *Advocate of Peace* (March–April 1864): 35.

34. "The Conscription," *Advocate of Peace* (March–April 1863): 255.

35. "English Views of Our Present Duty," *Advocate of Peace* (November–December 1862): 173.

36. "Misconceptions of Peace," *Advocate of Peace* (September–October 1861): 306–7.

37. "Peace and Rebellion: What Shall the Peace Society Do Now?" *Advocate of Peace* (September–October 1864): 140.

38. "Peace Compatible with Government," *Advocate of Peace* (November–December 1861): 330.

39. "The Bible on Peace and Government," *Advocate of Peace* (July–August 1863): 294.

40. "The Enforcement of Law Not War," *Advocate of Peace* (March–April 1863): 243.

41. "Criticisms of the Peace Society," *Advocate of Peace* (September–October 1862): 160–61.

42. "The Enforcement of Law Not War," *Advocate of Peace* (March–April 1863): 243.

43. "Retaliation in War," *Advocate of Peace* (March–April 1865): 239–41.

44. Howard Malcom, "Address," *Advocate of Peace* (May–June 1862): 72–73.

45. "What Is Proper at This Crisis?" *Advocate of Peace* (March–April 1863): 247–48.

46. "How to Close a Civil War," *Advocate of Peace* (November–December 1864): 172–74.

47. "The Treatment Due to Rebels," *Advocate of Peace* (March–April 1866): 50.

48. "Annual Report," *Advocate of Peace* (May–June 1865): 263–66.

49. "New Efforts for Peace," *Advocate of Peace* (May–June 1865): 272–75.

50. "Mr. Garrison's Speech at New York," *Liberator*, January 24, 1862, p. 14; "Drafting—What Is the Duty of the Abolitionists?" *Liberator*, September 19, 1862, p. 154.

51. Garrison, *Letters*, 5: 17.

52. "What of Your Peace Principles Now?" *Liberator*, June 14, 1861, p. 94.

53. Charles K. Whipple, "New Occasions Teach New Duties," *Liberator*, May 3, 1861, p. 70.

54. Alfred H. Love, "Thoughts on the War," *Liberator*, June 7, 1861, p. 91; "Fourth of July Celebration at Framingham," *Liberator*, July 12, 1861, p. 111.

55. Garrison, *Letters*, 5: 27.

56. "What of Your Peace Principles Now" *Liberator*, June 14, 1861, p. 94.

57. Samuel J. May, "A Sermon on Our Civil War," *Liberator*, May 24, 1860, p. 84.

58. "The Trial Hour," *Liberator*, August 21, 1863, p. 135; Garrison's *Letters*, 4: 591–92; Thomas, *Liberator*, p. 422.

59. Garrison, *Letters*, 5: 107; Garrison and Garrison, *William Lloyd Garrison: The Story of His Life as Told by His Children*, 4: 80, 84.

60. "Fourth of July Celebration at Framingham," *Liberator*, July 12, 1861, p. 111.

61. "Drafting—The Hour of Trial," *Liberator* September 19, 1862, p. 150.

62. Editor's note, *Liberator*, June 28, 1861, p. 106; "Does the Constitution Provide for Secession?" *Liberator*, July 19, 1861, p. 114; "Southern Secessionists and Northern Disunionists," *Liberator*, April 19, 1861, p. 62. See also Samuel J.

May, "Letter from Samuel J. May," *Liberator*, May 29, 1863, p. 85. May argued that "The grand doctrine of the Declaration of Independence is not a 'mere rhetorical flourish', a 'glittering generality'. It is a gospel truth; an eternal principle of the righteousness of God; and we are required, in the providence of Him who ruleth over all, to conduct a civil government *based upon that principle.* We cannot throw off or evade the obligation."

63. Garrison, *Letters*, 5: 164.

64. "The London Herald of Peace and the War in America," *Liberator*, June 21, 1861, p. 98; Garrison, *Letters*, 5: 221–223. See also Charles K. Whipple, "Correspondence with an Englishman," *Liberator*, August 28, 1863, p. 140.

65. "Secession and the War," *Liberator*, August 23, 1861, p. 134.

66. Charles K. Whipple, "Correspondence with an Englishman," *Liberator*, August 28, 1863, p. 140.

67. Abraham Lincoln, "Second Inaugural Address," in *God's New Israel*, p. 196.

68. Henry C. Wright, "Letter from Henry C. Wright," *Liberator*, November 7, 1862, p. 178.

69. Henry C. Wright, "Letter from Henry C. Wright," *Liberator*, April 24, 1863, p. 68.

70. See, for example, Alfred H. Love, "Moral Forces. No. I," *Liberator*, June 5, 1863, and "Moral Forces. No. II," *Liberator*, June 19, 1863.

71. E. H. Heywood, "The War Method of Peace," *Liberator*, July 17, 1863, p. 116.

72. "Mr. Heywood's Address," *Liberator*, July 31, 1863, p. 124.

73. "Mr. Heywood's Address," *Liberator*, July 31, 1863, p. 122.

74. Garrison, *Letters*, 5: 164.

75. "The War in America," *Liberator*, November 28, 1862, p. 192; "The Peace Society and the American Question," *Liberator*, November 7, 1862, p. 180; "Peace and Anti-Slavery in America," *Liberator*, August 30, 1861, p. 140.

76. "The Abolitionists and the War," *Liberator*, June 28, 1861, p. 102.

77. Charles K. Whipple, "Correspondence with an Englishman," *Liberator*, August 28, 1863, p. 140.

78. Ibid.

79. Ibid.

80. Henry Richard, "Correspondence with an Englishman," *Liberator*, August 28, 1863, p. 140.

81. "The New England Anti-Slavery Convention," *Liberator*, June 4, 1858, p. 90.

82. Lydia Maria Child, *The Collected Correspondence of Lydia Maria Child*, July 26, 1861.

83. "The Spirit of the South," *Liberator*, August 25, 1865, p. 134; Charles K. Whipple, "The Nation's Need," *Liberator*, June 10, 1864, p. 95.

84. "Fourth of July Celebration at Framingham," *Liberator*, July 12, 1861, p. 111.

85. William Lloyd Garrison, "Mr. Garrison's Speech at New York," *Liberator*, January 24, 1862.

86. "Reconstruction," *Liberator*, December 2, 1864, p. 194; Garrison, *Letters*, 5: 382. See also Henry C. Wright, "Letter from Henry C. Wright," *Liberator*, December 15, 1865, p. 200.

87. Charles K. Whipple, "More Light on the Situation," *Liberator,* September 1, 1865, p. 138.

88. Child, *Collected Correspondence,* May 8, 1868.

89. Garrison, *Letters,* 5: 383.

90. Garrison and Garrison, *William Lloyd Garrison: The Story of His Life as Told by His Children,* 4: 180.

91. Joshua P. Blanchard, "Separation," *Liberator,* February 24, 1865, p. 32, and "Political Liberty," *Liberator,* August 18, 1865, pp. 130–31; E. H. Heywood, "The Law of Liberty," *Liberator,* March 17, 1865, p. 44; "The Spirit of the South," *Liberator,* August 25, 1865, p. 134.

92. Many other Northerners agreed that the war was an apocalyptic struggle between good and evil. As Ernest Tuveson asserted in an incisive discussion, Julia Ward Howe captured that mood for the nation when she borrowed images from the Book of Revelation to write "The Battle Hymn of the Republic." The "coming of the Lord" was an allegory for the millennial triumph of Christian principles, and its "glory" was "the wonder and terror of the transition to the millennium." The "grapes of wrath" recalled Revelation 14:19, where the angel of God ordered the figure "like the Son of man" to gather with his sickle the grapes of the demonic Babylon and crush them in the "great winepress of the wrath of God." As Babylon fell and the reign of the Antichrist ended, the faithful shouted, "Aleluja; Salvation, and glory, and honour, and power, unto the Lord our God"—or, as Julia Ward Howe wrote it, "Glory, Glory, Hallelujah." The "terrible swift sword" recalled the horseman of Revelation 19. His name was the Word of God, and he wore clothes dipped in blood, while "out of his mouth goeth a sharp sword, that with it he should smite the nations." And so God was "sifting out the hearts of men" as the judgment preparatory to the dawn of the millennium. Thus, true believers would exhort, "Be swift, my soul, to answer him! be jubilant my feet!" (Ernest Lee Tuveson, *Redeemer Nation: The Idea of America's Millennial Role* [Chicago: University of Chicago Press; Midway reprint, 1980], pp. 197–202.)

93. Kelman, "Violence without Moral Restraint: Reflections on the Dehumanization of Victims and Victimizers," in George Kren and Leon Rappoport, eds., *Varieties of Psychohistory* (New York: Springer, 1976), pp. 290–91, 301–4.

94. Garrison, *Letters,* 2: 324–25.

95. Charles Sumner, *The Rebellion—Its Origin and Main Spring* (New York: Young Men's Republican Union, 1861), p. 14.

6. Conclusion

1. Friedman, *Gregarious Saints,* pp. 218–22.

2. "Peace Question before Massachusetts Ministers," *Advocate of Peace* (July–August 1866): 293–94.

3. "The Abolitionists and the War," *Liberator,* June 28, 1861, p. 102.

BIBLIOGRAPHY

A. Primary Sources

Archival and Manuscript Sources

Elihu Burritt Letter File. Library of Congress, Washington, D.C.

Child, Lydia Maria. *The Collected Correspondence of Lydia Maria Child.* Collected by Patricia Holland and Milton Meltzer. Millwood, N.Y.: KTO Microform, 1979.

The Elliott Coues Papers. Madison, Wisc.: State Historical Society of Wisconsin, 1971.

Holland, Frederick West. "The History of the Peace-Cause." Boston Public Library Archives.

William Ladd Letter File. Library of Congress Archives, Washington, D.C.

Minutes of the New York Peace Society, 1825–1828. Library of Congress Archives, Washington, D.C.

Records of the American Peace Society. Library of Congress Archives, Washington, D.C.

Henry Clarke Wright Scrapbooks. Boston Public Library Archives.

Newspapers and Journals

Advocate of Peace (Boston).

Advocate of Peace and Christian Patriot (Philadelphia).

Advocate of Peace and Universal Brotherhood (Worcester, Mass.).

American Advocate of Peace (Hartford, Conn.).

Bibliotheca Sacra (New York).

Calumet (New York).

Christian Examiner and General Review (Boston and London).

Christian Monitor and Common People's Adviser (Brooklyn, Conn.).

Christian Spectator (New Haven, Conn.).

Citizen of the World (Philadelphia).

Friend (Philadelphia).

Friend of Peace (Boston).

Harbinger of Peace (New York).

Herald of Freedom (Concord, N.H.).

Herald of Peace (London).

Liberator (Boston).

Liberty Bell (Boston).

Methodist Magazine (New York).

Methodist Quarterly Review (New York).

Military Magazine; and Record of the Volunteers of the City and County of Philadelphia (Philadelphia).

Moral Advocate, a Monthly Publication on War, Duelling, Capital Punishments, and Prison Discipline (Mt. Pleasant, Ohio).

National Anti-Slavery Standard (Boston).
New York Observer (New York).
Non-Resistant (Boston).
Oberlin Evangelist (Oberlin, Ohio).
Oberlin Quarterly Review (Oberlin, Ohio).
Peacemaker (Philadelphia).
Practical Christian (Hopedale, Mass.).
Quarterly Christian Spectator (New Haven, Conn., and New York).
Quarterly Review (Louisville).
Southern Quarterly Review (New Orleans and Charleston, S.C.).
Voice of Peace (Philadelphia).
Western Messenger: Devoted to Religion and Literature (Cincinnati).

Books, Pamphlets, and Articles

Alcott, Bronson. *The Journals of Bronson Alcott.* Edited by Odell Shepard. Port
    Washington, N.Y.: Kennikat Press, 1966.
————. *The Letters of A. Bronson Alcott.* Edited by Richard L. Hernnstadt. Ames:
    Iowa State University Press, 1969.
American Peace Society. *The Book of Peace.* Boston: George C. Beckwith, 1845.
————. *Peace Tracts.* Bound volume in the Library of Congress, n.d.
————. *Prize Essays on a Congress of Nations.* Boston: Whipple & Damrell, 1840.
Ballou, Adin. *Autobiography of Adin Ballou.* Completed and edited by his son-in-
    law, William S. Heywood. Lowell, Mass.: Vox Populi Press, Thompson &
    Hill, 1896. American Utopian Adventure, series 2. Philadelphia: Por-
    cupine Press, 1975.
————. *Christian Non-Resistance in All Its Important Bearings.* With an appendix by
    William S. Heywood. Philadelphia: Universal Peace Union, 1910; reprint
    edition, New York: Da Capo Press, 1970.
————. *History of the Hopedale Community.* Edited by William S. Heywood.
    Lowell, Mass.: Vox Populi Press, Thompson & Hill, 1897.
————. *Non-Resistance in Relation to Human Governments.* Boston: Non-Resistance
    Society, 1839.
————. *Practical Christian Socialism: A Conversational Exposition of the True System of
    Human Society.* Hopedale, Mass.: Adin Ballou; New York: Fowlers and
    Wells, 1854.
————. *Primitive Christianity and Its Corruptions.* Edited by William S. Heywood.
    3 vols. Lowell, Mass.: Vox Populi Press, Thompson & Hill, 1899.
————. *The Scriptural Doctrine of the Second Advent: An Effectual Antidote to Mill-
    erism, and All Other Kindred Errors.* Milford, Mass.: Community Press
    (Hopedale), 1843.
Beckwith, George. *The Book of Peace: A Collection of Essays on War and Peace.*
    Boston: George C. Beckwith, 1845. Facsimile reprint, Peace Movement in
    America, Jerome Ozer, 1972.
————. *Claims of Peace on Christians.* American Peace Society, n.d.
————. *The Peace Manual; or, War and Its Remedies.* Boston: American Peace
    Society, 1847.
————. *The Peace Manual, or War and Its Remedies.* Boston: 1848. With a new
    introduction by Alice Kessler Harris. Garland Library of War and Peace.
    New York: London: Garland Publishing, 1971.

———. *Safety of Pacific Principles*. American Peace Society, n.d.

Blanchard, J. P. *Communication on Peace. Written for the Christian Citizen*. Boston: C. P. Moody, 1848.

———. "League of Universal Brotherhood." *Christian Examiner and Religious Miscellany* 44 (May 1848): 356–67.

———. *Principles of the Revolution: Showing the Perversion of Them and the Consequent Failure of Their Accomplishment*. Boston: Damrell and Moore, 1855.

Burritt, Elihu. *Lectures and Speeches*. London: Sampson Low, Son, and Marston, 1869.

———. *Ten-Minute Talks on All Sorts of Topics*. With an autobiography by the author. Boston: Lee and Shepard, 1874.

———. *Thoughts and Things at Home and Abroad*. With a memoir by Mary Howett. Boston: Phillips, Sampson, and Company, 1854.

———. *The Works of Elihu Burritt*, London: Charles Gilpin, 1848.

C. H. "Non-Resistance." *Christian Examiner and Religious Miscellany* 41 (January 1848): 86–113.

Channing, William Ellery. *Discourses on War*. Boston: Ginn & Company, 1903.

Cherry, Conrad, ed. *God's New Israel: Religious Interpretations of American Destiny*. Englewood Cliffs, N.J.: Prentice-Hall, 1971.

Child, Lydia Maria. *Correspondence between Lydia Maria Child and Gov. Wise and Mrs. Mason*. Boston: American Anti-Slavery Society, 1860.

———. *Lydia Maria Child. Selected Letters. 1817–1880*. Edited by Milton Meltzer and Patricia Holland. Amherst: University of Massachusetts Press, 1982.

Collier, Rev. Joseph A. *The Right Way; or, the Gospel Applied to the Intercourse of Individuals and Nations*. New York: American Tract Society, 1854.

Commager, Henry Steele, ed. *Theodore Parker: An Anthology*. Boston: Beacon Press, 1960.

Coues, Samuel E. *United States Navy: What Is its Use?* American Peace Society, n.d.

———. *War and Christianity: An Address before the American Peace Society, on the Fourteenth Anniversary in Boston, Mass., May 23, 1842*. Boston: American Peace Society, 1842.

Curti, Merle. *The Learned Blacksmith: The Letters and Journals of Elihu Burritt*. Garland Library of War and Peace. New York: Garland Publishing, 1971.

Dawes, Thomas. *Address to the Massachusetts Peace Society, at Their Second Anniversary, Dec. 25, 1817*. Boston: Massachusetts Peace Society, 1818.

Dodge, David Low. *Memorial of Mr. David L. Dodge, Consisting of an Autobiography, Prepared at the Request of His Children: with a Few Selections from His Writings*. Boston: S. K. Whipple & Co., 1854.

———. *Remarks upon an Anonymous Letter, Styled, "The Duty of a Christian in a Trying Situation," Addressed to the Author of a Pamphlet, Entitled, "The Mediator's Kingdom Not of This World," etc.* New York: Williams & Whiting, 1810.

———. *War Inconsistent with the Religion of Jesus Christ* and *The Mediator's Kingdom Not of This World: But Spiritual*. Boston: Ginn & Company, 1905. Facsimile reprint, Peace Movement in America, Jerome Ozer, 1972.

Dodge, William E. *Memorial of William E. Dodge*. Edited by D. Stuart Dodge. New York: Anson D. F. Randolph and Company, 1887.

Dresser, Amos. *The Bible against War*. Oberlin, Ohio: for the author, 1849.

Dymond, Jonathan. *Causes of War*. American Peace Society, n.d.

————. *Efficacy of Pacific Principles.* American Peace Society, n.d.

————. *An Inquiry into the Accordancy of War with the Principles of Christianity.* With notes by Thomas Smith Grimke. Philadelphia: I. Asmead and Company, 1834.

————. *An Inquiry into the Accordancy of War with the Principles of Christianity, and an Examination of the Philosophical Reasoning by Which It Is Defended.* Philadelphia: Uriah Hunt and Son, n.d.

————. *Moral Results of War.* American Peace Society, n.d.

————. *Rights of Self-Defence.* American Peace Society, n.d.

Ebenstein, William, ed. *Great Political Thinkers: Plato to the Present.* New York: Holt, Rinehart and Winston, 1969.

Faust, Clarence H., and Thomas H. Johnson, eds. *Jonathan Edwards: Selections.* American Century Series, rev. ed. New York: Hill and Wang, 1962.

Faust, Drew Gilpin, ed. *The Ideology of Slavery: Proslavery Thought in the Antebellum South.* Baton Rouge: Louisiana State University Press, 1981.

Ferm, Robert L., ed. *Issues in American Protestantism: A Documentary History from the Puritans to the Present.* Gloucester, Mass.: Peter Smith, 1983.

Fitzhugh, George. *Sociology for the South, or the Failure of Free Society.* Richmond, Va.: A. Morris, 1854.

Gannett, E. S. "The Cause of Peace." *Christian Examiner and Religious Miscellany* 41 (September 1846): 173–92.

Garrison, Wendell Phillips, and Francis Jackson Garrison. *William Lloyd Garrison, 1805–1879: The Story of His Life, Told by His Children.* Vols. 1–4. New York: Century Company, 1885; reprint ed., New York: Negro Universities Press, 1969.

Garrison, William Lloyd. *The Letters of William Lloyd Garrison.* Edited by Walter M. Merrill and Louis Ruchames. Vols. 1–4. Cambridge, Mass.: Belknap Press of Harvard University Press, 1971.

Gibbes, George M. *A Letter to the American Peace Society, from a Member of Committee of Peace in Paris.* Paris: 1842.

Goen, C. C., ed. *The Great Awakening.* Vol. 4 of *Works of Jonathan Edwards.* New Haven: Yale University Press, 1972.

Grimke, Thomas S. *Address on the Truth, Dignity, Power and Beauty of the Principles of Peace, and on the Unchristian Character of War and the Warrior.* Hartford, Conn.: George F. Olmstead, 1832.

————. *To the People of the State of South Carolina.* n.p., n.d.

Hancock, Thomas. *The Principles of Peace Exemplified in the Conduct of the Society of Friends in Ireland: During the Rebellion of the Year 1798, with Some Preliminary and Concluding Observations.* American Peace Society, n.d.

Hemmenway, John. *The Apostle of Peace: Memoir of William Ladd.* Boston, 1872. Facsimile reprint, Peace Movement in America, Jerome Ozer, 1972.

Henry, C. S. "A Discourse Pronounced before the Hartford County Peace Society, December 25, 1833." *Principles and Prospects of the Friends of Peace.* Hartford, Conn.: J. Hubbard Wells, 1834.

Hickok, Rev. Laurens P. *The Sources of Military Delusion, and the Practicability of Their Removal.* Hartford: Connecticut Peace Society, 1833.

Jackson, John. *Reflections on Peace and War.* Philadelphia: T. E. Chapman, 1846.

Jay, William. *Inefficacy of War, or the Sword a Suicidal Resort.* American Peace Society, n.d.

————. *The Kossuth Excitement: A Letter from the Hon. William Jay, President of the American Peace Society.* Boston: American Peace Society, 1852.

————. *A Review of the Causes and Consequences of the Mexican War.* 2nd ed. Boston: 1849. Anti-Slavery Crusade in America. New York: Arno Press, 1969.

————. *War and Peace: The Evils of the First and a Plan for Preserving the Last.* Reprinted from the original 1842 edition with an introductory note by James Brown Scott. New York: Oxford University Press, 1919.

Judd, Sylvester. *A Moral Review of the Revolutionary War, or Some of the Evils of that Event Considered.* Hollowell, Maine: 1842. Facsimile reprint, Peace Movement in America, Jerome Ozer, 1972.

Ladd, William. *Address Delivered at the Tenth Anniversary of the Massachusetts Peace Society, December 25, 1825.* Boston: 1826.

Ladd, William [Philanthropos]. *A Brief Illustration of the Principles of War and Peace, Showing the Ruinous Folly of the Former, and the Superior Efficacy of the Latter, for National Protection and Defense.* Albany, N.Y.: 1831.

Ladd, William. *An Essay on a Congress of Nations.* With an introduction by James Brown Scott. Reprint of 1840 edition. New York: Oxford University Press, 1916.

————. *The Essays of Philanthropos on Peace and War.* Garland Library of War and Peace. New York: Garland Publishing, 1971.

————. *The Hero of Macedon, or History of Alexander the Great, Viewed in Light of the Gospel.* Boston: James Loring, 1832.

————. *Letters from an American.* London: Thomas Ward and Company, n.d.

Ladd, William [Philanthropos]. *On the Duty of Females to Promote the Cause of Peace.* Boston: American Peace Society, 1836. Garland Library of War and Peace. New York: Garland Publishing, 1971.

Leland, John. *The Writings of the Late Elder John Ireland.* Originally collected by Miss L. F. Greene. New York: 1845. New ed., New York: Arno Press, 1969.

Leopold, Richard W.; Link, Arthur S.; and Coben, Stanley, eds. *Problems in American History.* Vol. 1, 3rd ed. Englewood Cliffs, New Jersey: Prentice-Hall, 1967.

Love, Alfred H. *A Brief Synopsis of Work Proposed, Aided and Accomplished by the Universal Peace Union during the Last 31 Years (From 1866 to 1897) under the Direction of Its President, Alfred H. Love, of Philadelphia.* n.p., n.d.

————. *An Appeal in Vindication of Peace Principles, and against Resistance by Force of Arms.* Philadelphia: Maas and Vogdes, 1862.

Lovejoy, Joseph C., and Lovejoy, Owen. *Memoir of the Rev. Elijah P. Lovejoy.* Mass Violence in America. New York: Arno Press, 1969.

McLeod, Alexander. *A Scriptural View of the Character, Causes, and Ends of the Present War.* New York: n.p., 1815.

Mahan, Asa. *The Baptism of the Holy Ghost.* New York: George Hughes & Co., n.d.

————. *A Critical History of the Late American War.* With an introductory letter by Lieut.-General M. W. Smith. New York: A. S. Barnes & Co., 1877.

————. *Out of Darkness into Light; or, the Hidden Light Made Manifest.* Willard Tract Repository, 1876.

May, Samuel J. *Memoir of Samuel Joseph May.* Thomas J. Mumford, ed. Boston: Fields, Osgood, & Co., 1869.

————. *Some Recollections of Our Anti-Slavery Conflict*. Boston: Fields, Osgood, & Co., 1869.

"Memoirs of Worcester." *Christian Examiner and Religious Miscellany* 37 (November 1844): 371–80.

Minutes of the General Assembly of the Presbyterian Church in the United States of America from Its Organization A.D. 1789 to A.D. 1820 Inclusive. Philadelphia: Presbyterian Board of Publication, n.d.

Minutes of the General Assembly of the Presbyterian Church in the United States of America from its Organization A.D. 1821 to A.D. 1835 Inclusive. Philadelphia: Presbyterian Board of Publication, n.d.

Minutes of the General Assembly of the Presbyterian Church in the United States of America, with an Appendix, 1836–1841. Philadelphia: Stated Clerk of the Assembly, n.d.

Minutes of the General Assembly of the Presbyterian Church in the United States of America, 1842–1846. Philadelphia: Stated Clerk of the Assembly, n.d.

Minutes of the General Assembly of the Presbyterian Church in the United States of America, 1845–1849. Philadelphia: Stated Clerk of the Assembly, n.d.

Mott, Lucretia. *Lucretia Mott: Her Complete Speeches and Sermons*. Edited by Dana Greene. New York: Edwin Mellon Press, 1980.

Neckar on Peace. American Peace Society, n.d.

Noyes, John H. *The Berean: A Manual for the Help of Those Who Seek the Faith of the Primitive Church*. Putney, Vt.: Office of the Spiritual Magazine, 1847.

Obstacles and Objections to the Cause of Permanent and Universal Peace Considered, by a Layman. Boston: D. K. Hitchcock, 1837.

Paley, William. *The Principles of Moral and Political Philosophy*. British Philosophers and Theologians of the Seventeenth and Eighteenth Centuries. Rene Wellek, ed. New York: Garland Publishing, 1978.

Parker, Theodore. *Speeches, Addresses, and Occasional Sermons*. Vol. 1. Boston: Horace B. Fuller, 1871.

Peabody, Andrew P. *A Manual of Moral Philosophy Designed for Colleges and High Schools*. New York: American Book Company, 1873.

"Peace and War." *The United States Magazine and Democratic Review* (March 1839): 288–308.

Pease, William H., and Pease, Jane H., eds. *The Antislavery Argument*. Indianapolis: Bobbs-Merrill, 1965.

Peterson, Charles J. *The Military Heroes of the War of 1812; With a Narrative of the War*. 5th ed. Philadelphia: William A. Leary and Co., 1849.

————. *The Military Heroes of the War with Mexico: With a Narrative of the War*. 5th ed. Philadelphia: William A. Leary and Co., 1849.

The Question of War Reviewed. Tract number 3. New York: New York Peace Society, 1818.

Ramsey, Paul, ed. *Ethical Writings*. Vol. 8 of *Works of Jonathan Edwards*. New Haven: Yale University Press, 1989.

Read, Hollis. *The Hand of God in History; or, Divine Providence Historically Illustrated in the Extension and Establishment of Christianity*. Hartford, Conn.: H. Huntington, 1849.

Smith, H. Shelton; Handy, Robert T.; Loetscher, Lefferts A., eds., *American Christianity: An Historical Interpretation with Representative Documents*. Vol. 2. New York: Charles Scribner's Sons, 1963.

Smyth, Thomas. *The Sin and the Curse; Or, the Union, The True Source of Disunion, and our Duty in the Present Crisis.* Charleston, S.C.: Evans and Cogswell, 1860.

Society of Friends. *An Address on Peace.* n.p., New England Yearly Meeting, 1854.

Stein, Stephen J., ed. *Apocalyptic Writings.* Vol. 5 of *Works of Jonathan Edwards.* New Haven: Yale University Press, 1972.

Stone, Rev. Thomas T. *Sermons on War.* Boston: Peirce and Williams, 1829.

Sumner, Charles. *The Rebellion—Its Origin and Main Spring.* New York: Young Men's Republican Union, 1861.

———. *The True Grandeur of Nations.* Boston: William D. Ticknor and Company, 1845.

Upham, Thomas C. *The Manual of Peace; Exhibiting the Evils and Remedies of War.* Boston: American Peace Society, 1842.

———. *The Manual of Peace; Exhibiting the Evils and Remedies of War.* New York: Jerome S. Ozer, 1972.

Walker, Amasa. *Le Monde; or, in Time of Peace, Prepare for War.* American Peace Society, n.d.

War-Debts. American Peace Society, n.d.

"War in its Democratic and Economic Relations." *New Englander* 4 (July 1846): 368–80.

War Taxation: Consequent Diminution of National Wealth. American Peace Society, n.d.

Ware, Henry. *Memoirs of the Rev. Noah Worcester, D.D.* With a preface, notes, and a concluding chapter by Samuel Worcester. Boston: James Munroe and Company, 1844. Facsimile reprint, Peace Movement in America, Jerome Ozer, 1972.

Waste of Property by War. American Peace Society, n.d.

Wayland, Francis. *The Elements of Moral Science.* Boston: Gould, Kendall and Lincoln, 1835.

———. *The Elements of Moral Science.* 3rd ed. Boston: Gould, Kendall and Lincoln, 1836.

———. *The Elements of Moral Science.* 4th ed. Boston: Gould and Lincoln, 1856.

———. *The Elements of Moral Science.* Rev. and improved ed. Boston: Gould and Lincoln, 1865.

———. *The Elements of Political Economy.* 3rd ed. Boston: Gould and Lincoln, 1867.

———. *Sermons Delivered in the Chapel of Brown University.* Boston: Gould, Kendall and Lincoln, 1849.

Wayland, Francis, and Wayland, H. L. *A Memoir of the Life and Labors of Francis Wayland, D.D., LL.D.* Vols. 1 & 2. New York: Sheldon and Company, 1867. Reprinted by New York: Arno Press, 1972.

Weinstein, Allen, and Gatell, Frank Otto, eds. *American Negro Slavery: A Modern Reader.* New York: Oxford University Press, 1968.

Whelpley, Samuel [Philadelphus]. *Letters Addressed to Caleb Strong, Esq. Late Governor of Massachusetts: Showing War to Be Inconsistent with the Laws of Christ and the Good of Mankind.* Glasgow, 1819.

Whipple, Charles K. *Non-Resistance Applied to the Internal Defense of a Community.* Boston: R. F. Wallcut, 1860.

Williams, William R. *Miscellanies.* New York: Edward H. Fletcher, 1850.

Wilson, John F., transcriber and ed. *A History of the Work of Redemption.* Vol. 9 of *Works of Jonathan Edwards.* New Haven: Yale University Press, 1989.

Witnesses for Peace. American Peace Society, n.d.

Worcester, Noah. *Bible News of the Father, Son, and Holy Spirit.* Concord, N.H.: n.p. 1810.

———. *A Circular Letter from the Massachusetts Peace Society, Respectfully Addressed to the Various Associations, Presbyteries, Assemblies and Meetings of the Ministers of Religion in the United States.* Cambridge, Mass.: Hilliard and Metcalf, 1816.

———. *Circular Letter in Behalf of the Massachusetts Peace Society to the Friends of Peace of All Denominations.* Boston: John Eliot, 1817.

Worcester, Noah [Philo Pacificus]. *A Solemn Review of the Custom of War: Showing That War Is the Effect of Popular Delusion and Proposing a Remedy.* Boston: S. G. Simpkins, 1833. Facsimile reprint, Peace Movement in America, Jerome Ozer, 1972.

Wright, Henry Clarke. *Anthropology: or, the Science of Man; in Its Bearing on War and Slavery.* Cincinnati: E. Shepard, 1850.

———. *Dick Crowningshield, the Assassin, and Zachary Taylor, the Soldier: The Difference between Them.* Hopedale, Mass.: Non-Resistant and Practical Christian Office, 1848.

———. *Man-Killing, by Individuals and Nations, Wrong—Dangerous in All Cases.* Boston: 1841.

———. *The Self-Abnegationist, or the True King and Queen.* Boston: Bela Marsh, 1863.

Yoder, John Howard, ed. *The Schleitheim Confession.* Scottdale, Pa.: Herald Press, 1973.

B. Secondary Sources

Abzug, Robert H. *Passionate Liberator: Theodore Dwight Weld and the Dilemma of Reform.* New York: Oxford University Press, 1980.

Albrecht, Robert C. *Theodore Parker.* Twayne's United States Authors. Sylvia E. Bowman, ed. New York: Twayne Publishers, 1971.

Allen, Devere. *The Fight for Peace.* New York: Macmillan, 1930. Facsimile reprint, Peace Movement in America, Jerome S. Ozer, 1972.

Bainton, Roland H. *Christian Attitudes toward War and Peace.* Nashville: Abingdon Press, 1960.

Banner, Lois W. "Religious Benevolence as Social Control: A Critique of an Interpretation." *Journal of American History* 60 (1973): 23–41.

Barnes, Gilbert Hobbs. *The Antislavery Impulse, 1830–1844.* Gloucester, Mass.: Peter Smith, 1957.

Bartlett, Irving H. "New Light on Wendell Phillips: The Community of Reform, 1840–1880." *Perspectives in American History* 12 (1979): 1–57.

Beales, Arthur C. F. *A History of Peace: A Short Account of the Organized Movement for International Peace.* New York: Dial Press, 1931.

———. *A History of Peace: A Short Account of the Organized Movement for International Peace.* With a new introduction by Charles Chatfield. Garland Library of War and Peace. New York: Garland Publishing, 1971.

Beaman, Jay. "Pacifism and the World View of Early Pentecostalism." Presented to the Society for Pentecostal Studies. Cleveland, Tennessee. November 1983.

Bodo, John R. *The Protestant Clergy and Public Issues, 1812–1848.* Princeton: Princeton University Press, 1954.

Bolt, Christina, and Drescher, Seymour, eds. *Anti-Slavery, Religion, and Reform: Essays in Memory of Roger Anstey.* Kent, England: William Dawson & Sons; Hamden, Conn: Shoestring, 1980.

Booth, Ken, and Wright, Moorhead, eds. *American Thinking about Peace and War.* Sussex: Harvester Press; New York: Barnes and Noble, 1978.

Brock, Peter. *Pacifism in the United States from the Colonial Era to the First World War.* Princeton: Princeton University Press, 1968.

———. *Radical Pacifists in Antebellum America.* Princeton: Princeton University Press, 1968.

Brugger, Robert J., ed. *Our Selves/Our Past: Psychological Approaches to American History.* Baltimore: The Johns Hopkins University Press, 1981.

Chatfield, Charles, ed. *Peace Movements in America.* New York: Schrocken Books. 1973.

Clarkson, Jesse D., and Cochran, Thomas C., eds. *War as a Social Institution: The Historian's Perspective.* New York: Columbia University Press, 1941.

Cole, Charles C., Jr. *The Social Ideas of the Northern Evangelists.* New York: Columbia University Press, 1954.

Commager, Henry Steele. *Theodore Parker.* Boston: Beacon Press, 1947.

Connor, Seymour V. "Attitudes and Opinions about the Mexican War, 1846–1970." *Journal of the West* 11 (April 1972): 361–66.

Corey, Albert B. *The Crisis of 1830–1842 in Canadian–American Relations.* For the Carnegie Endowment for International Peace. New Haven: Yale University Press; Toronto: Ryerson Press; London: Oxford University Press, 1941.

Cross, Whitney. *The Burned-Over-District: The Social and Intellectual History of Enthusiastic Religion in Western New York, 1800–1850.* New York: Harper Torchbooks, Harper & Row, 1965.

Curti, Merle, *The American Peace Crusade, 1815–1860.* New York: Octagon Books, 1965.

———. "Non-Resistance in New England." *New England Quarterly* 2 (1929): 34–57.

———. *Peace or War: The American Struggle, 1636–1936.* New York: W. W. Norton, 1936.

Dayton, Donald W. "The American Holiness Movement: A Bibliographical Introduction." *Summary of Proceedings.* Twenty-fifth Annual Conference, American Library Association. June 14–18, 1973, Pasadena College, Pasadena, California: 71–97.

———. *Discovering an Evangelical Heritage.* New York: Harper & Row, 1976.

———. "The Holiness Churches: A Significant Ethical Tradition." *Christian Century* 92 (February 26, 1975): 197–201.

———. "Piety and Radicalism: Ante-Bellum Social Evangelicalism in the United States." *Radical Religion* 3 (1976): 36–40.

Dayton, Donald, and Dayton, Lucille S. "An Historical Survey of Attitudes toward War and Peace within the American Holiness Movement." Seminar on Christian Holiness and the Issues of War and Peace. Winona Lake, Indiana. June 7–9, 1973.

DeBenedetti, Charles. *The Peace Reform in American History.* Bloomington: Indiana University Press, 1980.

Demos, John. "The Antislavery Movement and the Problem of Violent 'Means.'" *New England Quarterly* 37 (December 1964): 501–26.

Dillon, Merton L. *Elijah P. Lovejoy, Abolitionist Editor.* Urbana: University of Illinois Press, 1961.

Dodd, W. E. "Investigation in American History." *American Historical Review* 18 (April 1913): 522–36.

Donald, David. *Charles Sumner and the Coming of the Civil War.* New York: Alfred A. Knopf, 1960.

————. *Lincoln Reconsidered.* New York: Alfred A. Knopf, 1956.

Elkins, Stanley. *Slavery: A Problem in American Institutional and Intellectual Life.* Chicago: University of Chicago Press, 1958.

Ellsworth, Clayton S. "American Churches and the Mexican War." *American Historical Review* 45 (January 1940): 301–26.

Fletcher, Robert Samuel. *A History of Oberlin College from Its Foundation through the Civil War.* 2 vols. Series 2, *American Education: Its Men, Ideas, and Institutions.* New York: Arno Press, 1971.

Foner, Eric. *Free Soil, Free Labor, Free Men: The Ideology of the Republican Party before the Civil War.* New York: Oxford University Press, 1970.

Forman, Sidney. *West Point: A History of the United States Military Academy.* New York: Columbia University Press, 1950.

Foster, Charles I. *An Errand of Mercy: The Evangelical United Front, 1790–1837.* Chapel Hill: University of North Carolina Press, 1960.

Fraser, James W. *Pedagogue for God's Kingdom: Lyman Beecher and the Second Great Awakening* Lanham, Md.: University Press of America, 1985.

Friedman, Lawrence J. *Gregarious Saints: Self and Community in American Abolitionism, 1830–1870.* Cambridge: Cambridge University Press, 1982.

Galpin, W. Freeman. *Pioneering for Peace: A Study of American Peace Efforts to 1846.* Syracuse: Bardeen Press, 1933.

Gardella, Peter. *Innocent Ecstasy: How Christianity Gave America an Ethic of Sexual Pleasure.* New York: Oxford University Press, 1985.

Gedell, Madelon. *The Alcotts: Biography of a Family.* New York: Clarkson N. Potter, 1980.

Gordon-McCutchan, R. C. "The Irony of Evangelical History." *Journal for the Scientific Study of Religion* 20 (1981): 309–26.

Graebner, Norman A. "Lessons of the Mexican War." *Pacific Historical Review* 47 (May 1978): 325–42.

Grevens, Philip. *The Protestant Temperament: Patterns of Child-Rearing, Religious Experience, and the Self in Early America.* New American Library. New York: Meridian Books, 1977.

Gribbin, William. *The Churches Militant: The War of 1812 and American Religion.* New Haven: Yale University Press, 1972.

Hamlin, Charles Hunter. *The War Myth in United States History.* New York: Vanguard Press, 1927.

Hammond, John L. *The Politics of Benevolence: Revival Religion and American Voting Behavior.* Norwood, N.J.: Ablex Publishing, 1979.

———. "Revivals, Consensus, and a Political Culture." *Journal of the American Academy of Religion* 46 (September 1978): 293–314.

Hardesty, Nancy. *Women Called to Witness.* Nashville: Abingdon Press, 1984.

Harlow, Ralph Volney. *Gerrit Smith: Philanthropist and Reformer.* New York: Russell & Russell, 1972.

Hatch, Nathan O., and Noll, Mark A., eds. *The Bible in America: Essays in Cultural History.* New York: Oxford University Press, 1982.

Haun, Cheryl. "The Whig Abolitionists' Attitude toward the Mexican War." *Journal of the West* 47 (May 1978): 260–72.

Hershberger, Guy F. "Some Religious Pacifists of the Nineteenth Century." *Mennonite Quarterly Review* 10 (January 1936): 76–86.

———. *War, Peace, and Nonresistance.* Scottdale, Pa.: Herald Press, 1944.

Hinckley, Ted C. "American Anti-Catholicism during the Mexican War." *Pacific Historical Review* 31 (May 1962): 121–37.

Hoblitzer, Harrison. *The War against War in the Nineteenth Century: A Study of the Western Background of Gandhian Thought.* Ph.D. dissertation, Columbia University, 1959.

Holifield, E. Brooks. *The Gentlemen Theologians: American Theology in Southern Culture, 1795–1860.* Durham, N.C.: Duke University Press, 1978.

Hovey, Amos Arnold, *A History of the Religious Phase of the American Movement for International Peace to the Year 1914.* Ph.D. dissertation, University of Chicago, 1930.

Howlett, Charles F. and Zeitzer, Glen. *The American Peace Movement: History and Historiography.* AHA Pamphlets, number 261. Washington, D.C.: American Historical Association.

Hughes, Richard T., and Allen, C. Leonard. *Illusions of Innocence: Protestant Primitivism, 1630–1875.* Foreword by Robert Bellah. Chicago: University of Chicago Press, 1988.

Irey, Thomas R. "Soldiering, Suffering, and Dying in the Mexican War." *Journal of the West* 11 (April 1972): 285–98.

Jeffrey, Kirk. "Marriage, Career, and Feminine Ideology in Nineteenth-Century America: Reconstructing the Marital Experience of Lydia Maria Child, 1828–1874." *Feminist Studies* 2 (1975): 113–30.

Johnson, Allen, and Malone, Dumas, eds. *Dictionary of American Biography.* 21 vols. New York: Charles Scribner's Sons, 1930.

Johnson, Paul E. *A Shopkeeper's Millennium: Society and Revivals in Rochester, New York, 1815–1837.* American Century Series. New York: Hill and Wang, 1978.

Kelman, Herbert C. "Violence without Moral Restraint: Reflections on the Dehumanization of Victims and Victimizers." In *Varieties of Psychohistory,* pp. 282–314. Edited by George Kren and Leon Rappaport. New York: Springer, 1976.

Kern, Stephen. "Explosive Intimacy: Psychodynamics of the Victorian Family." *History of Childhood Quarterly: The Journal of Psychohistory* 1 (1974): 437–61.

Kraditor, Aileen. *Means and Ends in Abolitionism.* New York: Pantheon Books, 1969.

Lane, Ann J., ed. *The Debate over Slavery: Stanley Elkins and His Critics.* Urbana: University of Illinois Press, 1971.

Lawson, David Clifton. *Swords into Plowshares, Spears into Pruninghooks: The Intellectual Foundations of the First American Peace Movement, 1815–1865.* Ph.D. dissertation, University of New Mexico, 1975.

Lipsitt, Lewis P. "Comment on 'A Case of Conviction.' " *Journal of Social History* 9 (Fall 1975): 35–43.

Lynd, Staughton, ed. *Nonviolence in America: A Documentary History.* Indianapolis: Bobbs-Merrill, 1966.

Mabee, Carleton. *Black Freedom: The Nonviolent Abolitionists from 1830 through the Civil War.* London: Macmillan, 1970.

McDonald, Clyde Winfield, Jr. *The Massachusetts Peace Society, 1815–1828: A Study in Evangelical Reform.* Ph.D. dissertation, University of Maine, 1973.

McLoughlin, William G. "Evangelical Child-Rearing in the Age of Jackson: Francis Wayland's View on When and How to Subdue the Willfulness of Children." *Journal of Social History* 9 (Fall 1975): 21–39.

Madden, Edward. *Civil Disobedience and Moral Law in Nineteenth-Century American Philosophy.* Seattle: University of Washington Press, 1968.

Mathews, Donald. *Religion in the Old South.* Chicago History of America. Martin E. Marty, editor. Chicago: University of Chicago Press, 1977.

———. *Slavery and Methodism: A Chapter in American Morality, 1780–1845.* Princeton: Princeton University Press, 1965.

Mayer, Peter. *The Pacifist Conscience.* New York: Holt, Reinhart and Wilson, 1966.

Mead, Edwin. *The Literature of the Peace Movement.* Boston: ca. 1900.

Meyer, D. H. *The Instructed Conscience: The Shaping of the American National Ethic.* Philadelphia: University of Pennsylvania Press, 1972.

Miller, Perry. "From the Covenant to the Revival." In *Religion in American Life.* Vol. 1, *The Shaping of American Religion,* pp. 322–68. Edited by James Ward Smith and A. Leland Jamison. Princeton: Princeton University Press, 1961.

Moorhead, James H. "Social Reform and the Divided Conscience of Antebellum Protestantism." *Church History* 48 (December 1979): 416–30.

Mulder, John M., and Wilson, John F., eds. *Religion in American History: Interpretive Essays.* Englewood Cliffs, N.J.: Prentice-Hall, 1978.

Murray, John Courtney. "Morality and Foreign Policy." *America* (March 26, 1960): 764–67.

Niebuhr, Reinhold. *Beyond Tragedy.* New York: Charles Scribner's Sons, 1937.

———. *Christian Realism and Political Problems.* New York: Charles Scribner's Sons, 1953.

———. *Christianity and Power Politics.* New York: Charles Scribner's Sons, 1940.

———. *An Interpretation of Christian Ethics.* New York: Seabury Press, 1979.

———. *Love and Justice.* Edited by D. B. Robertson. Cleveland: Meridian Books, World Publishing, 1967.

———. *Moral Man and Immoral Society.* New York: Charles Scribner's Sons, 1960.

———. *The Nature and Destiny of Man.* Vol. 2. New York: Charles Scribner's Sons, 1964.

Norton, Wesley. *Religious Newspapers in the Old Northwest to 1861: A History, Bibliography, and Record of Opinion.* Athens: Ohio University Press, 1977.

Oates, Stephen B. *To Purge This Land with Blood: A Biography of John Brown.* New York: Harper & Row, 1970.

Pease, William H., and Pease, Jane H. "Antislavery Ambivalence: Immediatism, Expediency, Race." *American Quarterly* 17 (1965): 682–95.

———. *Bound with Them in Chains: A Biographical History of the Antislavery Movement.* Contributions in American History, number 18. Westport, Conn.: Greenwood Press, 1972.

———. "Ends, Means, and Attitudes: Black–White Conflict in the Antislavery Movement." *Civil War History* 18 (1972): 117–28.

———. "Freedom and Peace: A Nineteenth-Century Dilemma." *Midwest Quarterly* 9 (October 1967): 23–40.

Perry, Lewis, and Fellman, Michael, eds. *Antislavery Reconsidered: New Perspectives on the Abolitionists.* Baton Rouge: Louisiana State University Press, 1979.

Perry, Lewis. *Radical Abolitionism: Anarchy and the Government of God in Antislavery Thought.* Ithaca, N.Y.: Cornell University Press, 1973.

———. "Versions of Anarchism in the Antislavery Movement." *American Quarterly* 20 (Winter 1968): 768–82.

Pessen, Edward. *Jacksonian America: Society, Personality, and Politics.* Rev. ed. Homewood, Ill.: Dorsey Press, 1978.

———. *Riches, Class, and Power before the Civil War.* Lexington, Mass.: D. C. Heath, 1973.

Quincy, Josiah P. "Memoir of Edmund Quincy." *Proceedings of the Massachusetts Historical Society,* 2nd series, 18 (October 1904): 401–16.

Richards, Leonard L. *"Gentleman of Property and Standing": Anti-Abolition Mobs in Jacksonian America.* New York: Oxford University Press, 1970.

Sager, Eric William. *Pacifism and the Victorians: A Social History of the English Peace Movement, 1816–1878.* Ph.D. dissertation, University of British Columbia, 1975.

Sandeen, Earnest R., ed. *The Bible and Social Reform.* The Bible in American Culture. Philadelphia: Fortress Press; Chico, Calif.: Scholars Press, 1982.

Sewell, Richard. *Ballots for Freedom: Antislavery Politics in the United States, 1837–1869.* New York: Oxford University Press, 1976.

Sibley, Mulford W. *The Political Theories of Modern Pacifism: An Analysis and Criticism.* Paullin, Theodore. *Introduction to Non-Violence.* Peace Section, American Friends Service Committee. *Pacifist Living—Today and Tomorrow.* With a new introduction by Mulford W. Sibley. Garland Library of War and Peace. New York: Garland Publishing, 1972.

Silberner, Edmund. *The Problem of War in Nineteenth-Century Economic Thought.* Translated by Alexander H. Knappe, with an introduction by Dennis Sherman. Garland Library of War and Peace. New York: Garland Publishing, 1972.

Smith, Timothy L. *Revivalism and Social Reform in Mid-Nineteenth-Century America.* New York: Abingdon Press, 1957.

Smith, Wilson. *Professors and Public Ethics: Studies of Northern Moral Philosophers before the Civil War.* Ithaca, N.Y.: Cornell University Press, 1956.

Sprague, William. *Annals of the American Pulpit.* New York: Robert Carter & Brothers, 1859.

Stewart, James Brewer. "Garrison Again, and Again, and Again, and Again . . ." *Reviews in American History* 4 (December 1976): 539–45.

———. *Holy Warriors: The Abolitionists and American Slavery.* American Century Series. New York: Hill and Wang, 1976.

"Sumner's Oration on the 'True Grandeur of Nations', July 4, 1845." *Proceedings of the Massachusetts Historical Society* 50 (April 1917): 245–307.

Takaki, Ronald T. *Iron Cages: Race and Culture in Nineteenth-Century America.* New York: Alfred A. Knopf, 1979.

Thomas, John L. *The Liberator: William Lloyd Garrison.* Boston: Little, Brown and Company, 1963.

Toes, Reg. "Can Mennonite Christians Govern?" *Festival Quarterly* 12 (Spring 1985): 7–9.

Tolis, Peter. *Elihu Burritt: Crusader for Brotherhood.* Hamden, Conn., Archon Books, 1968.

Trefousse, Hans. *Radical Republicans: Lincoln's Vanguard for Racial Justice.* New York: Alfred A. Knopf, 1969.

Tuveson, Ernest Lee. *Redeemer Nation: The Idea of America's Millennial Role.* Midway Reprint. Chicago: University of Chicago Press, 1968.

Tyler, Alice Felt. *Freedom's Ferment: Phases of American Social History from the Colonial Period to the Outbreak of the Civil War.* New York: Harper Torchbooks, Harper & Row, 1962.

Upton, James M. "The Shakers as Pacifists in the Period between 1812 and Civil War." *Filson Club Quarterly* 47 (July 1973): 267–83.

Walker, Peter F. *Moral Choices: Memory, Desire, and Imagination in Nineteenth-Century American Abolition.* Baton Rouge: Louisiana State University, 1978.

Walters, Ronald G. *American Reformers, 1815–1860.* American Century. New York: Hill and Wang, 1978.

———. *The Antislavery Appeal: American Abolitionism after 1830.* Baltimore: The Johns Hopkins University Press, 1976.

Wells, Ronald A., ed. *The Wars of America: Christian Views.* Grand Rapids, Mich.: William B. Eerdmans, 1981.

White, Stephen A. "The Nonresistance Philosophy of Adin Ballou." *Brethren Life and Thought* 24 (Spring 1979): 103–13.

Whitney, Edwin L. *The American Peace Society: A Centennial History.* Washington, D.C.: American Peace Society, 1928.

Wolf, Hazel Catherine. *On Freedom's Altar: The Martyr Complex in the Abolition Movement.* Madison: University of Wisconsin Press, 1952.

Wyatt-Brown, Bertram. "Prelude to Abolitionism: Sabbatarian Politics and the Rise of the Second Party System." *Journal of American History* 58 (September 1971): 316–41.

———. *Lewis Tappan and the Evangelical War against Slavery.* Cleveland: Case Western Reserve University Press, 1969.

———. *Yankee Saints and Southern Sinners.* Baton Rouge: Louisiana State University Press, 1985.

Yoder, John Howard. *The Christian Witness to the State.* Newton, Kans.: Faith and Life Press, 1964.

———. "The Experiential Etiology of Evangelical Dualism." *Missiology* 11 (October 1983): 449–59.

————. "The Hermeneutics of Peoplehood." *Journal of Religious Ethics* 10 (Spring 1982): 40–67.

————. "Jesus and Power." *Ecumenical Review* 25 (October 1978): 447–54.

————. *Nevertheless: The Varieties and Shortcomings of Religious Pacifism.* Scottdale, Pa.: Herald Press, 1971.

————. *The Original Revolution.* Scottdale, Pa.: Herald Press, 1971.

————. "The Otherness of the Church." *Mennonite Quarterly Review* 35 (October 1961): 288–96.

————. *The Politics of Jesus.* Grand Rapids, Mich.: William Eerdmans, 1972.

————. "Radical Reformation Ethics in Ecumenical Perspective." *Journal of Ecumenical Studies* 15 (Fall 1978): 647–61.

————. "Reinhold Niebuhr and Christian Pacifism." *Mennonite Quarterly Review* 29 (April 1955): 101–17.

————. "Response to Scott Paradise Paper: Vision of a Good Society." *Anglican Theological Review* 61 (January 1979): 118–26.

————. "The Unique Role of the Historic Peace Churches." *Brethren Life* 14 (Summer 1969): 132–49.

————. *What Would You Do?"* Christian Peace Shelf Selection. Scottdale, Pa.: Herald Press, 1983.

————. " 'What Would You Do If . . . ?' An Exercise in Situation Ethics." *Journal of Religious Ethics* 2 (Fall 1974): 81–105.

————. *When War Is Unjust.* Introduction by Charles P. Lutz. Minneapolis: Augsburg Publishing House, 1984.

Zikmund, Barbara. *Asa Mahan and Oberlin Perfectionism.* Ph.D. dissertation, Duke University, 1969.

INDEX

VALARIE H. ZIEGLER teaches in the Religious Studies department at Rhodes College. She has published articles on antebellum pacifism, women in the Southern Baptist Convention, and Elvis and the incarnation and is currently working on a book on the social construction of gender roles among American women pacifists.